THE MAGNIFICENT LIFE OF
MISS MAY HOLMAN

ABOUT THE AUTHOR

Dr Lekkie Hopkins is a feminist academic who researches the history of social protest and the lives of activist women. In 2010 she co-authored *Among the Chosen. The life story of Pat Giles* with Lynn Roarty. She coordinated the women's studies program at Edith Cowan University for twenty-five years and has received both local and national teaching awards. In the past decade she has collaborated with a group of peers and postgraduate students to pioneer innovative arts-based research methodologies for use in social science research. In 2011 she was among one hundred women to be inducted into the inaugural United Nations Western Australian Women's Hall of Fame, to celebrate the centenary of International Women's Day.

THE MAGNIFICENT LIFE OF MISS MAY HOLMAN

AUSTRALIA'S FIRST FEMALE LABOR PARLIAMENTARIAN

LEKKIE HOPKINS

This book is dedicated to my children's children – Harriet, Lily and Fergus – and to the children of their generation, in the hope that stories such as these will inspire them to live lives of integrity, dignity and purpose.

CONTENTS

Foreword by Professor Carmen Lawrence		7
Preface by Dr Judyth Watson		10
Prologue		13
Chapter 1	Here she is!	16
Chapter 2	'I can only say that her life was magnificent…'	42
Chapter 3	Honour thy father…	63
Chapter 4	… And thy mother	86
Chapter 5	The Entertainers	102
Chapter 6	The Honourable the Member for Forrest	119
Chapter 7	There's a woman in the House!	140
Chapter 8	League of Nations	158
Chapter 9	Let her story, then, be woven…	179
Epilogue		209
Endnotes		214
Bibliography		230
Acknowledgements		234

FOREWORD

In her concluding paragraph of this engaging biography, Lekkie Hopkins asks us to contemplate what we can learn from May Holman's trailblazing life as she 'charted new territory for women', demonstrating that a woman can be 'an excellent parliamentarian, a fine friend, a compassionate soul'. She asks us to remember that Holman achieved this while navigating the shoals of the 'almost impenetrable' masculine privilege which was part of her world and was (and remains) 'invisible to those who continue to enjoy it.'

Holman appeared to understand that men can't or won't see that their definitions of merit and their expectations about performance are nothing more than rules they have made up to protect their own positions, albeit often unconsciously. Rather than confronting this privilege head on (although she used wit to good effect to draw attention to it), Holman showed by her actions that what is required of a member of parliament has nothing to do with a person's gender. As John Stuart Mill said, what we require are 'enlightened individuals who will be mature and responsible because they reflect upon the issues that face them', a formula which could certainly improve the quality of our parliamentary representation today.

While Holman explicitly repudiated the description of herself as a 'feminist' she, nevertheless, epitomised the core of the feminist cause in the way she lived and worked. Lekkie Hopkins documents Holman's political development from her strong family roots in the Labor movement, through her experiences as a popular musical performer, to her feisty representation of her South-West constituency (leading to her being re-elected five times) and her understanding of the importance of speaking to people in terms they could easily embrace. The scope of her passionate, but practical, activism was enlarged and her commitment to improving the position of women deepened after her visit to Europe to observe the workings of the League of Nations. She continued to learn and adjust her thinking throughout her brief life.

Today Holman's example might give us pause to reflect on the fact that the journey to equality is far from over – women are still subjected to violence in their homes; too many exist on low incomes with poor employment prospects and, while more women occupy positions of power than in Holman's day, they are seen as fair game for misogyny and ridicule.

Behind the aggregate economic and social indicators is evidence that there is real disadvantage and distress in many Australian communities, despite the decades of sustained economic growth. While more women are in paid work, the majority still work in a range of low-paid, part-time and precarious jobs. Generally speaking, work is not structured to meet families' needs, but rather to suit the employer's. Equal pay remains an elusive goal – the gender pay gap has now hit a record high. The persistence of the gap indicates that the forces at play are deeply entrenched and difficult to eradicate – there is obvious prejudice in decisions about hiring, salaries and promotions. At the base of the problem is a persistent failure to properly value women's skills and 'women's work' as well as continuing occupational segregation. It doesn't help that women still bear the bulk of responsibility for caring for family members.

And violence against women remains a stain on our community; a series of horrendous murders and assaults of women and children has catapulted 'domestic violence' into the spotlight – again – but the issue waxes and wanes in political favour, with solemn pronouncements that 'we cannot tolerate violence against women' delivered against a backdrop of never-ending pilot programs. The deaths and injury of women are treated, for the most part, as inevitable, like the road toll.

In the face of these, and many similar affronts to equality and human dignity, May Holman would, no doubt, have rolled up her sleeves and organised. She would have confronted the problems squarely, and skillfully debated her opponents; she would have cajoled her supporters into more effective action, all the while smiling with the pleasure of working for her beloved people. We could do worse than remember and emulate this fine woman.

Professor Carmen Lawrence
The University of Western Australia
August 2015

PREFACE

May Holman (1893–1939) held the Western Australian State seat of Forrest for fourteen years from 1925 until her accidental death in 1939. She made history not only as the first Labor woman to be elected to an Australian parliament but also, in 1935, as the first woman parliamentarian in the entire British Empire to have served for a decade or more. These were turbulent times internationally and at home: at the time of her election Australians were still reeling from the impacts of the Great War; by 1930 the disastrous effects of a global depression were being felt; and at the time of her death, Australia was about to be swept into a second world war.

I first 'met' May Holman towards the end of my own parliamentary career when, as part of a nationwide attempt to encourage more Labor women into Australian parliamentary life, I researched and edited *We Hold Up Half the Sky: the voices of Western Australian ALP women in Parliament*, a collection containing short political biographies of each of the twenty-two Labor women elected to represent Western Australians in the seven decades since 1925.

What I learned about May Holman endeared her to me and to those assisting with the book's compilation. We saw in her a woman with a strong sense of loyalty to her own family and to the Great Labor Family; a woman with a clear political and personal ideology, one whom constituents could rely upon. She had amazing energy for organising events despite periods of ill-health and, in addition to her electorate advocacy, she demonstrated a strong sense of justice, particularly for women and for trade unionists.

PREFACE

There was no biography of this most deserving woman and I planned to write one. I began the research process by meeting with May's youngest sister, Sheila Moiler, who alerted me to the archives in the Battye Library. These included, among other things, letters and reports May had written while attending the 1930 Assembly of the League of Nations meeting in Geneva. May Holman had been appointed Australia's substitute delegate to the meeting. This was her first and only journey overseas.

In 1995 I published a collection of her private letters to family, together with the public reports of her experiences of her journey to Geneva commissioned by the Melbourne Herald Group, as *Remarks of an Inexperienced Traveller Abroad*. I was very taken with two things. One was the way both the letters and the reports revealed much about May as a curious, excited and inexperienced traveller. The other was the coincidence that she, like me, had attended a life-changing international forum. In September 1995 I attended the United Nations Fourth World Conference on Women in Beijing. When we returned, we Western Australian delegates published a view of our experiences and observations. The idea to publish in this way was directly inspired by May Holman's reflections on her 1930 trip to Geneva.

There were many parallels between May Holman's parliamentary life and mine. Although I entered parliament six decades after she did, we were both members of the Women's International League for Peace and Freedom. We shared a commitment to ensuring occupational health and safety for working people. While in the Western Australian State Parliament I spoke out frequently on that broad topic of women's interests, condemning all forms of violence against women and children, promoting an idea for paid housework, advocating research into HIV/AIDS, promoting peace, and suggesting ideas for making Parliament House what we would now call a family-friendly workplace. And like May Holman and every other Australian woman MP, I too suffered sexist taunts.

The early research I undertook about May gave wonderful glimpses into her life. Her younger sisters Sheila Moiler and

Eileen Thomson loved her dearly and were very happy to think that their sister, who died too young, would be remembered through a biography. They remained very proud of their big sister and recognised her place in history. Evelyn Coverley and Frances Shea were her young friends and colleagues and spoke warmly and fondly of the woman they knew. As I remember, each acknowledged that despite May's competence, it was hard for her. She had a commitment to family and to working people that in many ways took over her life. Her father was a hard man whom none of the family could fully understand, even though the two sisters in particular respected him for his life's work. He was such a dominant father and politician that even though Katherine, their mother, played an active leadership role in women's politics, it was hard for her daughters to give an adequate picture of who she was.

A few years ago I asked Lekkie Hopkins if she would consider reading my collection of May Holman papers with a view to writing her biography. I am so pleased she agreed and am delighted with the imaginative way she has used and added to that material to produce this book.

This long-overdue biography pays tribute to May Holman's contributions to Western Australia's political and industrial history, and brings her to life as a woman we would want to meet and know.

Dr Judyth Watson

PROLOGUE

'May Holman? Now that name's vaguely familiar. Who was she? Isn't there a building in Perth named after her?' These are the kinds of responses I've had from Western Australians during the writing of this biography. Even those committed feminist women who staffed the Women's Information and Referral Exchange in Perth during the 1980s and 90s, housed as it was in the May Holman Building, can produce only the sketchiest outline of her life when pressed.

And yet in the 1930s May Holman was a household name in Australia. She made history in 1925 when, at age thirty-one, she was elected to the Lower House of the Western Australian State Parliament in a by-election to fill the vacancy in the seat of Forrest left by the death of her father, John Barkell Holman. She was the first Labor woman ever to sit in an Australian parliament, and, unlike Edith Cowan whose stint in parliament lasted only three years from 1921 to 1924, May Holman was re-elected five times and remained in parliament for fourteen years until her untimely death by accident in 1939. We ought to remember her.

May Holman was vivacious and stylish, intelligent and articulate. Even before her election to parliament she was widely known in Perth circles as a brilliant musician and talented stage performer. Like her parents, she was a committed member of the Great Labor Family and quickly emerged as a leader in her generation. Her responses to the turbulent social and political periods that marked her lifetime – the Great War from 1914 to 1918 and the worldwide Depression of the early 1930s – give some indication of her calibre as a leader. Rather than succumbing helplessly to the devastating effects of the social disruptions that marked both of these periods, May Holman set out to make lives better for those worst affected. During the Great War and into the 1920s she assembled and led a hugely popular concert troupe of young women and men, known as The Entertainers, whose performances saw soldiers off to war and raised funds for worthwhile causes at home. Throughout the Depression, as a parliamentarian and as a leader of Labor women, she fought fiercely for the appropriate implementation of policies providing sustenance and government support for destitute workers and their families.

During her parliamentary career she remained a woman of the people. The issues she campaigned on – education reform, health reform, occupational health and safety reform in the mills and timber industry, equal pay for women and men, employment for young people – were issues that affected all phases of the daily lives of Western Australian citizens. During the 1930s, after the terrible hardships of the Great Depression, May Holman became intensely interested in bringing joy and intellectual nourishment to Labor women throughout the nation. The political slogan originating during the 1912 textile workers' strike in Massachusetts – *Hearts starve as well as bodies, Give them bread but give them roses* – may well have been hers. But her campaigning was not confined to ensuring the wellbeing of women and children. She was a formidable industrial advocate and, at the beginning of her career, she quickly established a reputation for intelligent and meticulous research and preparation when she gave the Second Reading Speech to introduce the widely acclaimed Timber Industry Regulation Bill.

None of this information would have been known to me without the intervention of Dr Judyth Watson. Judyth herself has had a distinguished career as a Labor politician. She was elected to the Western Australian Parliament in 1986 and served under the premiership of Dr Carmen Lawrence as minister for Aboriginal affairs, multicultural and ethnic affairs and seniors from 1991 to 1993, and as minister for women's interests from 1992 to 1993. She remained in parliament until 1996. During her parliamentary

PROLOGUE

career she became fascinated by the life of May Holman and researched it thoroughly, intending to write her biography. However, the writing process seemed daunting, and, a decade later, she invited me to take on the project. I'm so glad I did. I remain indebted to Judyth and her former staff for the extensive archive they have entrusted to me. And we are all indebted to those friends and members of May Holman's family who agreed to speak with Judyth and who supplied photographs, newspaper clippings and fascinating insights into the life of their famous relative and friend.

May Holman was a much loved public figure. But, as I have discovered in writing this biography, she was a complex and contradictory figure. She was intensely loyal and dignified, but also high-spirited and full of fun. She was sophisticated and charming and a brilliant scholar, but loved simple pleasures like having sing-alongs around the piano, and chatting in the kitchen over a cup of tea. She adored family life but, unlike most of her siblings, she did not create a conventional family of her own. She was widely admired for her immense energy and yet was plagued by ill-health and spent months at a time confined to her bed. She worked towards the creation of a new social order where poverty was eradicated and where women were seen as full human beings, but did not see herself as a radical or as a feminist.

When May Holman was killed in a car accident in 1939, the outpouring of grief across the nation was extraordinary. Press reports suggest that people everywhere responded personally to the news of her death and were genuinely heartbroken. John Curtin called her life *magnificent*. He acknowledged that her life was unfinished and inspiring. *Let her story, then, be woven into the tasks we will endeavor to do and in the lives we each have yet to live*, he wrote in a eulogy in 1939. *Let us take up the work that has been left yet unfinished, preserve the good that has been done, and in that way give fullness and completion to the glorified life of Miss Holman.*[1]

Seven decades later, it's time to remember her again.

Dr Lekkie Hopkins, Edith Cowan University

CHAPTER 1
HERE SHE IS!

May Holman pauses beside her mother at a side door to the chamber of the Legislative Assembly. It's just before three o'clock on the afternoon of Thursday 30 July 1925, and the ceremony to open the second session of the Twelfth Parliament of the State of Western Australia is about to begin. When she is sworn in this afternoon as the new member for Forrest, Miss Holman will become the first Labor woman in the nation to take a seat in parliament. She knows she is making history. She knows, too, that she is following in the footsteps of her beloved father, John Barkell Holman, whose unexpected death in February has rendered the seat of Forrest vacant.[1] She is thirty-one years old, younger by three decades than her trailblazing predecessor in this parliament, Edith Cowan.[2] We can imagine that she gives an involuntary shiver as she takes her mother's arm to enter the House.

Miss Holman's election has certainly captured the public imagination. Rarely has a routine opening ceremony of this parliament attracted so much attention.[3] High above her, the public galleries are packed. Curious onlookers spill over into the press gallery. The mood is festive. Necks crane and people jostle for position to watch the ceremony unfold. They see the speaker of the House enter in his wig and exotic regalia to occupy the one plush seat at the top of the room. They watch as the forty-nine members of the Legislative Assembly – all men – file in to take their places at two long tables facing the speaker's chair. They note the hush as the sergeant-at-arms announces the arrival of

The glamorous young Miss Holman.

the governor. But it is the glamorous young Miss Holman they have come to see.[4] Excitement makes them reckless. When her name is called for the swearing-in ceremony, those at the back abandon decorum and stand on their chairs to get a better view as she sweeps into the room to stand before the governor.[5] From the public galleries an excited whisper goes up: *Here she is! Here she is! Here she is!* [6]

I could hear them and I felt terrible, she later confessed to a journalist, *but all that is past now.*[7]

On that same afternoon May Holman gave her maiden speech in the Legislative Assembly as the address-in-reply to the governor's opening address. In a manoeuvre that was to become characteristic of her parliamentary manner, she began by warmly congratulating the government on its successes outlined in the Governor's speech, but then launched almost immediately into a plea that her listeners recognise the terrible conditions under which the timber workers in her electorate lived and laboured. The issues she raised – the need for an adequate basic wage, the need for legislation to ensure the health and safety of timber workers, the need for protection of foreigners in the timber industry, the need for improved sanitation, better housing, better water supplies, better medical services, better roads, better educational opportunities[8] – reflected concerns that threaded their way through her parliamentary speeches for the next fourteen years.

The public responded warmly to her parliamentary debut. Journalists reported that the politicians and the crowds in the public galleries were impressed. On 31 July *The Daily News* noted that the new member for Forrest *was attentively listened to throughout her twenty minutes effort and fervent applause marked the end of her remarks.*[9] The Brisbane *Worker* was even more explicit about the differences between what people were expecting and what they experienced, reporting that she drew most effectively on her father's reputation and on her own industrial experience to highlight the ongoing plight of the timber workers in her electorate. *It was thought in some quarters that the young lady might be no more than a novel adornment of the House, but now she is seriously regarded as a fine acquisition. May is of a refined, unobtrusive temperament, but she has had practical industrial experience, and should give a splendid account of herself as she gains confidence in her new sphere.*[10]

Those of us looking back at this history-making day from the vantage point of the early decades of the twenty-first century must surely wonder how it was possible for a woman of thirty-one to have acquired the confidence, the skill, the reputation and the nerve to chart such new territory for women, to successfully stand for election as an industrial advocate to a seat in parliament with a primarily male constituency. As we will see when we look closely at her family background and her own early experiences, May Holman was certainly an exceptionally intelligent and gifted young woman with an unusually specific suite of life experiences that equipped her well for the task that lay ahead. But it's too tempting to assume that hers was a lone voice in a sea of silenced and timid women. If we turn our attention to the activities of women from several generations and all walks of life in the Western Australian city of Perth in the mid-1920s, we begin to hear a cacophony of voices, some raised loud in anti-war protest, some demanding kindergartens and maternity hospitals in persuasively well-modulated tones, others weary from their behind-the-scenes battle to ensure the basic wage for women, some strident in their claims for equal pay for equal work, others loudly proclaiming the necessity of overthrowing capitalism, and still others asserting their independence as doctors, lawyers, journalists, teachers, nurses, poets, writers, seamstresses, shop assistants, factory workers, clerks, fashionistas. May Holman was unusual in charting new territory in the parliamentary sphere, but she was not alone, as a woman, in her social and political activism.

The world May Holman inherited as a young woman growing up in Perth was a world peopled with outspoken, determined, strategic activists – women and men – of her parents' generation. It was also a world of unevenly distributed privilege: some families lived in comfort and luxury in mansions lining the Swan River; others, like the families of timber workers in May Holman's electorate, lived in hovels with no sanitation, no access to clean water, and intermittent access to adequate health care. The Holmans were a staunch Labor family, and May's own mother, Katherine, emerged as a leader in Labor women's organisations from the early 1900s, working voluntarily alongside colleagues like Jean Beadle[11] and Ettie Hooton,[12] whose lives were dedicated to ensuring that women were included in the implementation of the great Labor ideals.[13]

The Labor women's organisations so dear to Katherine Holman's heart coexisted with, but remained largely separate from, the other influential women's groups that made up the social and political movement that we know, in hindsight, as the first wave of feminism.[14] The 1890s had been a particularly fertile period for women lobbyists in Western Australia. In 1900, after a long and carefully crafted campaign from three related women's groups established in the 1890s – the Women's Christian Temperance Union,[15] the Karrakatta Club,[16] and the Women's Franchise League[17] – Western Australian women were granted the right to vote.[18] Many of the women involved in the campaign for the franchise in Western Australia – Edith Cowan, Lady Madeleine Onslow, Emily Hensman, Lady Eleanora James – were educated women, well-connected to the colony's administration and to the conservative side of its political life.[19] By the time May Holman entered the parliament, they were aged in their fifties and sixties: they were clearly generationally and politically distinct from the young Miss Holman.

As a Laborite, May Holman was primarily concerned with bringing dignity and justice and a redistribution of wealth to the working classes; hers was clearly a party-aligned political process. In contrast, the women of the Karrakatta Club were determinedly non-party-aligned, and less interested in reforming the existing social order than in ensuring that women's needs were taken care of, whatever their social position. In this respect they were politically more conservative than May Holman; but the impact of their activism on the everyday lives of Western Australian women should not be underestimated. The issues that continued to concern them were social justice issues that went far beyond demanding the vote, and included women's right to access to the professions and to public life, to adequate reproductive health care, to just divorce laws, and to lives free from violence. The motto of the Karrakatta Club (*spectemur agendo*: let us be judged by our actions) emphasised that theirs was a practical idealism.[20] Throughout her adolescence and early adulthood May Holman must surely have been aware of the activities of the Karrakatta Club and the related Women's Service Guilds,[21] presided over by the indomitable self-avowed feminist Bessie Rischbieth[22] and co-founded in 1909 by Edith Cowan and Dr Roberta Jull.[23] She would have been in sympathy with their peace activism, and their defence of the rights of marginalised groups such as prisoners and prostitutes, and no doubt she would have admired their work in establishing crucial services for women and children in Western Australia, including the kindergarten system and the King Edward Memorial Hospital for Women.

For at least three decades before May Holman's entry into parliament, then, women had played an active role in publicly working for social change in Western Australia. There was no shortage of women lobbyists for May Holman to admire. She knew she was entitled to take her place in public life. But unlike the activist women of the previous generation and indeed of her own generation, May Holman eschewed the feminist label, seeing herself rather as a member of the Great Labor Family.[24] As John Curtin wrote in his tribute at the time of her death in 1939, *Her outlook was governed by the conviction that men and women are joint sharers of life's purpose... [and] fellow victims of injustice.*[25] Within the party itself, although she shared her mother's interest in Labor women's organisations, May Holman's political supporters were not primarily women. Rather, as we shall see, her early engagement with her father's world of trade unionism and party politics meant that for much of her young adult life she was the single woman in a company of men. And as a young woman, she worked alongside her father as a son might. When her father died, she set out to carry on his work. Her commitment was to the party process beyond an exclusive commitment to women's issues.

Herein lies the strange anomaly of May Holman's parliamentary success. The only other women elected to any Australian parliaments in the decade of the 1920s – Edith Cowan in Western Australia and Millicent Preston-Stanley in New South Wales – were quickly seen solely as women representing women's interests, and each lost her seat after serving one parliamentary term. In stark contrast, May Holman was seen to be carrying on her father's industrial reform agenda and held her seat of Forrest through five elections until her untimely death in 1939.

Edith Cowan, it seems, encountered hostility throughout her parliamentary term. Nobody was quite prepared for her entry into parliament in 1921. The legal bar to women entering the parliament was removed by legislation in 1920, after determined lobbying by Edith Cowan and her activist associates: she was one of five women candidates in this election, and ran a short election campaign. Like most of the other members of the Karrakatta Club, Edith Cowan was not immersed in a party process before her entry into the parliament, and she stood for election under the umbrella of the governing Nationalists, not because she was necessarily in sympathy with all their policies, but more because she took seriously their claim to be a non-party organisation.[26] Consequently, she had no existing body of supporters in the parliament. The men did not quite know what to do with this eloquent, intelligent and forceful woman who refused to dance to their tune. She had a tough time on the floor of the House: she was considered abrasive and lost the sympathy of her Nationalist colleagues almost immediately by refusing to vote with them, insisting that her constituents were the women of Western Australia, not the Nationalist supporters. Nor did the press know how to respond: during her election campaign Mrs Cowan was accused of being *a disgrace to women* and of *heartlessly neglecting her husband and children*. At the time, her youngest child was thirty, and her husband was out campaigning for her.[27] As a member of parliament she was admired for her success in opening the legal profession to women through introducing the Women's Legal Status Act 1923 as a private member, but she was frequently derided, and from the beginning she was lampooned by cartoonists.

By 1925, when both May Holman and Millicent Preston-Stanley stood for election, the public was fascinated with how women parliamentarians coped with what today we would recognise as sexism. The left-wing press was especially interested in observing how they fared. An amusing story recounted in the *Westralian*

Worker gives us a glimpse of the quick-witted Millicent Preston-Stanley, and of an appreciative crowd. It relates to a meeting in Townsville, where she was speaking outside, from the back of a lorry. *"How would you like to be a man?" an interjector called out. 'How would you?" was the prompt reply, which* (so the story goes) *caused discomforture to the man, and joy to the crowd. There were no further interjections.*[28]

But although Miss Preston-Stanley received some very favourable press at the time of her election, less than a couple of months into her parliamentary term *The Australian Worker* was predicting that she would serve one term only.[29] And just three months later, that same newspaper reported with grim satisfaction that *Miss Preston-Stanley receives more courtesy from her Labor colleagues in the Parliament than from the members of her own party, which only coldly welcomes her.*[30]

May Holman, however, entered the parliament on an entirely different footing. The welcome she received in the Women's Sphere pages of the *Westralian Worker* on Friday 10 April 1925 set the tone for much of what was to follow:

> *Congratulations are pouring in to Miss May Holman, MLA, who, having won the selection ballot for Forrest, has been returned unopposed for that seat. In this respect she shares the distinction with her late father, who won Forrest under similar conditions. "Long may she reign" is the wish of all who know her. That she will fill the bill is the opinion of all whom writer has come in contact with. Miss Holman knows the timber industry better than most of the officers of the Australian Timber Workers' Union: she knows the personnel of the union. Also she knows the intricacies of the award, of the union rules, and of every detail of the management of the organisation. In parliament the timber workers will have a capable representative, and their wives and youngsters will have an ardent advocate. When it comes to getting grants and concessions from Ministers, who is more likely to be*

successful than Miss Holman? Every Minister has known her from girlhood, and it is safe to say each is delighted with her success. Perhaps it would be wrong to say she will be welcomed into Parliament with open arms, but one can at least predict that both sides will express more than formal pleasure when she takes her seat. Of her many good qualities none is more outstanding than her happy knack of making friends, and within twelve months, if a vote were taken in Parliament for the most popular member, the result would be Miss Holman an easy first. Although she is not the first woman to be elevated to a seat in the Legislative Assembly, she is the first Labor woman to have that honour, and further she is the first Labor woman to take a seat in any Australian Parliament.[31]

It was not unusual for the newspapers of the day – *The West Australian*, *The Daily News*, *The Sunday Times*, the *Westralian Worker* – to carry stories of women's social and political activities. What was unusual, perhaps, was this article's assumption that a young woman – any young woman – would be so warmly welcomed into the all-male parliamentary sphere. But May Holman was already a well-known and much admired public figure, and her supporters were accustomed to seeing her operate at her father's side. In the months after her father's death but before her admission to the House, she was often in the news. The broad scope of her activities is evident in the publicity she received. After the flurry of articles commenting on her election to the seat of Forrest, *The Sunday Times* on 5 April published a flattering synopsis of her career as an entertainer.[32] Later, on Friday 1 May, the *Westralian Worker* published a feisty letter from May Holman in defence of her late father's reputation as a staunch advocate for the Timber Workers' Union. *My father earned his salt and so do I,* she wrote, *and I am sure that the timber workers as a body know that, from the hour my father entered their service, he spared neither health nor strength in fighting and working for their interests. His record in this respect cannot be besmirched by any innuendoes Mr Hughes is courageous enough to make over a dead man's tomb...*[33] On Saturday 2 May she opened the new Cottesloe sports oval;[34] and on Sunday 3 May she spoke before a crowd of one thousand people at the May Day rally at the Esplanade in Perth, expressing her support of a resolution to *abolish the capitalist system with its policy of production for private profit, and pledge itself to work for the establishment of a state of society wherein the means of production will be socially owned and operated for the benefit of all members of the community.*[35] In her speech she stressed that bloodshed would not be necessary, because transformation could be achieved by constitutional means.

Here then we have a young woman who is already an intriguing public figure. She is outspoken in her defence of her late father's reputation; she is politically revolutionary in her call for the end to capitalism and simultaneously pacifist in her insistence on avoiding bloody battle; and she is well known as an industrial advocate for the timber workers. But she is a curiosity, as the crowds at the opening of the parliament suggest. She is a woman, but she has been her father's *right hand man*.[36] She is a woman, but she is seen as his *political heir*.[37] She is a woman, but, as we have seen, she is perfectly positioned to take her place as a member of that exclusive men's club, the State Parliament. She's a woman, but her interest in the parliamentary process is genuine and her constituent base much broader and deeper than that of her two parliamentary sisters. It's no secret that she adored her father and was delighted to follow him and his much-admired predecessor, Peter O'Loghlen, into the parliament as the member for Forrest. Soon after her father's death she commented to a journalist on the *Westralian Worker, When I was a little girl there were two people in the world I thought were perfect – my father, and Peter O'Loghlen.*[38] But these heroes are dead and she finds herself as the lone woman in the parliament. To whom does she look for inspiration and guidance?

Enter Katharine Susannah Prichard. Of all the women who

were politically active in Perth in the 1920s, it was she who shared, specifically, May Holman's idealistic desire to seek genuine structural change through the overthrow of capitalism. In hindsight, Katharine Susannah Prichard emerges as a formidable dame of left-wing politics, a founding member of the Communist Party in Australia, and an internationally recognised and lauded literary figure.[39] But in the mid-1920s, although she had already seen some journalistic and literary success, her greatest works were still ahead of her, and her local reputation revolved around her success as an orator and political idealist.

Like May Holman, Katharine Prichard was an anomaly in conservative Perth. She was a political radical plunged into a deeply conservative milieu. Although throughout her life a segment of the community remained deeply suspicious of her,[40] she was renowned amongst her acquaintances for being readily able to befriend all who came into contact with her.[41] She had arrived in Perth from Melbourne in 1919 to live with her dashing young husband, Hugo Throssel, local war hero and beloved son of a former conservative state premier. At the time, two major industrial disputes – one on the Kalgoorlie goldfields and the other on the Fremantle waterfront – were reaching their climax. Trades Hall was flying a red flag, and Kalgoorlie miners who'd been arrested for striking were being brought to Perth for trial. These were politically turbulent times. The wharfies' strike in May 1919 resulted in the conservative Colebatch government ordering mounted police to advance on the barricaded strikers. One striker was killed and seven were wounded. Katharine Susannah Prichard, as one of the first Marxists to arrive in Perth, was quickly in demand as a public speaker. Her talks on the waterfront with the striking workers earned her wide admiration. Everyone listened to her. Her international outlook meant that, for her Perth audiences, the struggles of local workers were now linked to struggles of workers around the world.[42]

Katherine Susannah Prichard was ten years older than May Holman, much closer in age than many of the other activist women

May Holman could have seen as role models. In a city as small as Perth in the 1920s,[43] the two women could not have avoided knowing of one another. The young May Holman would surely have been enchanted. Here was a woman not much older than she, articulate and intelligent, fearless in her expression, who, even after joining the Communist Party in 1922, was simultaneously able to command the respect and admiration of those who met her, conservative and radical alike. Perhaps, for a young woman like May Holman, raised in the grudges and the barbs and the adversarial traditions of the trade union movement and the Labor Party, there was something here to learn.

For her part, Katharine would surely have admired the younger woman for her determination, her courage, her grace. She'd have known old Jack Holman as a fierce Labor man and trade unionist, uncompromising, intolerant of opposition, and, at times, violent. She'd have known the stories of the uproar he'd created in the parliament a decade or more ago when in a fit of rage at being gagged, he grabbed the speaker by the collar and threatened to hurl him out of the House. She'd have heard, too, of his eldest daughter's adoration of him and of her shared allegiance to the Labor cause, so that when Jack Holman died suddenly, Katharine would not have been as surprised as she otherwise might have been that young Miss Holman committed herself to the work he had begun and ran for election to the seat he'd vacated.

History does not relate whether the two women were confidantes. But in a fascinating twist of historical coincidence, their stories are forever linked by the publication, in 1926, of two internationally significant documents, each born of these two women's respective passionate concern with the plight of the timber workers in Western Australia. Katharine Susannah Prichard's novel, *Working Bullocks*, set in the karri forests of the South-West, detailed the appallingly harsh existence and living conditions of the timber workers and their families, and was considered by literary critics to be groundbreaking in its articulation of social conditions. It was hailed internationally as the first properly Australian modern novel.⁴⁴ And in that same year, May Holman's Timber Industry Regulation Bill, presented to the Western Australian Parliament in July, rightly received international acclaim for its meticulous outlining of measures to improve the occupational health and safety of timber workers. May Holman's attention to the detail of every stage of the process, from the research and drafting of the bill through to seeing its safe passage through the parliament, ensured that this is still held to be the greatest achievement of her fourteen-year parliamentary career.

Both May Holman and Katharine Susannah Prichard were intimately familiar with the lives they were writing about. For the past three years Katharine had visited the karri country often to gather material for her novel. She and her baby son had lived for long stretches with the timber workers and their families; she had felt the damp, the cold, the dark. She knew firsthand that timber cutting and mill work were dangerous. She knew the despair of women whose husbands were injured, and the rage of men whose livelihoods were threatened if they protested.

We know that May Holman read and admired *Working Bullocks* for its vivid portrayal of life in the timber country. The critic H. M. Green wrote of it as having ... *a kind of warmth and glow which seems to be a reflection of heat and light and the colour-effects of the landscape.*⁴⁵ Drusilla Modjeska, in her research into Australian women writers of the period, records that as early as 1925, writer Louis Esson wrote to colleague Vance Palmer that he and Hilda Esson were reading the manuscript of *Working Bullocks* and found it *astonishingly good. It is most unconventional, and it is less like an ordinary story than like actual life. You feel you are living in the karri forests.* On reading the novel himself, Vance Palmer wrote excitedly to the poet Frank Wilmot: *I hope the book gets a good spin in Australia, for something tells me it marks a crisis in our literary affairs.*⁴⁶ Nettie Palmer shared their excitement, giving it a more detailed assessment:

> Working Bullocks *seems to me different not only in quality but in kind. No one else has written with quite that rhythm, or seen the world in quite that way. The creative lyricism of the style impresses me more than either the theme or characters. From slang, from place names, from colloquial turns of speech, from descriptions of landscape and people at work, she has woven a texture that covers the whole surface of the book with a shimmer of poetry ...*[47]

But May Holman was also deeply attuned to the daily lives of the timber workers. It's a measure of her admiration for their resilience, perhaps, that Miss Holman felt that the novel did not do justice to the courage and tenacity of the real workers whose struggles are fictionalised here.[48] Nevertheless, *Working Bullocks* had clearly shone a spotlight upon the desperate living conditions of the families eking out a living in the timber country. Attention such as this must surely have been useful to May Holman's campaign to make their lives safer.

For more than a decade before the preparation of her Timber Industry Regulation Bill, May Holman had been immersed in the arcane world of the Timber Workers' Union. In 1910, aged seventeen, she went straight from school to Trades Hall to work directly with her father, who was at that time secretary of the Timber Workers' Union. For much of the Great War period she was employed elsewhere; but in 1918 she returned to work with her father as his personal clerk, gaining invaluable experience at his side in the state and federal arbitration courts as a trade union advocate. Her intense interest in timber workers' conditions meant that she was now ideally positioned to bring to fruition her father's preparatory work on a parliamentary bill to regulate the timber industry.

When on 19 October 1926 May Holman gave her Second Reading Speech for the Timber Industry Regulation Bill to her Western Australian parliamentary colleagues, it took two and a half hours to deliver. We know that its content is a history of every facet of the industry, a history of the international development of occupational health and safety legislation, and an account of timber-cutting at that time. Her research for this bill was characteristically detailed and thorough. She cited information from Australia – Queensland, Victoria, South Australia – as well as New Zealand, England, Switzerland, and the states of Arizona and Washington in the United States of America. The detail of her argument demonstrates an intimate knowledge of the daily lives of workers. She recounted information from the timber mills at settlements throughout the forest with an ease that speaks of close familiarity:

> *At Holyoake the accident rate is very high. Returns put in to the Arbitration Court showed that over one particular period there were 51 accidents over 12 months among the 104 men who were employed there. There are records of accidents in which the men's hands were caught in ropes or their legs were jammed... Also there is a bad stretch of line. It was badly laid and on one occasion the men had to get off the train and pack the sleepers with bark. During stormy weather trees may fall across the line or washaways may occur... At Nanga Brook there were 16 accidents in five months among the 80 men employed there giving a percentage of 47. At Nanga Brook bush landing seven accidents occurred within four months among the 45 men employed there. Regarding the accidents at Pemberton, the details I have were compiled from the doctor's figures. These show that from March 1925 to May 1926 there were 83 accidents including 13 on the group settlements, seven on railway construction and 63 at the mill. There are about 200 men employed at the mill and the percentage of accidents worked out at about 25. The small benches have guards and covers for the saws but the big benches have not.*[49]

She argued that inspectors were badly needed in the industry, concluding: *As the Minister proved the other night, the inspection of machinery in this industry is practically nil, and there is no protection for the men who operate the saws and woodworking machinery.* Ultimately, in her attempts to persuade her fellow parliamentarians to support her bill, Miss Holman was strategically modest in her appeal for a small measure of protection for workers. In a manoeuvre that became characteristic of her parliamentary demeanour, the tone of her appeal – moderate, reasonable, measured, sensible – tempered the passion she brought to her defence of her constituents, and invited reciprocal compassion from her fellow parliamentarians based in a common concern for the wellbeing of Western Australian citizens: *Any member who considers the terrible percentage of accidents in this industry will, I am sure, not refuse his assistance to get those men a small measure of protection.*[50]

It is extraordinary enough that two such groundbreaking documents detailing the lives of timber workers in the South-West of Western Australia – one a novel, the other a crucial piece of legislation – should emerge from the pens of two activist women in Perth in 1926, at a time when women were only just beginning to take their places in the public arenas of literature and parliamentary debate. It would be more extraordinary still, surely, if these two documents emerged completely independently of each other.

Katharine Susannah Prichard would no doubt have supported Miss Holman's proposal to regulate the industry through legislation: machinery inspections must be compulsory; the safety of workers in mill and forest must become the primary obligation of employers. These were crucial issues in the struggle for workers' rights, and it was important that the bill that eventually went before the parliament was thoroughly researched and forcefully argued. Given Katharine Prichard's intense interest in the party political process, and her concern for the plight of the timber workers and their families in May Holman's electorate, why would she not suggest they meet? Surely she would want to offer support and encouragement to the younger woman.

Let's imagine them in a tearoom in West Perth in the winter of 1925, in the year May Holman first takes her seat in parliament. Here they are, two women seated at a table beside the window. Katharine is pleased that May has accepted her invitation to meet. She smiles, congratulates, calls for tea. Today she wants to offer support and encouragement to the young woman seated across the table. They have much to discuss.

Initially their talk is of the parliament, of the honour of being the first Labor woman elected here, or, indeed, anywhere in this vast country, of the thrill of entering the parliament for the first time.

Their talk turns to courage and honour and duty, and May, emboldened by the graciousness of the older woman, inclines her head to ask quietly about Katharine's own road to political activism. And so Katharine tells her about her awakening to the wider world of radical politics, first as a young journalist in 1908 when she was sent to London to cover the Franco-British exhibition for the Melbourne *Herald*. This taste of cosmopolitan life exhilarated her, and in 1912, aged twenty-nine, she returned to London, hoping to find ways of living professionally and independently in the comparative freedom of that city. She acknowledges to May that life was hard, but that it was a life full of the passionate exploration of ideas. She became part of a circle of artists and writers, and embarked upon a systematic study of socialist ideas, which provided a fertile context for her later study of Marxism. At this time, too, she became an outspoken pacifist: from childhood she had felt that war was wrong, but her pacifism was confirmed when she travelled to northern France and saw at firsthand the atrocities of war.

As a writer, she tells May, the climax of her London stay came in 1915 when she won the prestigious Australian section of the Hodder & Stoughton All Empire novel competition with *The Pioneers*. For this she won two hundred and fifty pounds, a considerable sum, and with renewed confidence in her Australian future as a radical writer, she says, she returned to Melbourne. Here, in spite of her clearly articulated controversial views, she was warmly welcomed back by her family. It was here that she gained the love and support she needed to continue her political work. The crucial turning point came in 1917. She was greatly affected by news of the Russian Revolution. 'That the revolution was an event of world-shaking importance, I didn't doubt,' she tells May. 'Press diatribes against Lenin, Trotsky and Bolshevism indicated that they were guided by the theories of Marx and Engels.' She sips her tea and laughs in anticipation of the story of her own audacity. 'I lost no time in buying and studying all the books of these writers available in Melbourne. Discussion confirmed my impression that these theories provided the only logical basis that I had come across for the reorganisation of our social system.'

May is fascinated by the combination of playfulness and passion in the older woman's story. Katharine looks directly at her, eyes alight. 'My mind was illuminated by the discovery,' she continues in a rush. 'It was the answer to what I had been seeking: a satisfactory explanation of the wealth and power which controlled our lives – their origin, development, and how, in the process of social evolution, they could be directed towards the wellbeing of a majority of the people, so that poverty, disease, prostitution, superstition and war would be eliminated.' Katharine pauses, glances out the window to the wintry world outside, then turns her gaze once more upon her companion. The gaiety of the moment before is gone. She's reflective, sombre now. 'The works of Marx and Engels all made such sense to me,' she says. 'Here at last was a blueprint for life: peoples of the world would live in peace, and grow towards a perfecting of their existence on this earth.'[51]

May listens intently. She is not new to idealism, nor to political talk. Her own family life has been immersed in it. Her very earliest memory has political overtones: she pictures her father riding his bicycle home to their little house in the goldfields at Cue, bottle in one hand, drunkenly celebrating his win for the miners in a stoush with employers. Family history relates that he had won yet another round of the battle and whisked his wife around the room in a celebratory dance, with three year old May still safely in her mother's arms.[52] May recalls images, smudges, smells: her mother's face glowing with surprise and delight; a spinning room; a whoosh in her head; the smelly breath of her beloved father as he bellowed his joy. But May is captivated now by Katharine Susannah's gentle manner and generous ways. Perhaps here there's something for her to learn. Perhaps one can be committed without being divisive or aggressive. Perhaps ...

‡

As the afternoon light fades into a wintry dusk, we'll leave them there now in the tearoom, heads bent together, talking earnestly and animatedly. The extraordinary contributions of these two women to political life in Western Australia have earned them each an honoured place in history. But information about the detail of their everyday lives in the 1920s is relatively slight. Did such a meeting ever occur? History does not relate. What we do know, though, is that they shared that *happy knack of making friends* noted so enthusiastically by the journalist in the *Westralian Worker* of 10 April 1925. In political terms, what this means is that when we look back at their political lives, we see that they shared an unusual strength in shunning adversarial politics in favour of the politics of cooperation and reconciliation. Without ever resiling from their firmly held ideals, each was able to command the respect of her political opponents and supporters alike.

‡

If, as we might suppose, these two women did meet to discuss their political passions, we must also suppose that Miss Holman's admiration for Katharine Susannah Prichard would have been tempered with apprehension about her political strategies. Although Katharine herself was warmly admired in Perth circles, the Communist philosophy was not. Meeting with her in a public place may have been a risky undertaking for this first Labor woman parliamentarian. Rather than openly courting Communists, Labor parliamentarians, especially those closely aligned with the trade unions, had been at pains to establish distance from them. May was keenly aware of this. In 1923 her father John Barkell Holman brought a libel suit against *The Sunday Times* Publishing Company for alleging that he was a Communist. The suit was widely reported in newspapers around the nation. In October 1923 a special jury, that is, one drawn from *a class which usually belonged to a certain political section which was believed to oppose the Labor Party*,[53] awarded him damages and costs. An appeal before the Full Court eight months later was lost and Holman was paid three hundred pounds and costs. Most importantly, Jack Holman's reputation remained officially untainted by Communism. As is clear from the newspaper coverage of the case, public attitudes in Australia in this period following the Great War often aligned Communism with treachery. Katharine Susannah Prichard may well have been inspired by the Russian Revolution of 1917, but for the majority of Australians this event was hazy and dark: accounts of its violent upheaval of an established order induced fear rather than admiration. During the libel trial, Jack Holman was required to prove his distance from Communism by vouching for his own and his family's patriotism, as the excerpts from newspaper reports of the case make clear. On Wednesday 17 October 1923 the South Australian newspaper *The Register* reported that:

> In the Supreme Court [in Perth] *today, before Mr Justice Burnside and a special jury, a case was commenced in which J. B. Holman, secretary of the Australian Timber Workers' Union, claimed damages from The Sunday Times Publishing Company for libel alleged to be contained in a*

Federal Election paragraph which appeared in that paper on November 9, 1922, stating "Carpenter has pulled out of the contest for Fremantle. This will [leave] it to Hedges and Watson to down the co-unionist candidate. Perhaps you did not know that Holman is a member of the disgruntled council of action which is affiliated with the Moscow revolutionaries. It is true that the workers of the east are deserting the council; but that does not alter the fact that Holman had gone the whole hog for the German-made conspiracy against British industry and survival."

Plaintiff gave evidence that he and his son offered themselves for service in the Great War; but were rejected, and his daughter endeavoured to enlist as a nurse. Witness also took the platform in support of conscription.

The case stands part heard.[54]

The next day, Thursday 18 October 1923, Melbourne's daily *The Argus* carried a similar report under the heading *Union Official Sues Newspaper*.[55] *The Brisbane Courier* also got into the action, reporting from Perth on 16 October under the headline 'Libel Action. Election Sequel. Union Secretary Sues Newspaper' that Mr Holman considered his reputation had been damaged by the libellous claim that he was a Communist supporter.[56] As with the initial reports of the case, this article emphasised that Jack Holman had proffered as evidence of his unquestioned loyalty to King and country the fact that he and a son and daughter had all offered themselves for war service but had been rejected. For the twenty-first century reader, the foregrounding of his nationalism and loyalty provides a glimpse of the abhorrence with which Communist sympathies were regarded in Western Australian society at that time.

So controversial was this case that *The West Australian* of Friday 19 October 1923 ran a long and detailed article entitled 'Holman Libel Claim: Third Day's Hearing: An Editor's View', in which an exchange between Mr W. Dwyer, lawyer for Holman, and Alfred Thomas Chandler, editor of *The Sunday Times*, was outlined. The Supreme Court debate as recorded in this article centred around whether or not Chandler meant to defame Jack Holman by calling him a Communist, and the relationship between avowed Communists, trade unions and the Australian Labor Party. Precisely ninety years later, it's impossible not to be fascinated by the discussion of the libellous nature of being called a Communist. As revealed in the following excerpt from that Supreme Court debate, Mr Dwyer's argument that, in the popular imagination, Communists were guilty of *advocating the overthrow of Parliamentary Government*, was by implication a self-evident horror:

> *His Honour asked, what is the harm in calling a man a Communist? Mr. Dwyer said that if the word were construed in the dictionary sense the use of it would not be libellous, but the "Sunday Times", as its articles indicated, used it in a different sense which meant a good deal more.*
>
> *"He means a Nihilist, anarchist, of some other 'ist'?" his Honour suggested.*
>
> *Mr. Dwyer said that the word as generally accepted meant more than the dictionary meaning. It meant a man advocating the overthrow of Parliamentary Government.*

This same account of the Supreme Court debate examined in some detail the extent to which the Trades Union Congress of 1923 and its Council of Action could be seen to have been affiliated with Communism:

> *Cross-examination proceeded on the subject of the Melbourne Trades Union Congress. "Conference on two occasions," Mr. Dwyer put it, "threw out resolutions that would overthrow the authority of Parliament." "Yes," witness returned, "but they adopted the revolutionary preamble."*
>
> *Asked what were his grounds for asserting the affiliation*

of the Council of Action with "Moscow revolutionaries," witness cited "the affirmation of the revolutionary preamble at the Melbourne Congress at which the Council of Action was appointed": the fact that on each of the two councils there were declared Communists – Messers. Garden and Howie – both of whom visited Moscow: and the statement, already quoted, from "Smith's Weekly" [of 11 November 1922, in which Mr A. C. Willis, secretary of the Council of Action, was quoted as saying that at the Congress "Communists were to join up with the ALP"].

The witness was still in the box when the court adjourned till this morning.[57]

The case was still being reported on Saturday 19 October 1923 in the Adelaide *Advertiser*. Mr Philip Collier, leader of the Labor opposition in Western Australia, spoke in Holman's defence, so reinforcing the public perception that Communists were traitors deserving of condemnation, and strongly arguing that neither Jack Holman nor the Labor Party was aligned with them.

‡

May Holman knew her father's view on the need to be distant from the radicalism of Communists. But Jack Holman was now dead and his daughter was a parliamentarian in his stead. She might be taking on his seat, but her tactics were her own. She would chart her own path. In her first couple of terms in parliament it seems she embodied Labor philosophies and political stances. As we have noted, in the mid-1920s when she entered the parliament she might well have been a man, her father's son rather than his beloved daughter.

But later, in the 1930s, after her horizons were widened by European travel and international experience, and after the rupture caused by the terrible hardships of the Depression in the early 1930s, we see a new sense of independence emerge in May

Holman's political views. In this period of her life she crossed paths often with Katharine Susannah Prichard,[58] and found her fascination with Russia's social and educational policies to be thought-provoking, at times challenging. She was especially fascinated by the notion that the promotion of pacifism in schools could be adopted as public policy.[59] A deep respect for Katharine Susannah Prichard, in combination with a respect for the views of women she had met at the League of Nations meeting in Geneva in 1930, would perhaps begin to explain May Holman's outspoken defence of freedom of speech and freedom of political allegiance in the 1930s, when Communism was on the brink of being outlawed, and when most Labor parliamentarians were afraid to speak in defence of such freedoms. Hansard records her saying to the parliament in 1932: *I understand there is now a possibility of the setting up of a reserve police force to deal with these terrible Communists. But I say the people of this State, when unemployed and hungry and suffering unjust conditions, should not be characterised as Communists merely because they kick and refuse to be treated like dogs.*[60] Further, in the lead-up to the Second World War in the late 1930s, May Holman held to what she called the *Great Peace Ideal* and opposed conscription: not always a popular stance within her beloved Labor Party, but a stance she took nevertheless. Was she influenced in these views by an ongoing respect and admiration for the pacifism of Katharine Susannah Prichard?

We know that Katharine Susannah Prichard emerged as a leader of the radical left in Perth and in the late 1930s gathered a group of intelligent women around her – Margaret Green, Irene Greenwood, Jean Beadle – to establish the Modern Women's Club in Perth in May, 1938.[61] We know, too, that May Holman became a deeply respected leader of Labor women, but this does not explain her independence of thought and action in the 1930s. Perhaps it is enough to argue that the very presence of the more radical but widely respected Katharine Susannah Prichard in Perth made it possible for May Holman as a young woman in parliament to remain fearless in her determination to fight injustice for workers and for other oppressed groups wherever she found it. The meeting in the tearoom in West Perth that we imagined would have been at the very beginning of May Holman's life as a parliamentarian. If she were to seek womanly support for her parliamentary career, she would certainly have to seek it outside the House. She was to remain the only woman in the parliament in Western Australia for the next eleven years until the election of the conservative Florence Cardell-Oliver to the Western Australian Legislative Assembly in 1936. Miss Holman's long stint as a woman member of parliament was as unusual as her initial election to the parliament itself. In 1935 she was celebrated widely as being the only woman ever to have served a decade in parliament not just in Australia but indeed in the British Empire.[62]

May Holman remained the only Labor woman in the Western Australian parliament until her sudden death in 1939. The issues she campaigned on – education reform, health reform, occupational health and safety reform in the mills and timber industry – were issues that affected all phases of the daily lives of Western Australian citizens. She remained passionate about ensuring the health, comfort and wellbeing of the men, women and children in her electorate throughout her parliamentary career. As a reformist politician, it seems, she had few aspirations to grandeur. Hers was a temperate, practical idealism. People respected her for her hard work, her generosity, her willingness to engage fully in the worlds of the people she represented in the parliament.

But wait: this picture of her is altogether too serious. Far from being unequivocally earnest and restrained, May Holman had a warm and vivacious personality for which she was widely admired. We've already noted her style as she swept into the chamber of the House to be sworn in as the Member for Forrest in July 1925. Add to this a certain *je ne sais quoi* – a presence, a sense of fun, a love of frivolity and of performance, all of which we'll see more fully as we explore her life as a young adult during the Great War and afterwards – and we begin to understand the affection she generated in the hearts of those who knew her. As we shall see, her sudden death in 1939 left a devastated circle of family and close friends and caused a bewildered grief in the wider community for which nobody seemed prepared.

The seasoned politician: Miss May Holman arriving for the opening of Parliament, 1936.

CHAPTER 2
'I CAN ONLY SAY THAT HER LIFE WAS MAGNIFICENT ...'

May Holman's public popularity seemed to reach new heights in the lead-up to the 1939 state election. She had been in the parliament for almost fourteen years; she had conducted an energetic and strenuous election campaign and was *popularly tipped as certain to receive Ministerial honours*[1] following her re-election. But on Friday 17 March 1939, on the eve of the election, she was involved in a horrific car accident in her electorate. She and her sister Iris Demasson were on their way to one last political meeting in the small settlement of Brookhampton. Iris was driving. Their car skidded in loose gravel after rounding a hazardous bend. The steering rod broke. The car continued on for about forty yards, ran off the road and overturned when it hit the bank of a drain six feet deep. Iris was thrown clear but May was pinned underneath the wreckage. Her injuries were severe: she *suffered fractures of both legs, an arm and several ribs, and internal injuries.*[2] Both women were taken by ambulance to St John of God Hospital in Bunbury.

The accident was widely reported in the local and national press[3] and for the next three days detailed updates were given on Miss Holman's condition. She was on the *danger list*;[4] *in a critical condition* though slightly better after *a fair night*;[5] *much weaker* after a bad night;[6] and *so gravely injured that she has not yet enquired as to whether her constituents re-elected her.*[7] On Tuesday 21 March 1939 *The Daily News* reported that *In spite of her desperate condition ... Miss May Holman smiled her pleasure when told yesterday that she had won the Forrest seat again.*

'She seemed to be waiting for something all the time,' said her brother, Mr. W. Holman today. 'When she was told that she had been elected she smiled wanly and seemed satisfied.'[8] On the afternoon of Monday 20 March 1939, just three hours after the declaration of her re-election to state parliament, she died. She was forty-five years old.

The outpouring of grief that occurred across the nation was unprecedented in Labor circles. At first the newspapers carried single-paragraph announcements of her death, staccato whimpers of disbelief. It was as if even the press were too stunned to do more than report its own shock. And then came the deluge: long, lingering tributes to the life and work of May Holman began flowing in before her body was buried.

But who was the woman they were mourning? Why the tidal wave of grief at her passing? If we look at the tributes and eulogies, remembering that their sentimentality was characteristic of the writing of the time, we are presented with a complex and brilliantly talented woman of charm, grace and fierce loyalty to the Labor cause.

One of the first and most deeply felt public statements was from Labor politician John Curtin, then leader of the opposition in the Commonwealth parliament. On Tuesday 21 March 1939, *The West Australian* carried the speech he had given on the previous evening when he heard of her death. Under the headline 'Labour Was Proud of Her', John Curtin's speech held traces of the shock that he and others still felt at the loss of Miss Holman:

> *Realisation seems impossible. All of us seem stunned by a sense of overwhelming loss. Miss Holman was Australian Labour's pioneer woman parliamentarian. But she was far more than that. There was not a phase of our work which she did not share and strengthen. The Labour movement was proud of her. As organiser, persuader, friend and comrade her name became a household word. In timber camps, in the small mill towns, no less than in the great cities there are sad hearts tonight. I can only say that her life was magnificent;*

it was gallant and gracious and every day had its good deed. Her memory will have a precious place in the annals of our cause.⁹

On that same day, Tuesday 21 March, Brisbane's *Worker* carried a sympathy statement from Mr C. G. Fallon, Branch Secretary of the Australian Workers Union and President of the Federal ALP:

It is with a sense of profound sadness that I received this morning the news of the tragic death of Miss May Holman, M.L.A. The circumstances surrounding Miss Holman's

Westralian Worker, 24 March 1939.

death ... are poignantly sorrowful, followed, as they are, by her signal victory at the polls, and the sense of loss which Western Australia and the Labor Movement feels is intensified by the knowledge that this cultured woman had not yet reached her prime, and gave promise of so much splendid work in the cause of humanity in the future. Miss Holman was a brilliant speaker, a woman of great cultural attainments, and possessed a profound knowledge of the Labor Movement and Australia's requirements, and a personality of charm and distinction which will be greatly missed by all sections of the community, and particularly the Labor Movement, which she loved and which she served so well. I extend my deepest sympathy to her bereaved relatives and friends in their tragic hour of sorrow.[10]

The Western Australian premier, John Willcock, newly returned to office in the state election, also gave a heartfelt tribute to May Holman on the evening she died. His words, recorded in *The Daily News* of 21 March, draw attention to the deep and long-term connections amongst Labor families, connections abiding over several generations:

'It is difficult amply to express my regret at the loss of Miss May Holman both as a stalwart of the Labor Party and a personal friend. I knew the Holman family 40 years ago in Cue, where they were in the forefront of everything which tended to bring success to the Labor movement. May Holman was a little girl then. But I've seen her carry on the traditions of the family with conspicuous ability. With the death of her father, by representing Labor in the State Parliament, the line of succession fell naturally on her shoulders. We all know the wonderful way any humanitarian effort met with ready response from the late Miss Holman and also the way she was always prepared to take her part in the leadership in work for the uplift of the people. The late

> Miss Holman has an Australia-wide, in fact a world-wide, reputation, having represented her country in international conferences. Her death will be mourned by thousands of personal friends and tens of thousands of others who had not the privilege of knowing her personally, but who admired her work.' Mr. Willcock said he had received literally hundreds of telegrams of sympathy from all over the State and Australia.[11]

The West Australian of 22 March 1939 carried an elaboration of Premier Willcock's tribute:

> Today I have received many messages of sympathy and regret from all parts of Australasia, including telegrams from the Premier of Queensland (Mr. Forgan Smith), the Leader of the Opposition in South Australia (Mr. Richards), the Minister for Labour in New Zealand (Mr. P. Webb), the Speaker of the Victorian Legislative Assembly (Mr. T. Tunnecliffe), Senator J. M. Sheehan (Victoria), the Mayor of Kalgoorlie (Mr. Moore), and from the Democratic Women's League of South Australia.

That same article in The West Australian acknowledged the grief being expressed across the nation in Labor circles:

> Grief over the untimely death of Miss May Holman, M.L.A., was widespread in the Labour movement, said the secretary of the State Executive of the Australian Labour Party (Mr. P. J. Trainer) yesterday. During the day, Mr Trainer said, he had received scores of telegrams of condolence from all parts of Western Australia, and from all States of the Commonwealth.[12]

As the news spread, from around the country came reports

of meetings that began in silence to acknowledge the tragic end of the life of May Holman. Imagine that: in Trades Halls and timber mills, in factories and private houses, in arbitration courts and council chambers and schools, groups of working men and women bowed their heads to remember her, before going on with their business. Some groups went further and postponed their meetings in order to give participants time to grieve.[13]

One group devastated by their loss was the WA Timber Workers' Union. On 24 March their secretary, Mr G. Foley, captured the personal nature of her political commitment when he wrote:

> *In the tragic loss of May Holman, the timber workers, the Labor Party, and the State have been bereft of a great personality. Accomplished, brainy and cultured, she was possessed of an abundance of energy that only a burning enthusiasm for a Cause could inspire.*
>
> *From the foundation of a grand Labor tradition, May's inherent qualities were ever directed to the promotion of those ideals she loved – the cause of the worker, the cause of women, education, and the lot of the bush folk. Possessed of an organizing ability far beyond ordinary standards, the diversity of interests she successfully undertook was amazing. Withal, she was a radiant personality, loved life and remained always a charming lady, girlish, yet womanly, cheerful, though carrying the troubles of others in addition to her own full share.*
>
> *Old timber workers sought her because they loved her, and were proud of her – she was a daughter to them all. In her cultured way she rose far above the little vanities that success sometimes brings. With equal grace she could talk over their problems with the workers in the bush camp, or act as hostess on a big social occasion. The bulk of her electorate was industrial, and yet I know of no man who could represent the workers more ably.*

> Miss Holman spent a noble, useful life in the cause of the people. She will long be remembered.[14]

On 21 March, the day after her death, *The West Australian* carried a long and detailed eulogy titled 'Miss Holman's Death. Car Smash Proves Fatal'. If we read this carefully, we uncover not only the chronology of her life but also some of the reasons she was so widely admired.

IN HER FATHER'S FOOTSTEPS

Miss Mary Alice Holman, who was more generally known as Miss 'May' Holman, was born at Broken Hill (New South Wales) on July 18, 1893, and she came to this State with her mother when only two years old, her father, the late Mr. J. B. Holman, having arrived almost two years earlier. The eldest of a family of eleven, she was educated at a convent in Cue, where they made their home, and later at the Sacred Heart High School, Perth. Her education completed, she became a typist at the Perth Trades Hall and, in her leisure hours, she continued her musical studies, attaining the degrees of L.AB. for singing, and L.AB., L.T.C.L, and A.T.C.L. for piano. Her musical ability was quickly recognised and she became greatly in demand at concerts for her impersonations at the piano and her singing. During the war she used her talents freely both to entertain invalid soldiers and in raising money to relieve war distress. In 1918 she became assistant secretary to the then State branch of the Australian Timber Workers' Union, and it was the ability she displayed in this position, coupled with the popularity which she quickly earned for herself, which paved the way for her entry into Parliament. Her father, whose name will always be remembered as one of the outstanding men of the early days of the Labour Party in this State, had long been prominent in the timber workers' organisation and was a member of Parliament

> *for various terms between 1901 and his death in 1925. It was only natural that the timber workers should see in his daughter a fitting successor to his seat and she had little difficulty in gaining it in 1925.*
>
> *When she won the seat Miss Holman achieved the distinction of being the second woman, and the first woman representing the Labour Party, to sit in an Australian Parliament. In the succeeding years she had no trouble in retaining her seat. She was not a frequent speaker in the House, but when she did rise her words were listened to with the closest attention as she invariably spoke upon subjects of which she had a thorough knowledge, particularly the development of the South-West and the timber industry, and questions related to women's interests. Less than a year after she entered Parliament she successfully sponsored the Timber Industry Regulation Bill and she surprised many members with the knowledge she showed of the industry and the calm and clear way in which she presented the facts. Her sincerity earned her the respect and esteem of her fellow members on both sides of the House and her untimely death will be deplored by them all.*

Under the headline 'Work for Many Organisations' the article continues:

> *Miss Holman was always deeply loyal to the Labour Party and her outstanding services to the party were recognised in 1933, when she had the distinction of being elected as secretary to the Parliamentary Labour Party, a post she held until the time of her death. She was delegate to several State A.L.P. congresses and to the interstate A.L.P. congress at Canberra in 1930; past-president and secretary to the Perth Labour Women's Union; and Labour representative on the Adult Education Board. She helped to form the Labour Women's Central Executive and the Labour Women's Interstate Executive; and was first*

president of the Labour Women's Central Executive of Western Australia from 1927 to 1930 and secretary in 1932–33. She was the representative of the Labour women on the Economic Council and a director of the "Westralian Worker" newspaper.

In 1930 she was appointed substitute delegate for the Commonwealth to the League of Nations Assembly at Geneva, but her influence in this sphere was diminished by ill-health, which forced her to spend much of the following year in hospital. Miss Holman was also keenly interested in the West Australian Federation of Parents and Citizens' Associations and she was general president at the time of her death, having filled the position for a number of years.

On the death of her mother, to whom she was very devoted, Miss Holman became the guardian of three young sisters. As one who knew her well said: "She was a splendid woman who deserved all she attained, for both in her public and private life she aimed at very high ideals and was a very courageous and womanly woman."

She is survived by three brothers [John, Ted and Bill Holman] and five sisters [Maude Corboy, Winnie Burge, Iris Demasson, Eileen Thompson and Sheila Holman.] She will be buried in the Karrakatta Cemetery tomorrow.[15]

‡

May Holman's funeral was held on Wednesday 22 March 1939, two days after she died. A requiem mass was held at St Mary's Cathedral in Victoria Square, Perth, at 9 o'clock in the morning, and the funeral cortege left from the Cathedral at 3.15 pm, arriving at the Karrakatta Cemetery at 4 pm.

Picture, if you will, hundreds of people crammed into St Mary's Cathedral for the mass in the morning, and hundreds more spilling out into the gardens.[16] By the afternoon, huge crowds had assembled to watch the funeral procession. This was no ordinary funeral. Working people had downed tools and had

'I CAN ONLY SAY THAT HER LIFE WAS MAGNIFICENT ...'

spontaneously flocked to the city to attend. Men and women had poured in from the timber country, from the Goldfields, from the Wheatbelt and from the farming country to the south, travelling in whatever vehicle was available.[17] In an unprecedented display of grief and affection, crowds six people deep lined the streets along the forty-five minute route to Karrakatta Cemetery, bowing their heads as the half-mile-long cortege passed. Thousands more had travelled by train from the city to be present at her graveside.[18]

At the cemetery there was scarcely a union in the country that was not represented by at least several members, and women and girls were legion. Everywhere, as the procession passed, one could hear hushed whispers. *The usual funeral is a silent affair, but these mourners seemed so overwhelmed that they had to talk about the great loss they all had sustained.*[19] In a deeply moving gesture, as the cortege made its way slowly to the graveside, the call went out to Labor women to identify themselves, and hundreds of women stepped out from the crowd to walk beside the hearse and mourning coaches.[20] After the interment, hundreds and hundreds of wreaths were laid.[21] The crowd lingered, reluctant to turn its back on this momentous day.

Almost six decades later, the image of *hundreds and hundreds of wreaths heaped high* was still carried by May Holman's niece, Kathleen Corboy, who was a child at the time. She remembered that she and her younger brother were taken to the cemetery the day after the funeral by their mother Maude (May's next sister) to see the wreaths. She was very aware that her Aunty May was special and was deeply respected and loved.[22]

The funeral was widely acknowledged as being extraordinary, and it was hailed as *a people's tribute to a great woman.*[23] Detailed reports were immediately carried by local city and regional newspapers. A sample of the eloquent statements of admiration and regret was carried by the *Mirror* of 25 March 1939. Under the heading 'A Courageous Fighter. A Staunch Friend', the statement reads:

> When the late Miss May Holman M.L.A. was laid to rest in the Karrakatta Cemetery this week, there were widespread expressions of regret that death had claimed a talented woman who had devoted years of unselfish service to others.
>
> Brilliantly accomplished on the musical side, deeply imbued with Labor principles, possessed of a womanly intuition and sympathy wherever there might come to her notice reports of cases of distress, and boasting a heart virtually as big as one of those magnificent forest giants in the timber country she loved so deeply, May Holman was a courageous fighter for the under-dogs of the community, a staunch friend, and a tireless worker.
>
> Amongst all shades of political opinion she commanded the highest respect, and the many spheres of community life represented at the graveside mirrored the general regret that an accident had, in its fatal consequences, robbed the State of a great woman![24]

Her funeral was still being discussed weeks after it happened. On March 30, a week after the funeral, under the headline 'Last Respects', the *Western Mail* carried a large photograph of *mourners preceding the hearse from the main entrance of the Karrakatta Cemetery at the burial of Miss May Holman on March 22.*[25] Almost three weeks later, a newsreel of the event was broadcast at the Ambassador Theatre in Perth.[26]

This was not a state funeral – only ministers of the Crown were entitled to such formal recognition, and Miss Holman had not yet made it to the rank of minister – but it had the trappings of one. May Holman's official status as a public figure was explicitly stated in the funeral notice: *The Friends of the late Miss May Holman of 3 Ida-street, Bassendean, and Member of the Legislative Assembly for Forrest, are respectfully invited to follow her remains to the place of her interment, the Roman Catholic Cemetery, Karrakatta.*[27] The attendance list certainly read like that of a state funeral. On the afternoon of the funeral *The Daily News* ran the headline 'State's Last

Tribute to Miss Holman', in which it reported that *a representative of the Lieutenant-Governor, in addition to the Premier, the Leader of the Federal Opposition and the President of the State Arbitration Court were among the pall-bearers at the funeral of the late Miss May Holman, M.L.A. this afternoon; and eight women representing the Labour women's organisations in this State formed a guard of honour* outside the Cathedral. The article named all pallbearers and their official capacities: Colonel C. H. E. Manning representing the lieutenant-governor; Premier Willcock; Mr John Curtin, then leader of the federal opposition; Mr Dwyer, president of the State Arbitration Court; Mr Millington, the minister for works; Mr Wilson, member for Collie; Mr Trainer, the secretary of the state executive of the Australian Labor Party; Mr P. J. Mooney, the secretary of the metropolitan council of the ALP; Mr H. Sweeney, the president of the WA Timber Workers' Union; Mr G. Foley, the secretary of the WA Timber Workers' Union; Mr O. Walters from the *Westralian Worker*; and Mr A. W. Dedman. The article also named the women who formed the guard of honour: Mrs F. Mason, Mrs Carter, Mrs H. Styants, Mrs J. Curtin, Mrs P. J. Trainer, Mrs J. Kent, Miss Molly Holmes, and Miss E. Hooton. The premier, Mr Willcock, was reported as saying that *many additional messages of sympathy were received by the Government today from this and the Eastern States, revealing the esteem in which the late Miss Holman was held.*[28] In listing with such attention to detail the names and positions of those who attended, it was as if the newspaper were according recognition of the national importance of the occasion on behalf of their community of readers.

Next day, on Thursday 23 March 1939, *The West Australian* ran a long article headed 'The Late Miss Holman' in which, in addition to remarking on the large crowds providing a *striking demonstration of the affection and esteem in which the late Miss May Holman* was held, it named the pallbearers, the members of the guard of honour, the chief mourners (May's sisters and brothers and their spouses and her aunt) and went on then to list specific members of the large attendance, which included *parliamentarians, members of the civil service, professional men, and representatives of employees and employers' organisations.* The list of mourners reads like a *Who's Who* of Perth public life in 1939: in addition to the premier and the chief secretary and ministers of agriculture, mines, and railways, parliamentarians included the leaders of the opposition and the National Party, senators, and members of the Legislative Council and of the Legislative Assembly. In addition, the clerks of those two bodies, the sergeant-at-arms, and the chief Hansard reporter were present. Other elected public figures included the lord mayor of Perth and the mayor of Fremantle. Amongst the civil servants were the auditor-general, the chairman of the Agriculture Bank, the public service commissioner, the under-secretary for works, the under-treasurer, the crown solicitor, the superintendent of technical education, the conservator of forests, the under-secretary for water supply, the workshops manager of the WA Government Railways, the chairmen of the WA Transport Board and the Perth Hospital Board, the director of public works, the industrial magistrate, the inspector of factories, and representatives from the Arbitration Court, the Adult Education Board, the Teachers' College, the Education Department, the Electoral Department, the Department of Labour, the Sawmillers' Association, the WA Employers' Federation, the WA Fire Brigades, the Police Department, the Wyalkatchem and Bassendean Road Boards, the Licensing Branch, the Midland Railway Workshops and the Lotteries Commission. From the broader community there were representatives from the Fremantle Trades Hall, the Australian Journalists' Association, the *Westralian Worker* office, the Primary Producers' Association, the Parents and Citizens' Federation, the University Labor Club, the Women's Christian Temperance Union, the Sacred Heart High School Parents and Friends Association, the Old Aquinians, the Braille Society, the National Council of Women, the Labor Women's Organisations, the Returned Soldiers' League, the Amateur Swimming Association, the Perth Life-saving Club, the Trotting Association, the United Ancient Order of Druids, the Australian Natives' Association, the Pensioners'

League, the Dominions League, the Young Labor League, and *numerous trade unions and several business houses, and well as a large crowd of private citizens.*[29]

The relentless detail in these reports attests to the desire to ensure that the breadth and depth of Miss Holman's influence be acknowledged. There is no doubt that May Holman herself would have been gratified at the notion that her life had affected so many. As one of her close associates observed, *One felt that nothing would have pleased May Holman more in life than to know that so many people understood that her mind was set on being of real service to humanity.*[30]

On Sunday 26 March, *The Sunday Times* in Perth wrote of the *widespread sorrow and regret felt* at her death, of her *varied and colourful career*, of the *thousands of people* she had been in contact with during her political life and of the many *in needy circumstances* she had personally assisted.[31] This article specifically pays tribute to her organising abilities:

> *Many organisations with which she has worked in the capacity of president or secretary will sadly miss her inspiration to their activities, and the understanding which she always manifested in administrative matters. She was president of the Parents and Citizens' Association, and president of the Sacred Heart High School Old Girls' Association, at which school she completed her education. She was also president of the Perth Labor Women's Organisation, and secretary of the Labor Women's Central Executive ... and was conductor and secretary of the W.A. Labor Choral Union.*

Perhaps the most deeply felt and insightful comment comes from the *Westralian Worker* of Friday 31 March 1939. May had a long association with this newspaper and sat on its board at the time of her death. The details suggest that the writer had an intimate knowledge of May's inner life:

> *A great inspirational spirit has passed from us into the unknowable, and we are left with an indescribable sense of loss.*
>
> *May Holman was above all intensely a human being. She thrilled to life's joys and walked bravely through some of its darkest sorrows. She had a deep realisation of the brevity and uncertainty of our tiny circlings here, and frequently, in different ways, voiced the conviction that we cannot afford to be other than kind to each other.*[32]

Twenty-first century readers of these eulogies will be struck first by their sentimentality, and next perhaps by some of the telling observations made here. If we peep through the cracks in the smooth surface of sentimental gloss we glimpse the specificity of a woman whose life had touched the lives of so many. She was clearly recognised as a crucial figure in the Labor Family. She was trusted to carry on the work of her esteemed father to such an extent that, as John Curtin said, it was *only natural* that, in 1925, she take his seat in parliament – an extraordinary observation, surely, when only one other woman had ever been elected to an Australian parliament before her. If the sense underpinning these eulogies gives us access to the feeling that propelled them, the picture that emerges is of a woman very much of the people, but simultaneously more than that. She was admired for her capacity to rise above the drudgery of daily life and to bring sparkle, wit, and glamour into the lives of those around her. But we learn that her own life has its *darkest sorrows* too: as we will discover later in uncovering the course of her life story, these darkest sorrows related both to the emotional turmoil generated by complicated relationships with each of her deeply admired parents, and also to recurring bouts of physically debilitating illness that dogged her throughout her life.[33] But in spite of these sorrows, or perhaps because of them, she was known as a woman who brought courage to adversity, and compassion to the struggles of others. Her talent for music, for performance, above all for organising people and events and for galvanising people into action, positioned her as a leader in the circles she mixed in. Perhaps the most telling observation made in the eulogies is the one made by her friend and colleague at the *Westralian Worker* where she insists on the need for kindness to one another. Without doubt, kindness and genuine concern for the wellbeing of others in a public figure makes a deep impression. In this isolated corner of the continent, kindness seems to have been the currency of many activist women in the decades during and after May Holman's lifetime: Katharine Susannah Prichard was renowned for it;[34] Irene Greenwood[35] and Joan Williams[36] actively promoted its value to the women they worked with; Elsie Gare[37] was propelled by it. Clearly, May Holman was imbued with it. It's no wonder people saw her as much more than a conscientious politician.

In addition to local expressions of sorrow, grief and regret, tributes flowed in from across the nation. On March 22, the Melbourne paper *The Argus* cited Miss Jean Daley, secretary of the Labour Women's Interstate Executive, who declared:

> *The death of Miss May Holman M.L.A. of Western Australia, has caused an irreparable loss to the Labour movement. The creation of the* [interstate] *executive was due largely to her influence and ability, and the inter-dominion conference of Labour women, to be held in London, originated from a suggestion made by Miss Holman. Miss Daley said Miss Holman had a charming personality, and not only was she a gifted musician but she was also a splendid organiser.*[38]

In Adelaide, the *Advertiser* of 22 March noted that:

> *Deep regret was expressed in Trades Hall and Labor circles yesterday at the death of Miss May Holman, Labor M.L.A. of Western Australia. Telegrams of sympathy were sent to her relatives by the State A.L.P. branch, State Parliamentary*

Labor Party, Labor Women's Central Organising Committee and several trade unions.[39]

On 21 March the *Border Watch* from Mount Gambier acknowledged that *news of her death was received with deep sorrow*.[40] Similar articles were carried by the Burnie *Advocate*[41] and the Launceston *Examiner* in Tasmania,[42] the Broken Hill *Barrier Miner*,[43] the *Sydney Morning Herald*,[44] the *Geraldton Guardian and Express*,[45] the Hobart *Mercury*,[46] the Brisbane *Courier-Mail*,[47] *The Townsville Daily Bulletin*,[48] the *Kalgoorlie Miner*,[49] and the Lismore *Northern Star*.[50]

A more personal lament came from the members of her old school, Sacred Heart in Perth:

[Miss Holman] *was proud of her School and her School was proud of her... She had a radiant personality, loved life and remained always a charming lady, girlish yet womanly – cheerful, though carrying the troubles of others in addition to her own full share. Miss May Holman is an abiding memory, an inspiration. May she rest in peace.*[51]

On Saturday 1 April 1939, almost a fortnight after her death, *The Australian Women's Weekly* ran an article that hailed May Holman as glorious in death, and painted her as the quintessential ideal of the charming, domesticated, intelligent Australian woman in life.[52] The article was headed 'May Holman's triumph at hour of death', and subtitled 'Moving drama of woman who was elected six times to Parliament'. It begins with a tone that's more dramatic than that of the eulogies from the newspapers: *This is the simple, moving story of May Alice Holman, the girl from Broken Hill, elected to the West Australian Parliament for the sixth time last week – one hour before she died*; and could well stand accused of inaccuracies, hyperbole and, in parts, of plagiarism.

However, one of the insightful features of this article, perhaps in response to the all-female readership of this magazine, is its vivid articulation of the ways May Holman interacted with her electorate, and the associated implication that her womanliness made this kind of engagement possible:

> *No member of Parliament has ever been more closely identified with the life of an electorate.*
>
> *Did a timber man's daughter go to Perth to work, Miss Holman kept a sisterly eye on her. Did his wife want to match a pattern or shade in Perth, May would gladly undertake the task. If a timber man wanted advice about improved conditions, more pay, or a new job, he never hesitated to go along to her.*
>
> *She sang at their concerts, spoke at their gatherings, and went right into their lives and hearts.*
>
> *She had an amazing grasp of industrial problems, yet she could discuss recipes, babies, and house-work with the housewives in her electorate.*
>
> *Once in an interview she said that the woman Member of Parliament has an advantage over the man Member.*
>
> *"A woman Member can walk straight into the kitchen to see her constituents," she said, "but the man has to sit in the front room."* [53]

Perhaps it's this evocation of the informality and genuine sincerity of May Holman's engagement with the people in her electorate that holds the key to her success as a politician. She entered their kitchens; they took her into their hearts.

News of her death was registered, too, in the international arena. On 29 May 1939 the *Recorder* in Port Pirie carried a letter of condolence from the International Labour Office in Geneva to the Western Australian Branch of the Australian Labor Party. The letter states that the International Labour Office learned with deep regret of her passing, and proceeds:

> The late Miss Holman was a staunch supporter of the International Labor Organisation and of the ideals for which it stands. For many years she was in touch with the office on industrial problems, particularly those dealt with by the correspondence committee on women's work, of which she was an active and valued member. We are also aware of the part she played in her own country in the improvement of labor and social conditions, including the promotion of legislation for the protection of workers in the timber industry.[54]

May Holman remained in the hearts of her colleagues and constituents and communities long after her death. Her brother Ted was elected in her place to the seat of Forrest in the by-election that followed. Much was made of the line of Holman succession in the seat of Forrest which dated from 1923 when John Barkell Holman first held that seat. When the seventeenth parliament sat for the first time on 3 August 1939, a posy of violets wrapped with purple ribbon was placed on the bench in front of May Holman's old seat in the Legislative Assembly chamber at Parliament House to honour her memory, and that seat was formally allocated to her brother.[55]

On 8 August 1939 the Legislative Assembly agreed to a motion moved by the deputy premier Mr Millington, recording its sense of loss at the death of Miss Holman. Members stood in silence while the motion was put. The motion noted that *Her life was so bright and of such value to the community that it was a cause of very great sorrow and enduring regret that it should be so cut off… She was the friend of everyone and everyone's friend.* The leader of the opposition said that she *had endeared herself to all in the House*, and the leader of the National Party said that the *tragic accident had cast a gloom over the entire community*.[56] That gloom and sense of community loss was invoked in July that year in a more popular forum by *The West Australian* newspaper's gossip columnist, 'Hepzibah', when she announced that the July wedding of May's youngest sister Sheila to the popular and well-known footballer

Tom Moiler, would be *a quiet family affair, as the former head of the Holman family since their parents' death, the late Miss May Holman M.L.A., is still too poignantly missed.*⁵⁷

In the months following Miss Holman's death, the communities whose lives she had touched so deeply honoured her memory in a number of specific and moving ways. At the annual general meeting of the Sacred Heart Old Girls' Association in April 1939 it was announced that arrangements had been made for a life-sized portrait of the late Miss Holman to be hung in the school's entrance hall, and for the school's new swimming pool to be named in her honour.⁵⁸ When Western Australian Labor Women met for the Fourteenth Annual Conference at Trades Hall in Perth on Tuesday 26 September 1939, a portrait of May Holman, decked with purple pansies, was prominently displayed on the chairman's table.⁵⁹ At some time in the months following her death the Labor Women's Organisation decided to raise funds for a children's memorial ward at the Dwellingup Hospital in the timber country of the Forrest electorate, dedicated to May Holman. *The West Australian* reported on a bridge and rummy party being held at the North Perth home of May's dear friend Molly Holmes in late October 1939 to raise funds for the new hospital ward;⁶⁰ and a month later it reported that the ALP Labor Choral Union had travelled by bus from Perth to Holyoake in the timber country to sing at a social and dance, again to raise funds for the May Holman Children's Memorial Ward at Dwellingup Hospital.⁶¹

In the cynical twenty-first century, it is perhaps difficult to imagine that a groundbreaking woman politician could be so treasured by her community. To a certain extent one can expect that the sudden death of any public figure will generate expressions of sorrow, shock, surprise. May's father, John Barkell Holman, for example, was respected by his Labor colleagues as a stalwart, a Labor fighter, a fierce advocate for the workers under his watch. On his death there were expressions of sorrow, of respect for his public works, of admiration for a life dedicated to the Labor cause. But the responses to May's own death go further than admiration. A funeral attended by thousands, an outpouring of grief at every turn: these are personal responses that surely attest to the depth of connection she forged with those around her. She emerges from the archives generated at the time of her death as that rare public figure who is deeply admired for her capacities and talents, and genuinely loved for the person she was.

Who exactly was May Holman? John Curtin had said that her life was *magnificent*; but others had referred to sorrows, and persistent ill-health, and distress when her younger siblings left home. Here surely is a complex personality. If we look beneath the shimmer of adoration we find a tangle of fascinating contradictions. Here is a woman who is intensely loyal and dignified, but also high-spirited and full of fun. She's clearly adores family, but remains Miss Holman until her death. She charts new territory for women in politics but eschews the feminist label. She works towards the creation of a new social order but denies she's a radical. She's widely admired for her immense energy and yet she spends months and months at a time bedridden. The wellbeing of children is her avowed propelling impulse, but she has no children of her own. She's hailed as a brilliant scholar yet is equally at home chatting over a cup of tea in the kitchens of the timber worker's families. She's a gifted musician but chooses politics over the stage. She's sophisticated and charming but takes simple holidays where she can go fishing. She is close to her mother yet makes no secret of her exasperation with her for her unreliability. She idolises her father yet in one memorable episode she's prepared to defy him. It's to that episode in the year of her twenty-first birthday that we now turn.

CHAPTER 3
HONOUR THY FATHER ...

Picture this: It's 18 July 1914 in Perth, Western Australia, and Mary Alice Holman, favourite eldest daughter of the Honourable John Barkell Holman MLA, is celebrating her twenty-first birthday with a party at McLeod's Hall in Grosvenor Road, Mt Lawley.[1] Everyone is here: all the old Labor families, the trade union officials, her father's parliamentary colleagues, her mother's Labor Women's committee, her aunts and uncles, her sisters and brothers, her workmates, her special friends. It's a grand turnout. The hall's bedecked with streamers, and trestle tables are laden with food. Little girls in party frocks and new hair ribbons squeal with delight as they slide recklessly across the slippery dance floor, dragging little boys behind them. Sturdy Labor women smooth their skirts and tidy their hair on the way from the kitchen into the hall, pausing to glance around the room to see who else has arrived.

In one corner, near the kitchen, men cluster about the bar. In another, there's the table piled high with birthday gifts. People have been generous, for everyone knows that May is the apple of her father's eye, and this event has been long planned. There's a buzz of excitement, abandonment almost. For once, they can forget all this talk of the war that they are told is looming in Europe. Besides, it's not every day that the Holmans throw a party for the world. The band starts up. May herself takes her seat at the piano on the stage. Her father beams with pride, shaking hands and slapping backs as he strides about the room. His May is a good girl, no doubt about that. She's loyal and charming, and talented to boot. The dance floor fills. The party's begun. Shy young men sidle up to pretty young women to ask for a dance, or hang about the door, smoking, waiting for courage to appear. Matrons prise their husbands from the bar for the Pride of Erin or the Gypsy Tap. The air is thick with laughter and good cheer.

Jack Holman is standing with a group of friends, leaning in to hear the words of a woman beside him. Then suddenly above the noise, a roar, then a shout. 'May, May! What's this I hear?' Jack Holman is alarmed, panicked almost. His eyes are wild, bewildered. 'What's this I hear May? Is it true?' He pushes through the crowd to the piano where May, ashen, stands to meet him. The whole room stops. 'Married? May? Married to Joe Gardiner? Tell me it's not true, girl.' May looks at him steadfastly and says in a clear strong voice, 'Yes, Father, it's true.' For a moment Jack Holman's body crumples. He looks winded. Then, with a bellow of rage, he turns on his heel, stumbles down the stairs of the stage, rushes to the doorway and returns with an axe. Women scream as he lifts it high above his head and smashes it into the table of birthday gifts. Again and again he brings it down. A jardinière shatters. The table sags drunkenly. Gifts clatter to the floor. Some of the children stare, wide-eyed and afraid; others whimper into a shocked silence. Who is this monster come to replace Uncle Jack? But he's not finished yet. 'Over my dead body,' he rages. 'I'll run him out of town!' Men rush to restrain him.

The party is over. So too is the two-month marriage of Mary Alice Holman to Joseph Peter Gardiner, parliamentarian, gambler, bachelor, family friend. And so too, is the stability of the Labor government, because Jack Holman does run Joe Gardiner out of town, and within a year Joe's seat of Roebourne is lost to the opposition and Labor's eight-year hold on power in the West under Premier Jack Scadden is over.

A secret marriage, a father enraged, a government brought down.

There are several versions of this story. In some versions,

Joe Gardiner himself is at the birthday party and flees the scene before Jack Holman kills him. In others, he's still up north in his electorate, waiting for the opportune moment to reappear and to fetch *the best little wife in the world*.[2] In most versions, Joe is a shadowy figure, considered unsuitable perhaps because he was a gambler and almost certainly because he was *much older* than May, *almost of the same generation as her father*. But in all versions, there's the axe, the shattered jardinière, and the terrified husband who is run out of town.

What these stories all omit is the preamble: although their marriage was clearly a shock to May's father, her association with Joe Gardiner was not. They had become engaged in January of that year.[3] Why, then, his very public rage at their secret marriage?

What we do know for certain is that Mary Alice Holman married Joseph Peter Gardiner on Saturday 9 May 1914 at the Perth Registry Office.[4] She was twenty years old, just two months short of her twenty-first birthday. He was twenty-seven (clearly *not* the same generation as her father). Five years later, on 3 September 1919, Mary Alice Gardiner of 616 Beaufort Street, Perth, petitioned Joseph Peter Gardiner of Melbourne, Victoria, in the Supreme Court of Western Australia to appear in a suit for *dissolution of marriage by reason of desertion for five years and upwards without cause*. In an affidavit issued the previous day, Mary Alice Gardiner had sworn that:

1. *At no time have I lived or cohabited with my said husband.*
2. *My said husband has never contributed in any way towards my support but upon enlisting with the AIF in Victoria about March 1916 he was obliged under military regulations to make an allotment in my favour.*
3. *My husband wilfully and continuously deserted me for a period of five years and upwards without just cause or excuse.*
4. *My said husband has lately returned to Victoria and is living in Melbourne.*

5. *No collusion or connivance exists between me and any other person.*

The case was undefended and on 2 December 1919 the court costs were paid by Joseph Peter Gardiner, the respondent. The following day a *decree nisi* was issued, and on 18 July 1920, a *decree absolute* was issued, meaning that the marriage was formally over.[5] The marriage was never discussed in the family, and May Holman remained single for the rest of her life.

Whatever possessed the young May Holman to marry in secret? Clearly, this one act cost her dearly. Although her marriage was dissolved five years later, she appeared to consider herself not free to marry again. Anecdote and archive combine to suggest that she was forced to choose between her father and her husband. But why was Jack Holman so enraged? What was the nature of his relationship with his daughter that he so fiercely insisted on her purity? Was May coerced into filing the affidavit that implied her sexual innocence? For the answers to some of these questions we can turn to an extensive report in *The West Australian* on 4 December 1919:

A SECRET MARRIAGE. PETITION FOR DIVORCE.
EX-MEMBER OF PARLIAMENT RESPONDENT.

Secretly married at the Perth Registry Office in May, 1914, the former member for Roebourne in the Legislative Assembly, Joseph Peter Gardiner, never lived with his wife, according to evidence related in the Divorce Court yesterday. The Chief Justice (Sir Robert McMillan) was petitioned by Mary Alice Gardiner, daughter of Mr. J. B. Holman. M.L.A., for a dissolution of the marriage on the ground of desertion.

Mr. W. M. Nairn, for the petitioner, said that in 1914 the respondent had taken to drink, and the petitioner's parents would not approve of the proposed marriage until he had made some attempt to provide a home. Accordingly the parties were married at the registry office and parted at the door. A few days later respondent went to the North-West. His idea was to resign from Parliament, and to go on a pearling venture, and, when he was established, to send for his wife. When he reached his constituency, he was persuaded to stand again for Parliament. He returned to Perth in July, 1914, and took up a totally different attitude towards the petitioner. He called at the house of her parents in a state of drunkenness, and showed complete indifference. He made appointments with the petitioner, but never kept them. He shortly afterwards returned to the North-West to contest the election without saying good-bye. Having won the election, he again returned to Perth in November, 1914. The petitioner saw him at the Trades Hall and Parliament House, and on one occasion she saw him take a number of her unopened letters out of his pocket, and he said that he did not have time to read them. The respondent disappeared from the State, and his seat was declared vacant. He was ultimately found to be in South Australia. The petitioner had no communication from the respondent until March, 1916, when he wrote from Victoria, stating that he had enlisted, and had made an allotment in her favour. He declared his intention not to live with the petitioner, and said that if he got through he intended to go to England. He mentioned that he had loved her all along, and still did so, adding that she was a girl of unblemished character, and that he had been of no use to himself and a burden to others. The respondent's father was in Melbourne in July and August last, and served the citation on the respondent, who had returned from Europe. He repeated that it was his intention to leave Australia at the earliest opportunity, and said that his decision to leave the petitioner was final and unalterable.

The petitioner, in giving corroborative evidence, said that the respondent was a native of South Australia. Her father did not find out about the marriage until the middle of August, 1914.

> *J. B. Holman, M.L.A, in the course of evidence, said that when he was in Melbourne recently he endeavoured to induce the respondent to honour the marriage contract, but he refused.*
>
> *His Honour, having commented on the unusual nature of the case, said that he had only to be satisfied that the respondent had deserted the petitioner without any good cause. The respondent made no suggestion whatever against the petitioner, but spoke of her as a girl of unblemished character. It seemed to be quite clear from the evidence that the respondent never had any real intention of living with the petitioner. The marriage was a very unfortunate one. It was a secret marriage, because, for very good reasons, the parents objected to it at that time. There would be a decree nisi, returnable in six months with costs.*[6]

This report is both puzzling and intriguing. Clearly, it provides an explanation of sorts for May's entry into a secret marriage: her parents did not approve of her choice of husband on account of his alleged instability. But the report sheds no light on why Joe Gardiner ran away and stayed away. There's no mention of an axe, a shattered jardinière, or a father enraged. There's no mention of that father vowing to run him out of town, or threatening to kill young Joe if he returns to Perth. His absence from parliament, surely a peculiarity, is unexplained. And why, if Joe had wittingly and wilfully deserted May, did he claim later (presumably at the time he met with Jack Holman in Melbourne in August 1919) that he had loved her all along? Was he coerced into saying he intended to return to Europe, and that his decision to leave May was final and unalterable? Finally, whose idea was it to claim May's sexual innocence?

> *At no time have I lived or cohabited with my said husband*

the affidavit claims: and yet we know from a series of letters exchanged between the pair in the two months following their marriage that they certainly intended to be together.[7] A letter from Joe to his *sweetest girl* written from Shark Bay and dated 15 May 1914, six days after their marriage, indicates that Joe had left Perth to travel north three days before, on Tuesday 12 May, and was ... *now anxiously awaiting arrival in Carnarvon in order that I may hear from you.* But for the twenty-first century reader, the letter is mysterious. Joe is clearly apprehensive about something: *Has anything leaked out about that little affair?* he asks. *I am very anxious about that.* Could he be referring to their clandestine marriage? But if so, why call it THAT *little affair*? Why not OUR *little affair*? But on paper at least he is gallant, aware that he could be seen to be running away but wanting to reassure her that he is not: *It seems that I am running away while you remain behind to bear the brunt. However dear it will all come right in the end* ...[8] Is this perhaps one of the telltale signs of the gambler's blind optimism that May's father despised?

Five weeks later, on 24 June 1914, another letter from Joe to *the best little wife in the world* is full of optimistic plans for their reunion, but this letter, too, remains similarly enigmatic. It appears that Joe had considered resigning from his parliamentary seat of Roebourne, but was persuaded otherwise for the good of the Party: *Am afraid I will have to contest again,* he writes. *The Party insist that it would be most unfair for me to refuse on this occasion.* Were they each so afraid of Jack Holman that they considered running away? Perhaps distance and a little time had given Joe Gardiner courage to face his father-in-law's anticipated wrath: *I intend returning by the "West" on her downward trip and we can insist on an immediate settlement* (is Joe angling here for money from May's father?) *and then my little wife can return with me at the earliest opportunity and we can have our honeymoon travelling in a motor car on an electioneering trip. That was one of the promises made by the Party. They decided to supply me with a car to travel the whole district.* This letter clearly attempts to allay May's own fears of *discovery,* presumably by her father of their secret marriage: *I can quite understand how nervous you must be dearest but I do not fear discovery now. It seems to me that if we were going to be found out it would have been in the earlier stages.* Once again, Joe Gardiner's optimism allows him to reassure her breezily: *However let us hope for the best.*⁹

This letter contains additional enigmatic references to *private affairs* which he cannot fully disclose, it seems, even to May:

> *Since arriving here so far nothing has been settled in regard to private affairs. If I were going out of politics of course it would be easy... but the way things are it is impossible to disclose the identity of my partner's partner. However we will pull through alright... Do not worry until my return and we will make some arrangement. I am not telling you as much as you should know in your position but there are some things I am afraid to write about and you know the reasons.*¹⁰

Three weeks later, another letter dated 12 July 1914 similarly acknowledges May's nervousness and attempts to reassure her that all will be well when he returns to Perth: *... yes my dear I can quite understand your nervousness and hope the trouble will soon be terminated. It must be a great strain on you. However we must come to a definite understanding* (with May's father, about money and marriage perhaps?) *on my arrival in Perth.*¹¹

In this letter Joe Gardiner jokes about his place in parliament and speculates on what his absence from the opening of the midyear session of parliament under the Scadden government might mean: *I hope dearie that you watched that no one usurped my seat when you went to the House... I wonder what they thought of my not turning up to the opening of Parliament.* He understands, too, May's commitment to election campaigning in this reference to the Federal election scheduled for 5 September 1914: *No doubt you are up to your neck in work over the next fed election.* For his part, he says that he is attending public meetings and looking round mines. He concludes: *Hope you will receive this* [letter] *on your 21ˢᵗ birthday...*¹²

The final letter in this series is written from Roebourne on 18

July 1914, May's birthday, clearly contradicting the version of the twenty-first birthday story that claims Joe Gardiner was present at McLeod's Hall and fled the scene in fear of his life. Rather, his letter from the safe distance of Roebourne is full of tenderness and the talk of intimate gifts and of their impending reunion: *I have had a silk suit of pyjamas made ... and I have also pearls for setting in a lovely blister ... which I will bring down with me.* His letter then turns to political talk which, again, alludes to incidents that are unclear, not because Joe himself is being enigmatic this time, but rather because the correspondence to which we have access remains one-sided: *I received your wire re being defeated in a selection ballot and hastened to contradict the report. As a matter of fact it was impossible for me to get opposition otherwise I would not be a candidate at the forthcoming election ... I desire to retire next year.* Here too Joe refuses a request May has made of him, claiming: *am a victim of circumstances, therefore it is impossible to comply with your request.*[13]

Was May asking Joe to hurry down to Perth to stand by her side while she told her father of their marriage? Was Joe hoping they could run away from the West to his hometown of Adelaide, perhaps, or further east to Melbourne?

Only two further letters from Joe Gardiner remain. The first, dated 28 March 1916 and written to May from the Military Court, Broadmeadows, Victoria, tells her that he is about to leave Australia with the AIF for overseas service. He is aware that *you have no further desire to see me and* [I] *have made army allotment in your favour.* This presumably is the 1916 allotment mentioned specifically in the affidavit of 2 September 1919, which Mary Alice Holman provided in her suit for *dissolution of marriage by reason of desertion for five years and upwards without cause.* But his statement that *you have no further desire to see me* implies, surely, that it's May herself who is rejecting Joe, rather than Joe deserting May. Is this because she is completely shattered by his earlier desertion? Or is it because she's been persuaded or coerced by her father to turn her back on Joe Gardiner forever?

The final letter, written on 19 August 1919 by Joe Gardiner from his military position in the 11th reinforcements Second Divisional Signals Company to his erstwhile father-in-law, John Barkell Holman, who was in Melbourne at the time, asks him to tell May that it was not his intention to return to her. *I sincerely regret that it is necessary for me to adopt this attitude but during my absence certain things have happened to me, which will render it impossible for me to meet her...* He says he has plans to leave Australia and concludes with the reassurance that *May is and always was a girl of unblemished character*.[14] The motivation for this letter, enigmatic as ever, remains a mystery. Did John Barkell Holman insist that Joe Gardiner write it when they met to discuss the dissolution of the marriage in August 1919, in order for May to be able to file her suit for dissolution of the marriage? If so, did he also insist that Joe Gardiner include a statement to the effect that May was a young woman of *unblemished character*? For whose eyes was this letter intended? Did John Barkell Holman have an eye to the future? Was he cooking the books, doctoring the records? Was this the clincher he needed in order to seek not just dissolution of the marriage but an annulment in the eyes of the Catholic Church? If so, why would he seek this? Although May and her eight living siblings had been raised in the Catholic faith by their mother, John Barkell Holman himself remained nominally aligned with the Salvation Army until his conversion to Catholicism on his deathbed in 1925.

The question perhaps of most fascination to twenty-first century readers concerns May's sexual conduct, not for moralistic reasons but simply because if, in defiance of the sexual standards she was expected to adhere to in 1914, she was not the virgin bride, this would unsettle the public persona of the pure, undefiled, obedient daughter of the Great Man that was carefully crafted during her lifetime. What sort of young woman was she? Was she indeed of *unblemished character*? What were her passions? Why did she marry in secret? What kind of thrill did secrecy

May Holman, aged 25, 18 September 1918.

provide? Was she afraid of her father? Was she among the young women of the early twentieth century who were charting new sexual territory? We know from the research of Susan Magarey and others that first-wave feminists were *passionate, challenging convention on every side, visionary, and centrally preoccupied with sex.*[15] We know that May herself did not identify as a feminist. But was she a daredevil, a risk-taker, a flamboyant young woman who took danger in her stride? We know that she was high-spirited and that she was renowned for her style and flair. Was it Joe Gardiner's cowardice in the face of her father's wrath, rather than her own fear of her father, that persuaded her to abandon hopes of living openly as his wife? Did she honestly believe that she had been abandoned by Joe, *deserted for five years and upwards without cause*? Was being run out of town and threatened with death *without cause*? And whose idea was it that the affidavit should so clearly insist that *At no time have I lived or cohabited with my said husband*? Did she intend the affidavit to imply that she was a virgin, or was it a simple statement of truth, that she and Joe had never set up house together?

Almost a century after the Western Australian Supreme Court handed down its finding that the marriage be dissolved and a *decree absolute* be issued, the jury is still out on whether or why she allowed herself to be coerced into renouncing Joe, and on why she remained single for the rest of her life. Her much younger sister Eileen confirms that May never talked about her marriage and Eileen herself did not even know Joe's name till she read it in a book somewhere much later.[16]

Anecdotal records suggest that May's friends knew more than her younger sisters did. May's friend Evelyn Cloverley, for example, remembers that May and Joe would *take long train trips in trains with no corridor*.[17] Presumably this was before their marriage. And we know that in the two years immediately following the revelations of her secret marriage May went (or was sent?) to work in the country on a farm and then to Kalgoorlie where she worked as a cinema pianist. We don't know whether she was escaping, or whether she was banished. Perhaps she went away to give her father time to recover from his murderous rage. Or perhaps the family was colluding to hide something. It might have been May's own idea to go to the country so she could escape the surveillance of her father and continue to meet with Joe. After Joe was known to be living in Melbourne, May travelled there several times, first to the Arbitration Courts as a trade unionist and later, when she was an MLA, to promote Labor women's organisations. By 1922, though, within two years of their official divorce and well before May's entry into the parliament, Joe had remarried. Given what we know of May's loyalty and character, it is unlikely that she'd have crossed that boundary.

But in the broader context of May Holman's life and career, the questions that hover and circle around this twenty-first birthday scene and demand to be asked are: is this a pivotal moment in May's life? What was the impact of Jack Holman's blind fury, his uncontrollable rage, on May and the family? Is this the kind of father May adored? What does it tell us about her personality, her psychological makeup, that she bowed to his will, that she allowed her husband to flee? May's silence about her marriage and its dissolution throughout her life suggest that she accepted the veil of secrecy that the rest of the family seemed to throw over the affair. But did she try to resist? What hold did her father have on her, and she on him? Would he have been as enraged if another daughter had deceived him in this way? What was the cause of his rage? Was he simply vexed that his daughter acted without his permission? Was he jealous of the man she chose to marry? Was he distraught because he felt the match not suitable? Did he want a more brilliant man to wed his daughter? Did they discuss the possibilities for her future, or did they maintain a tight-lipped silence? Did she remain unmarried as a covert act of resistance, defiance even?

At this distance there's no way to explore the father–daughter relationship in specific detail. At best we can circle around it, shed light from various directions. And perhaps the clearest way to do this is to shine our light directly upon John Barkell Holman himself for a time. Thus far we've met him at a party with axe in hand, we've seen him successfully bring a libel suit against the most powerful newspaper in town, and we've glimpsed him almost three decades earlier wobbling home on his bicycle to whisk up his wife and small child in a celebratory dance. He's a man of passion, and violent rage, and brute strength. But who else was J. B. Holman? History suggests he was a thoughtful, strategic politician, and a committed advocate for social justice. Was he charming, a magnetic personality? Or was he simply a bully? We know that May adored her father, and that as a small child she had thought him perfect.[18] She kept a photograph of him on her desk at Parliament House for the fourteen years of her parliamentary career, and throughout her adult life she always wore a large opal ring that, when opened, contained his photograph.[19] What were the qualities she so admired?

‡

Bromide Street Broken Hill, 1893. House of May's birth.
John Barkell Holman is third from left.

We first meet John Barkell Holman, or Jack, as he was known, in February 1893. He was almost twenty-one years old and had just married the seventeen year old Katherine Mary Rowe. They were living in Broken Hill, and Katherine was already pregnant with their first child, a daughter who arrived on 18 July 1893, and whom they registered as Mary Alice. They didn't know it yet of course, but over the next two and a half decades they would have another ten children together, six daughters and five sons in all. But it was Mary Alice, their firstborn, who would be famous.

John Barkell Holman with May and Katherine, 1894.

Jack was a miner of Cornish stock. He had mining in his blood. His father Edward was a miner before him in the goldfields at Clunes, just north of Bendigo, in the colony of Victoria. Jack himself had been working down the mines since he was fourteen years old. He started out at Bendigo, working to a depth of eighteen hundred feet. Now he was in Broken Hill where they were mining for silver and lead. Like his father, he was a fighter for miners' rights. He was intelligent, articulate and an excellent sportsman. Already he'd been swept up in trade union politics. He'd been an active unionist since he was sixteen and joined the Bendigo Miners' Association, but this past year at Broken Hill had deepened his resolve to fight for better working conditions for his comrades. Broken Hill already had a reputation as a radical union town. Miners had long considered managerial policy to be negligent. Conditions below ground were dangerous. Above ground, toxic dust from the huge piles of tailings left lying around town carried the threat of lead poisoning. It's not surprising that, since 1886 when only four hundred of the three thousand miners were non-unionists, the push had been on to achieve one hundred per cent unionism.

Jack cut his activist teeth during the one-week strike in Broken Hill in 1889 to protest against the employment of non-unionised workers. Passions ran high, and during that week the Women's Brigade was formed to demonstrate solidarity for the striking miners. Jack was inspired. In 1890 when Jack was just eighteen, major strikes of the maritime and shearing unions erupted throughout the colonies in an attempt to ensure that every Australian worker was a unionist. The mines at Broken Hill closed for a month when supplies were cut off by striking wharf workers. That strike was defeated, but miners were militant. When in 1892, in direct contravention of the 1890 Trades Agreement, the Broken Hill mining companies decided to employ non-unionised contract workers, the miners responded with outrage. On 3 July that year, a meeting of six thousand workers at the Central Reserve voted to strike immediately – a strike that lasted for the next sixteen weeks. During that time Jack was caught up in violent clashes between miners and strike-breakers. On 25 August a crowd of ten thousand had assembled to deter newly arriving potential strike-breakers. There was a brass band and a street march and speeches, and the womens' brigade, armed with sticks and axe handles, set upon any man attempting to pass through the picket lines. The first train-load of contract workers arrived on 10 September, and in the following days, armed police clashed with protesters. Seven strike leaders were arrested and charged with conspiracy and inciting a riot. All were imprisoned.[20]

We don't know the extent to which Jack Holman incited violence or riot, but we do know that during these turbulent times he was appointed a special officer of the Labour Defence Committee.[21] Although he was not among the seven strike leaders imprisoned, he was sufficiently involved to be *driven out of town*.[22] In 1893, just one week after the birth of his baby daughter, he borrowed money and, leaving his young wife and child behind in Broken Hill, he moved to Western Australia to work at the Murchison goldfields near the mining town of Cue.

These were surely formative experiences for young Jack Holman. On the one hand the strike had been crushed, and conditions for workers deteriorated, with a ten per cent decrease in wages and the restoration of the forty-eight hour working week. People were dispirited and, within two years, union membership at Broken Hill had fallen from six thousand to three hundred. But on the other hand, Jack Holman had tasted the thrill of union solidarity and he knew that, although it was foolish to place all faith in direct action methods, another kind of solidarity – between the unions and the Australian Labour Party – was emerging. From this time onwards his union activism went hand in hand with an intense interest in the party political process.

Archival records tell us that Jack Holman became involved in trade union activism immediately on reaching the Murchison. In 1894 he successfully negotiated a reduction of working hours to forty-four; and in 1896 at the Day Dawn mine site just south of Cue he successfully led a strike against a proposed reduction of wages to five shillings per week. But although he remained actively involved in the union movement for the rest of his life, first representing miners and later, from 1908 until 1925, representing timber workers, it was soon clear to him that it was not enough to be a union advocate, and so, additionally, he sought election to the parliament. In 1901 after several attempts at gaining endorsement for ALP seats, he was elected to the WA Legislative Assembly as the Australian Labor Party member for North Murchison. When in 1902 that seat was abolished he successfully stood for the new seat of Murchison, a seat he retained for the next seventeen years. He was an MLA for much of the remainder of his adult life until his unexpected death in 1925, with a short interlude away from parliament from 1919 until his re-election to the seat of Forrest in 1923.

Here then is a portrait of a passionate man, an idealist perhaps, committed to fighting for his fellows through the unions and through the parliamentary process; a man committed to solidarity, to the dignity of workers; a resourceful and adventurous man, not reluctant to face the challenges of moving vast distances to find work, and not slow to take up the reins of leadership once there.

Given what we already know about Jack Holman's rage at his daughter's twenty-first birthday party, it should not surprise us that, earlier in his life, he had a reputation as an aggressive man. Between 1907 and 1910 Jack had been suspended on numerous occasions from the WA parliament for *abusive, offensive and unparliamentary language and abusing the privileges of the House.*[23] His reputation for being harsh certainly followed him beyond the grave. As recently as 1997, in an interview with Judyth Watson, Mrs Frances Shea (who had been born into a Labor family in 1909 and whose father, Edmund Harry Gray, was in parliament with Jack Holman from 1923), said of Jack Holman, *I never knew the man, but gossip was that he was hard as nails...*[24] The incident that is often cited as illustration of his aggressive tendencies occurs at the end of February 1917, and was reputedly so scandalous that it was cited forty-five years later in an article in Perth's *Daily News* as an example of bad behaviour in the House when numbers are close. In this article, Jack Holman is painted as an out-of-control strongman who, in a fit of rage, threatened the newly appointed speaker of the House with bodily removal and refused to be restrained. *Pandemonium broke out.* A policeman was called to restore order but even though he was *six feet tall with massive shoulders* he failed to do so and was locked out by Jack's Labor colleagues. The division bells rang for over an hour without a division being taken on the motion, and the speaker was so distraught that he resigned his post the following day, only sixteen days after taking it up.[25]

There's no escaping the drama of this incident as recounted in the *Daily News* of 1962. But if we search other sources we find a slightly different picture. Political historian David Black, for example, in an article published in 1981, situates the incident so differently that Jack Holman emerges as a man of principle, rather than as a thug and a bully who unnecessarily frightens a timid speaker out of his seat. Black's understanding is that Holman's rage was fuelled by a righteous sense of betrayal of the Labor Party by the newly appointed speaker, Edward Bertram Johnston. Johnston (known as Bertie), a farmer who had been a Labor Party member for the country seat of Narrogin under the Scadden Government since his election in 1911, had resigned from the Labor Party in 1915 in protest at Premier Scadden's failure to keep a promise to lower the price of Crown land. His resignation effectively meant that the Scadden government did not have the numbers to continue to govern, and in mid-1916 the conservative parties took the reins of government. Johnston, meanwhile, had been re-elected to the parliament in 1916 as an Independent. In February 1917, Labor moved a motion of censure against the government, and Bertie Johnston indicated his intention to move an amendment. Much hung on this censure motion. If it passed, the conservative government would be defeated and Labor would regain power. But, in addition to the support of Bertie Johnston, the Labor members needed one more vote to ensure victory. Consequently, the speaker, a Labor man named Troy, assuming that Bertie Johnston would vote with the Labor members to support the censure motion and ensure the fall of the conservative government, resigned his position as speaker in order to add his vote to the Labor count, thus ensuring the defeat of the government. However, the conservatives too were plotting and scheming, and at the last moment persuaded Bertie Johnston to accept the role of speaker. This meant that Bertie Johnston's vote was lost to the Labor Party and the government was then able to defeat the censure motion by a single vote. Not surprisingly, the Labor members saw Johnston's actions as an overt betrayal, and they refused to accept Johnston's authority as speaker of the House. This was the context in which Jack Holman threatened to remove Bertie Johnston from the House.

Hence in David Black's version of events, we see that Jack Holman was acting on principle. He and his party felt betrayed and from this perspective we might conclude that it's this – the unjust betrayal – rather than a petulant self-righteousness or bullying tendency – that fuelled Jack's rage. Perhaps this was what his daughter so admired: his refusal to be cowed by place or circumstance into betraying his own deeply held principles.

When she was interviewed in 1997, Sheila Moiler – who was born in 1916 and was Jack Holman's youngest daughter – had sketchy memories of her father.[26] She was twenty-three years younger than May, and was only nine years old when her father died. He was clearly a man in full flight during Sheila's childhood. She remembers her father's tremendous energy. In this interview, her sense is that it was her father who was the *driver in the family. I can't remember Mum doing much,* she says, *but he was the one who got the family to do things.* She remembers leaving 616 Beaufort Street and moving with the family as a two year old to the Bassendean house with its extensive gardens. She has two enduring images of her father. The first is as a worker, a labourer, a gardener. *He worked so hard in that place,* she recalls. *It was like a miniature farm with racehorses, cows, turkeys, chooks, pigs, you name it. We used to kill our own pigs. And he worked so hard.* Sheila's second image of him is as a toff, an urbane gentlemen heading in to town: *He always looked, I can remember him going in to Parliament House – he'd catch the train – and he always had a flower, a white carnation or something, in his lapel…* Without prompting, Sheila goes on to recount the story that she's heard of her father's violence in the House:

> *I don't know whether you heard about the time when he pulled the speaker Johnston out of the chair at Parliament House? I think it was 1917. Apparently Johnston was handing on a bit, and father went up to him and said, 'I'm going to yank you out of your chair' (except he would have said something different – Father could put it on a bit – swear) and they called for the constable to come in and he came in to get them all, and then the Labor members locked everybody out. They could neither get in nor out. And apparently Johnston resigned. He made the first disruption.*

Fascinatingly, when asked whether this incident reflected her father's *volatile nature, his quick temper,* Sheila replies, *I don't think he had a quick temper but when he'd had enough, he'd had enough, you know?* This view, of a man to be respected for his principles rather than feared for his temper, is supported in a eulogy in *The Daily News* of 23 February 1925: *John B. Holman, though vigorous in debate, and a foeman worthy of any man's steel, never carried any animus.*[27]

John Barkell Holman died unexpectedly in 1925, following complications of an appendectomy several years earlier. He was fifty-two years old. On his deathbed, May promised to continue his work, and to be responsible for the education and upbringing of her four youngest siblings, Bill, Iris, Eileen and Sheila. His funeral was widely attended. The flag flew at half-mast at Parliament House.[28] This report in *The West Australian* on 27

February 1925 gives an indication of the depth and breadth of his connection to the decision-makers and the workers in this city, and reflects a world that his daughter May was prepared to inherit.

THE LATE MR J. B. HOLMAN.
LARGELY ATTENDED FUNERAL.
The funeral of the late Mr. J. B. Holman, M.L.A., yesterday, was the occasion for an impressive tribute by representatives of several sections of the community. There had been a postponement to permit of the attendance of representatives of branches and sub-branches of the Timber Workers' Union (of which the deceased was general secretary), and very many of these were present. The cortege was a long one and the gathering at the graveside in the Roman Catholic portion of the Karrakatta Cemetery was very large. Moving from Messrs. Bowra and O'Dea's private mortuary, in Pier Street, in the afternoon, the cortege halted for one minute at Holman House, in Stirling Street, where the offices of the Timber Workers' Union are situated, and for a similar period at Parliament House. At Karrakatta the last rites were conducted by the Rev. Father O'Neil, assisted by the Rev. Fathers Lynch and Crowley. The chief mourners were: – Mrs. K. Holman (widow), Messrs. J. B. Holman, E. J. F. Holman, and W. T. Holman (sons). Misses M. Holman, K. Holman, W. Holman, I. Holman, E. Holman, and S. Holman (daughters), Mr. Jos. Holman (brother), Mrs. J. Holman (sister-in law), Mr. E. Holman (nephew), Mrs. D. Campbell and Mr. P. Johnson. The pall-bearers were: – The Acting Premier (Mr. W. C. Angwin), Mr. S. W. Munsie (Honorary Minister), and Messrs. D. Watson, A. J. Watts. J. Gallagher, E. McAlister, E. Barker, and W. D. Johnson, M.L.A. Other members of the State Ministry present were: – The Minister for Works (Mr. A. McCallum), the Minister for Railways (Mr. J. C. Willcock), the Minister for Lands (Mr. M. F. Troy),

the Colonial Secretary (Mr. J. M. Drew), and Mr. J. W. Hickey (Honorary Minister). The assemblage included also Senator Lynch, many members of both Houses of Parliament, and officers of Parliament; a large number of Perth and Fremantle A.L.P. and union officials; the executive of the Timber Workers' Union, Mr. N. Temperley (president of the Sawmillers' Association and general manager of Millars' Timber and Trading Company), Sir Edward Wittenoom (chairman) and Mr. W. Macmurtrie (director of Millars' Co.); directors, editor, and staff of the 'Worker' Newspaper; Captain Wheeler (representing the British Labour Party), Mr. W. Somerville (Arbitration Court): and representatives of the Celtic Club Licensed Victuallers' Association, Perth Hospital, Children's Hospital, Fire Brigades' Board, Labour Women's Organisations of Perth and Fremantle, the Police Department, Commercial Travellers' Club, and the Perth M.U.O.F.S.[29]

It's clear that Jack Holman's influence spread wide in the community. And it's also clear that, in spite of his very complex personality, or perhaps even because of it, May Holman revered her father. Apart from her clandestine marriage, she seemed to do his bidding, to support his ideals. Her pledge to carry on his work industrially and personally in supporting her younger siblings throughout their schooling was a pledge made openly and celebrated by her siblings and her political colleagues alike.

But what of her mother? Was May also her mother's daughter? We'll soon see that her relationship with her mother was every bit as complicated as that with the father she adored.

CHAPTER 4
... AND THY MOTHER

Katherine Mary Rowe was only seventeen years old and already pregnant when she married the charismatic young miner, John Barkell Holman, in Broken Hill on 14 February 1893.[1] What was she thinking about on that hot summer afternoon? We can only imagine what kind of life she was anticipating. Was she mature enough to imagine that hardship, isolation and grief might sit alongside joy and fame? Perhaps she was swept up in some kind of romance in which her dashing Prince Charming would lead her into a life of unmitigated happiness. Perhaps she aware that, across the world in the land many still called Home, the young Princess Victoria Mary of Teck, later to become Queen Consort and royal matriarch, grandmother of the young Princesses Elizabeth and Margaret, was similarly choosing her own Prince, so creating yet another version of the fairytale romance for the civilised world to follow.[2] Perhaps she knew with a sense of foreboding that the world was brinking on depression, and that the prolonged strikes of 1892 augured badly for the miners in this ten thousand-strong once-thriving community.[3] Presumably she understood that five months after her wedding day she would be the mother of a tiny baby, but she could not have known that, a week after that, her young husband would board a train on the first leg of his westward journey to the remote goldfield region of the Murchison, to the resounding cheers of his beloved football team.[4] Nor would she have known then that she would not see him again until her daughter was two years old.[5] What hopes did she hold for this first child? Could she imagine a future in which she gave birth to ten more babies over the next twenty-five years?[6] Could she imagine the black grief that would stalk her for decades after the loss of not one but two baby boys?[7] Surely not. On that afternoon the sun was shining and the world was hers. Let's leave her there, for a moment, on the threshold of life, eager, strong, radiant, certain in her love for this strapping young man.

Katherine Holman with Maude and May, 1900.

Not surprisingly perhaps, we know more about her young husband at this time than we do about Katherine herself, and can only surmise through what we see of him what kind of young woman would have been attracted to him. Newspapers tell us that even outside his trade union activism he was a leader of sorts amongst the young men in this mining community. He had arrived in Broken Hill at age seventeen after four years already down the mine near Ballarat, and as a sportsman he quickly became involved in establishing a junior cricket team.[8] But his primary sporting love was football. Local newspapers list him as one of the local team. In March 1893 he was re-elected as secretary of the Victoria Football Club in Broken Hill, and was one of three delegates from the team to the Victorian Football Association. In his role as secretary he regularly rallied the lads, through notices in the *Barrier Miner*, to attend meetings of the Association.[9] But it's the football scandal of 1893 that throws the most telling light on the character of the young Jack Holman.

This saga of the apparently 'rigged' football match demonstrates not only young Jack's moral integrity but also the moral code of the community in which the event occurred. The story begins with a report in the *Barrier Miner* of the match between Victoria and the South Australians of 1 July 1893, in which several players on the home side appeared to be playing 'cronk' or deliberately trying to lose the game, presumably for some monetary gain. There was outrage amongst onlookers. The paper reports:

> *So disgusted were the officials of the Victorian club who were witnesses of the contest that the secretary (Mr. Holman) walked on to the field and requested that the members of the team who were not "tied up" should abandon the match. The assertion was made, alike by players and spectators, that the strange loss of form by several of the leading Vics was due to an absence of desire on their part to score a win.*[10]

Two days later, on 3 July 1893, the *Barrier Miner* published the following letter to the editor, in which young Jack Holman, as *worthy secretary of the Vics*, was praised for his *manly protestation*. The letter was written under the pseudonym *Manly Sport* and reads:

> *Would that my pen were steeped in gall; or, better still, in the "gore" of certain barefaced swindling footballers whom I could name. Your paper richly deserves the thanks of the whole sporting community of the Barrier for the severe strictures passed in your last issue on the "reversal of form" of certain socalled but mis-named "sports," who, up to Saturday last, had the honor (?) of playing for ... the Victorians. To think that the noble and manly game of football should be dragged into the mire of public contempt by such mean, ignoble, and mercenary devices is enough to make one's blood boil. I am glad that you noted Mr. Holman's (the worthy secretary of the Vics.') manly protestation, and I, for one, shall use whatever little influence I may possess in helping that gentleman to secure the immediate expulsion of the delinquents aforesaid.*[11]

Expel the delinquent 'cronk' players they did. On Wednesday 12 July the *Barrier* reported on a meeting of the Broken Hill Football Association held the previous night where Mr Holman had brought a letter from his club instructing him to bring the club's decision to expel the cheats to the notice of the association. A lengthy discussion followed during which it was acknowledged that the actions of the miscreants brought the game of football into disrepute. There was some questioning of the severity of the penalty exacted upon them, but the meeting agreed that there was no way for the association to overturn the decision of the club to expel these men for life.[12]

On Friday 21 July a meeting of the club was called to accept the resignation of Secretary Holman because of his impending departure for WA; and a discussion was again had about the severity of the sentences meted out to the 'cronk' players. It was decided to try to reduce their sentences to expulsion for a season or two, rather than for life, because the public exposure of their crime had already done much to chastise them.[13]

In all these discussions and newspaper reports, Jack Holman

emerges as a hero, a man of principle, a fair man who was not afraid to stand up for what he knew to be right, and a man who was prepared to fairly represent his committee. Are these the qualities that attracted Katherine to him? Was he her hero? Certainly he was given a hero's farewell by his football mates, as the following article in the *Barrier Miner* of Saturday 29 July relates. It's titled *Valedictory*, and records:

> *A large number of the members of the Victorian Football Club assembled at the Sulphide-street station on Tuesday night to wish their late honorary secretary (Mr. J. B. Holman) "goodbye". Mr. Holman goes to Nannine, a new township on the Murchison (W.A.) under engagement to a local gold-mining company. On behalf of the club, Mr. J. B. Murphy presented the late secretary with a handsome pair of gold solitaires, engraved, and a horn silver pendant, mounted with gold. The recipient thanked the members for their handsome present and the kind wishes expressed for his future. He had tried to do his best for the club, and was sorry that anything should have occurred to endanger its chance for the premiership of 1893. However, he hoped they would stick together like true footballers, and still make a bold try for the premiership. As the train left the station three hearty cheers were given.*[14]

And so Jack Holman left Broken Hill a hero. But was his young wife Katherine among the cheering crowd assembled at Sulphide Street station to see him off, with their one week old baby wrapped snugly against the winter cold? Or was she still recuperating from the birth, tucked up in bed at her mother's house and resting? History does not relate. What we do know is that Jack Holman travelled alone to Nannine, quickly became absorbed into the community, and sent for his wife and child almost two years later, in 1895. We know too, that towards the end of that first year on the goldfields, the nineteen year old Katherine Holman, one of the few non-Aboriginal women in the district, gave birth to a stillborn son.

What can life have been like for Katherine and her daughter on the Murchison goldfields? Today Nannine is a ghost town, but in 1895 it was poised ready to prosper. Gold had been discovered in the Nannine area in 1890, and by the end of 1891 about seven hundred men had arrived to seek their fortunes. Like all mining settlements, it was a man's town. There were five hotels. The townsite of Nannine was gazetted in April 1893; in 1895 Katherine and May arrived to a tent settlement. However, early in 1896, handsome stone buildings began to replace tents and in that year the post and telegraph office, the mining warden's court, and the police station were built. The town was connected to the rest of the world by twice-weekly Gascard coach from Yalgoo, and, from 1894, by telegraph. There was no town water supply, and no school. It was 1903 before a railway line connected Nannine to its neighbouring town, Cue. Cue, meanwhile, had overtaken Nannine as a boom town, and by 1900 boasted a population of ten thousand.

To a twenty-first century city dweller, the Nannine of 1895 sounds hot and remote and blokey, but Katherine had grown up in Broken Hill amongst miners, and was accustomed to a harsh climate. The isolation of Nannine, though, seems to have presented deeper challenges than she was prepared for. When she found herself to be with child for the third time, not twelve months after the birth of her stillborn son, she was clearly unwilling to face the prospect of giving birth alone on these goldfields again. She and four year old May made the long journey home to Broken Hill by road and sea and road again in order to have her mother's help in the birthing. Here, surely, is a young woman who is simultaneously strong and vulnerable. She knew what she needed – a return to the mother – and she was prepared to endure the long trip home in order to do so. As we shall see, these qualities – personal strength, and vulnerability – are coupled in her life as she ages.

Katherine's second daughter, Kathleen Maude, was born in Broken Hill on 6 August 1897. When mother and two small daughters returned to the goldfields at the Murchison the following year, they brought with them Katherine's mother, Mary Anne Rowe, who soon became the midwife for the entire district. No doubt Grandmother Rowe provided stability and good sense. Perhaps she recognised Katherine's need for female company; perhaps she recognised her daughter's emotional vulnerability, her grief for the child she had lost. Perhaps she loved her new life as midwife to women birthing hard and lonely in this remote region. Whatever the case, Grandmother Rowe did not return to Broken Hill. She lived with the family for the next twenty years, first at Cue on the Murchison goldfields, then in Perth from 1905. She died in 1918 just before the family moved from their first Perth house at 616 Beaufort Street to their big ten-acre property at 3 Ida Street in Bassendean. Even in death, Grandmother Rowe made a strong impression. The earliest memory of her youngest granddaughter, Sheila, who was two years old at the time her grandmother died, is the sight of her grandmother's dead body, laid out in a brown cloth in the front room of the Beaufort Street house, hands crossed over her chest.[15]

The family lived at Steward Street in the township of Cue from the time Katherine and her mother arrived back with two little girls in tow.[16] Jack Holman was thriving on the goldfields. He was an athlete, a champion fire brigade man – the family still has his medals – and a deeply respected trade unionist. He had opened a tobacconist shop, was a secretary to the Australian Workers' Association, and wanted to open a weekly newspaper. By 1901 he had fulfilled his ambition to be elected to the Legislative Assembly as a member of the Australian Labor Party, and for one year from 1904 to 1905 he was minister for railways under the short-lived Labor Daglish government.

Three more children were born to Katherine and Jack on the goldfields before they moved to Perth in 1905. A son, John Barkell Jnr, was born on 17 June 1900, when Mary Alice was almost seven and Maude was almost three. Two years later, Winifred Lillian was born on 18 May; and two years after that, on 9 August 1904, another son, Edward Frederick Joseph, was born. When the family left the goldfields for the city, eleven year old Mary Alice, or May as she was known, was the eldest of five children. Her life as big sister, always ready to help, and always with one small child or another on her hip, had begun.

Although we might imagine what life in a remote goldfield region might be like, there are few archival documents that provide stories of Katherine's daily life. We can imagine that she worked hard, as all women with young children must do, and that even with her capable mother at hand, life would be tough. However, one newspaper article from 1902 recounts a story that has gained the status of family legend, and shines some light momentarily on Katherine's life as a mother. The article is from *The West Australian* of 19 September 1902.

> CUE.
>
> CUE, SEPTEMBER 18.
>
> *A four years' old daughter of Mr. J. B. Holman, M.L.A., was lost in the bush at Milly Soak yesterday, and was not recovered until 2 o'clock this afternoon. The child was at an Anglican Sunday school picnic, and wandered away picking wild flowers. She was missed very shortly afterwards, and a search was instituted. The searchers were unsuccessful until to-day, when Mrs. Holman found her daughter about twelve miles from Cue near Jack's Well.*[17]

It's a good news story, for sure, and the family remembers it thus. But the drama of it, the anxiety, the terror of wondering whether this little child would ever be found: these are barely hinted at. We can imagine that the entire town turned out to search for little Maude. But we cannot know how distraught her mother felt, or how long she searched. Did she return to the family home exhausted late at night on the seventeenth, to set out again at dawn? Or did she search and continue searching all night? How long did it take her to walk the twelve miles to Jack's Well? We know that in September 1902 May had just turned seven, and there were now two children younger than four year old Maude. Little Jack had just turned two, and baby Winnie was four months old. But Katherine already knew the heartbreak of stillbirth, and Maude was the next child born after the baby she had lost. She could not afford to lose this child too. We can imagine her grit, her determination to find her child alive. She certainly did not stay passively at home while others searched.

But what else do we know of Katherine? Her life, as usual for the times, was not recorded in as much detail as her husband's life. At some time during her life on the goldfields she must have become interested in Labor women's politics, because almost immediately on the family's move to Murchison House at 616 Beaufort Street, Perth, in 1905, we find records of her becoming central to the activities of Labor women. What's more, like her husband, she was

Eight Hour Day Commitee, 1909. Katherine Holman seated, second row, third from right.

a leader. By 1906 when she was thirty years old, we find that she was president of the North Suburban Women's Political League. By 1910, she was an active member of the Labor Suburban Social Club and president of the newly formed Women Workers' Union. In 1912 she was a delegate to the first Labor Women's Conference in Perth. Her nineteen year old daughter, May, was minutes secretary to that meeting. Katherine was also a member of the combined Perth and Fremantle Eight Hour Day Committee. Clearly, Katherine was steeped in Labor women's politics. She was also involved in civic affairs more widely. For example, she was one of the first members of the board of King Edward Memorial Hospital, alongside joint convenors Edith Cowan and Jane Scott. This board began meeting in 1909. A *Daily News* report of 13 January 1913 notes that Katherine Holman, along with two other prominent women, Edith Cowan and Bessie Rischbieth, had been returned to the board of the Perth Hospital.[18] Katherine, like her husband, was a Labor stalwart. No doubt she was his helpmeet in every way.

Astonishingly, amidst a busy public life, Katherine also gave birth to five more children between 1908 and 1918. William Thomas was born on 16 August 1908. His biggest sister, May, was by then fifteen years old. Iris Monica was born on 6 April 1911, Eileen Veronica on 22 August 1914 (just after May's twenty-first birthday fiasco), and Sheila Josephine on 22 July 1916. Katherine's eleventh child, her last, Richard, was born on 8 March 1918. Katherine was by now forty-two years old. Her beloved mother, old Grandmother Rowe, died the year Richard was born. Richard lived for ten months, and died in November.

Imagine Katherine's distress: her eldest daughter, May, had earned the wrath of her adoring father and been banished to the country for a time, to atone for her sin of marrying without permission. Katherine's mother was dead, her new baby boy dead too, and although Maud and Jack had finished school, she still had six children under sixteen to raise. She must have been tired, exhausted even. Was it at this point that she took to the bottle?

Family discretion has ensured that not much is written about

Katherine and alcoholism, but if with hindsight we acknowledge it as a medical affliction, many puzzling comments, images and stories fall into place. For a start, there's May's ambivalence towards her mother. As the first child, four years older than her next sister Maude, May was doted on, adored, invited into the adult world of her parents. She was admired for her brilliance at school, and her talents for music and performance were early recognised and encouraged by both parents. In her teens she was invited to share her mother's passion for Labor Women's Organisation activities and her father's passion for trade unionism and Labor politics. In public she spoke loyally and lovingly of her mother and of family life; and after May's death her close friend Molly Holmes wrote *She was devoted to her mother, and nobody could have wished for a better daughter, sister or friend.*[19] But at times in private letters and diaries

Holman family, 1911. May, John, Maude (back row). Winnie, John, Bill, Ted, Katherine, Iris.

May seemed deeply disappointed or dismissive of her mother.[20] Was this because Katherine became increasingly unreliable, unable to cope? If we accept the alcoholism story, Sheila's comment that 'Mother never seemed to do anything much' when reflecting on family life in Bassendean, makes some kind of sense. Sheila was only two years old when her grandmother and her baby brother died. Perhaps her mother was deeply depressed. Perhaps she was finding oblivion in the bottle. And if this is the case, it can perhaps explain why the thirty-one year old May was prepared to agree to the requests her father made of her in 1925 on his death bed. Not only was she to carry on his work for the timber workers, but she was charged with the responsibility of caring for her younger siblings, seeing them all through school. This she agreed to do, publicly. But why was this not the responsibility of Katherine as the children's mother? Only if we take into account the notion that Katherine was somehow unfit to be mother and father both to her children does it make sense that May agreed to act as the responsible parent to her younger siblings.

There is another story in the Holman family legend that, like the story of May's secret marriage, and the story of Katherine's drinking, is a story that was hushed up, rarely discussed in the family. It's the story of Jack Holman's will. What we know now is that, in a thoroughly baffling gesture, Jack Holman insisted that May take over as head of the household, and made provision in his will for an allowance of a mere thirty shillings per week to be paid to Katherine as his widow, for the rest of her life. As an indication of the value of this amount, for much of the 1920s the average wage of a worker supporting a wife and three children was nine pounds ten shillings per week, that is, 190 shillings, or more than six times the amount allocated to Katherine. In 1925 Jack Holman knew that he was gravely ill. It is almost certain that his will was made deliberately and with full awareness of its implications for Katherine. Consider this: in 1925 Katherine was forty-nine years old. She had borne eleven children in twenty-five years. In addition to raising her children, she had devoted her entire life to the support of her husband and the Labor movement. At the time of her husband's death, their youngest daughter, Sheila, was only nine years old. Eileen was eleven, Iris – Cis – was fourteen, and Bill had just turned seventeen. They were all still at school. Katherine, as their mother, would have dependent children to support for much of the coming decade. Clearly, a will that gave her a meagre weekly sum would actively write her out from her role as mother and head of the household in the event of her husband's death. It must surely also have set up tensions between May and her mother. If May had agreed on her father's deathbed with his wish that she take responsibility for the younger children, surely she must have seen that she usurped her mother's position?

In 1926, Katherine took the unusual step of contesting the will in the courts. The family was scandalised, but Katherine, it seems, was determined to assert her rights. In effect she was challenging her eldest daughter's right to the overall control of the family finances. There appear to have been two points at issue. The first was that the allowance made to Katherine was inadequate. The second was that the availability of even this small amount of money was now in doubt. The allowance was to be paid out of the proceeds of sale of the family property at Beaufort Street, Perth but,

> *in an affidavit produced before Mr. Justice Burnside in Chambers yesterday,* [the widow] *set forth that the testator sold the property in question, under contract and she was now informed she would be no longer entitled to this money when the amounts due under contract had been paid.*

She had no other interest under the will except for the weekly payment of thirty shillings. The affidavit claimed that *Mr Holman had real and personal estate valued at £4,123 6s 8d.* It also dealt with the various ways in which she had assisted her husband during his lifetime, and stated that she had had eleven children, nine still living, four of whom were still dependent. The argument put by Katherine Holman's counsel was that the allowance made to her was *entirely inadequate*,[21] and the outcome of the court case was that Mr Justice Burnside ordered the weekly allowance to be doubled, to three pounds per week.

The case made headlines in *The Brisbane Courier* (Monday 18 January 1926),[22] The Adelaide *Advertiser* (Saturday 16 January 1926),[23] the Adelaide *Register* (Saturday 16 January 1926),[24] the Ipswich *Queensland Times* (Monday 18 January 1926),[25] Melbourne's *The Argus* (Monday 18 January 1926),[26] and Kalgoorlie's *Western Argus* (Tuesday 19 January 1926)[27] but *The West Australian* buried its report under a general column called *News and Notes* on page ten of its Saturday edition of 16 January.[28] All reports are short and provide the merest hint of what family struggles might have existed. The Holman family was widely admired and Katherine seen as an exemplary wife and mother. But at what point did Katherine become a liability? What does this will suggest about her relationship with her husband, and about her role in the family? One can imagine that she felt sidelined, erased by her husband's will, ignored by her family, under siege. Was she so enraged by its terms that she decided to go public? Or was her legal challenge merely an avenue to ensure that the family could provide an adequate allowance for her without defying the terms of the will?

The wording of the affidavit clearly suggests that Katherine Holman felt the need to justify her request for an increase in her allowance by stressing her role as helpmeet to her husband during his lifetime and as mother to their large family, and sought just reward for her crucial contributions to the family wellbeing. She employed a Queen's Counsel, Sir Walter James, to argue her case. The executors of the will were represented by family friend Mr Dwyer. Even though Katherine's allowance was increased by the courts, the fact that she was given an allowance and not a central role in the administration of her husband's estate was surely a public signalling that her role as mother and guardian was over. Family legend has it that Katherine's public challenge to the terms of the will was experienced as distressing and bewildering by her children, as too was her completely unexpected journey to New Zealand immediately after the court case was concluded. We know, too, that the three young schoolgirls – Iris, Eileen and Sheila – were packed off to Sacred Heart Convent as boarders as soon as their father died. Only if we acknowledge that Katherine had already begun to drink too much and too often does this story begin to make sense. With May as their guardian absorbed in her work as a politician all day, and Katherine as their mother unfit to parent them, boarding school would have been a sensible option.

Katherine Holman lived for another decade. She died on 20 March 1935. She was fifty-nine years old. Although family members remember her as *a fine old lady*,[29] she seems by the time of her death to have faded from public view, and her funeral rates barely a mention in the local press.

Ultimately, Katherine Holman emerges from the archival records towards the end of her life as a tragic figure, broken, shadowed, hidden from view, displaced in her role as mother and protector, yet resilient enough to fight for her legal rights, and unafraid of besmirching the family reputation in doing so. The fact that she employed a Queen's Counsel to fight her battle in court in 1926 suggests that she felt entitled to the best representation possible; at the same time it suggests that she knew she was up against tough adversaries. That these adversaries were her own children, particularly her beloved eldest daughter May whose career as a politician was in its infancy, is a horror she could surely never have imagined in her younger days.

No doubt the deep distress of the situation was felt on both sides. May herself would surely have been torn between wanting to honour her beloved father's instructions, and wanting to honour the mother whose energy, intelligence, resilience, and independence of thought she had so admired as a child and as a young woman. We don't know whether May was able to view her mother's increasing lassitude after the death of Grandmother Rowe and baby Richard as a medical condition. We don't know precisely when Katherine

Holman's alcoholism began to take its toll on family life. The glimpses we do get – of a listless mother in Bassendean in the early 1920s, seen through the eyes of her youngest daughter, Sheila; of a vociferous defender of her own rights in the newspaper records of 1926; and of a mother who has all but faded from public view by the beginning of the 1930s, but who continues to elicit tenderness and care from her eldest daughter as indicated in public reporting of May Holman's connection with her mother – combine to provide a distressing and multifaceted view of the slide from public admiration to private disgrace that the illness of alcoholism evoked at this time. Fascinatingly though, these qualities of vulnerability, resilience and deeply felt emotional connection can be seen to be amplifications of the Katherine we met first in the goldfields of Cue, and later in her public life in the Labor Women's Organisations in Perth. It is fortunate that May's emotional bonds with her mother were forged long before Katherine's fall from grace; and that the qualities that May so admired in her mother – her energy, her intelligence, her willingness to take the initiative, her loyalty to the Labor cause – were qualities that the young May Holman had plenty of opportunity to observe, embody, and take into her own life.

CHAPTER 5
THE ENTERTAINERS

One of the keys to understanding May Holman's popularity with her electorate and with the Western Australian public more generally is found in the story of her role as an entertainer. From the time she was a little girl, May adored music. She loved to sing, but her first love was the piano. She simply loved to play and to perform for an audience, and throughout her life she was widely admired for the sheer effortlessness and charm of her music-making. At times she was saucy, at times demure. She was always stylish, and during a long performance career she perfected the witty art of musical monologue. In her performances she combined her love of music and theatre with her love of politics. As historian Daphne Popham writes, *The stage enchanted her: she had a radiant personality that reflected the great love she had for people and her desire to uplift their spirits and conditions.*[1]

May Holman frequently declared that if she had not been a politician she'd have gone onto the stage.[2] This was no idle fantasy. Her parents and her teachers early recognised her talent for music and for dramatic performance, and encouraged her to take lessons in music and elocution and drama during her school years. She became so passionate about music that, during her adolescence and into her early adulthood, she undertook the most advanced musical studies available to brilliant young Australian music students at that time, through a system of exams conducted annually in Australia by Trinity College of Music in London. By age twenty-seven she had gained degrees

May Holman in costume, 1924.

in both singing and pianoforte. Passing this series of exams was reverently called 'getting your letters' in musical circles around the country. The letters she could now put after her name were

LTCL and ATCL (singing and pianoforte) and LAB (singing), which translate as Licentiate of Trinity College London and Associate of Trinity College London, and Licentiate of the Associated Boards.[3]

Even as a child, May loved to organise, and she loved to entertain. Family legend has it that from about the age of eight, while the family was still on the Murchison goldfields, she was involved in concert preparations and performances for family and an extended circle of friends. We can imagine her planning concerts, writing programs, issuing invitations, organising her brothers and sisters into their acts, saving the juiciest and most complicated parts for herself.

Many little girls plan and perform at family concerts, but it was the combination of high quality performance, organising, and fundraising that set her apart from her contemporaries. Her first sortie into the world of fundraising through concert performance happened in 1907. May was fourteen years old. She knew from family discussions that the timber workers in her father's union were being punished by their employers by being locked out from their workplaces, and that their families were in deep distress. She responded to the injustice of the situation by organising and performing in a fundraising concert to benefit the timber workers' children. The concert was hailed as a *wonderful show*. Perhaps the youth of its organiser and star performer was novelty enough to draw a big crowd. Whatever the case, the concert was extremely well attended, and was not easily forgotten. Indeed, three decades later, in an article in the *Westralian Worker* following May Holman's death in 1939, we learn that the *large amount of money raised* [at the 1907 concert] *was still a source of wonder to many of the old Labor stalwarts*.[4]

We get a sentimental but vivid picture of the young performer a year later, in this same article written for the *Westralian Worker* in 1939. The sense of theatre and dramatic effect in this description foreshadows the kind of entertaining she was to do for the rest of her life:

At 14 years of age May was nearly as tall as when fully grown. The writer well remembers her appearance at a social given by the women's section of the A.N.A. At that time she was a very shy schoolgirl, whose light nut-brown hair fell in a shower to her waist, being brushed back from her face, while side strands were tied with a blue ribbon near the crown of her head. She gave what was probably the first rendering in W.A. of a new and dainty little song which had a world vogue at the time, entitled "Meet me where the Lanterns Glow". It was given with lights down; the singer and a chorus carried lighted Chinese lanterns, and glided mysteriously about as the item proceeded, finishing with further mystery tunes.[5]

Although she had such early success as an entertainer, it was not until the years of the Great War, when May was in her twenties, that she began to perform publicly in earnest. The pleasure she took in organising concert parties and performing in them eclipsed the other pleasures of her busy young adult life. In retrospect we can see that a series of life events conspired to facilitate this wholehearted engagement with the stage.

In 1910, aged seventeen, May had left school after a brilliant career and, instead of taking a course in teaching or nursing as seen to be expected of a clever young woman, she enrolled immediately in a course of shorthand, typing and stenotypy. She then went to work at Trades Hall, as a clerk and personal secretary to her father, who at that time was general secretary of the Amalgamated Timber Workers' Union and Musicians' Union. This was an unusual position for a young woman – she was for many years the only woman working at Trades Hall – but was consistent with the role her father seemed to have carved out for her, as his helpmeet and protégé. These were turbulent times industrially and politically, and Jack Holman did not shrink from confrontation either in the Parliament[6] or within the union movement.[7] He had steered the timber workers through the disputes of 1907, and by 1911 could boast that under his stewardship the union had moved from being one of the weakest to one of the strongest in the state.[8] He was proud of the industrial peace that had reigned during this time: *Prior to 1907 a stoppage took place at least once a year, causing loss to all*, but since June 1907 no serious stoppage had occurred.[9] His views on the positive benefits of unionism were deeply ingrained, and no doubt readily transmitted to his talented daughter:

> *The fact that unionism as it becomes stronger not only protects the worker but brings industrial peace should teach those who are continually opposing unionism and condemning the officers and leaders as agitators that the best possible protection for industrial peace is perfect organisation.*[10]

Although no doubt the young May Holman admired her father's skill in ensuring industrial peace, she would also have been aware that this was exhausting work. She'd have been aware that, by the end of 1911, not long after she had joined him at Trades Hall, her father was tired. In spite of his successes on behalf of unionists, there was disquiet in the ranks. He had been publicly accused in a long-running battle in the newspapers of making inflated claims about his effectiveness as union organiser.[11] In a moving statement to the fifth Annual Conference of the Amalgamated Timber Workers' Union he announced his decision to retire from his position as secretary:

> *After five years of the hardest work of my life, I find it necessary to have a spell, for a time at least. To organise and keep together a few thousand men is no light task, especially when they are scattered over a large area, and the nature of their calling renders it necessary for them to shift to many different places. At times it has been a difficult matter to keep things going smoothly. I am, however, pleased to say my term of office has been fairly successful. Many advances have been secured, and much-needed reforms brought about; and it is gratifying to know that I can leave the timber workers*

in a strong position. Though many improvements have been secured, there is yet much to do, and I hope to see greater progress made in the near future. Since my connection with the timber workers I have often been accused of causing trouble, and have often been termed an agitator, but I am pleased to say that although my connection with the workers in this State dates back to 1893, when we were successful at Nannine in securing, after eight weeks, the increase of wages of £4 per week after reductions had been made to £3 3s. and £3 10s., and although since that time I have been engaged in many serious troubles, strikes, and lock-outs, I have never been the cause of a single employee ceasing work. After that step was taken, however, I never hesitated to take a definite stand, and have almost without exception, had the pleasure of leaving the workers better than I found them. While it may not, for private reasons, be possible for me to take the same active interest in the timber workers as hitherto, still I will be pleased at all times to give them any assistance that is in my power.[12]

In spite of this heartfelt speech, or perhaps because of it, Jack Holman was persuaded to withdraw his offer of resignation, and continued in his position as union secretary until 1914.

Imagine May's world: at work she was immersed in the rough and tumble of trade union politics, and from her beloved father she learned that tenacity, optimism, hard work and crafty politicking sat alongside the raw pain and exhaustion of the fight for workers' rights; at home in the big old house at 616 Beaufort Street she was her mother's confidante, and the house was full of Labor women dropping in for tea, to chat and to plan for, discuss, arrange the next event; and of course every day after work, even though Grandmother Rowe was always on hand, there was a string of younger siblings to attend to, to play with, to raise. The children clearly admired and depended on May. Was something broken? May would fix it. Did someone need her swimsuit mended? May would do it. Her next sister Maude had just started high school, but the younger ones – Jack, Winnie, and Ted – were at primary school, and little Bill was a toddler. Within a year of May leaving school there would be another baby, a girl, Iris, to care for. It was a full and busy life, but May relished it. She was still taking piano and singing lessons and soon she was accompanist for the Sacred Heart Ladies' Choir.[13] But she hadn't ever considered taking her performance career more seriously. There simply wasn't time. She was deeply interested alongside her mother in the affairs of Labor women, and in 1912 at age nineteen she had attended the first Labor Women's Conference in WA as note-taker. She had found some chums, Molly Holmes and Freda Wilson in particular, amongst the young women involved in Labor circles. And within another year or two she was in love, and she and Joe Gardiner announced their engagement in January 1914.[14]

We already know the story of her short-lived, secret marriage in the middle of 1914. Presumably the birthday party fiasco was enough to keep May and Joe apart forever. We can only guess at the impact this had on each of them. It's at this point that details of May's working life become shadowy. The Great War had begun and the everyday lives of Perth residents were already in turmoil. At home her newest baby sister, Eileen, was born a month after May's twenty-first birthday. Jack Holman had finally resigned as secretary of the Timber Workers' Union and May was working as a clerk in the office of the People's Printing and Publishing Company, which produced a Labor daily paper, and of which her father was promoter and chairman of directors. She continued to live at home with the family, but she must surely have been in shock. In one dramatic moment her father took to her birthday gifts with an axe, and her entire future was rearranged.

At some time in 1915, perhaps to regain some emotional equilibrium after the turmoil of the previous year, perhaps to rethink her relationship not just with her father or with Joe but with the world, May went to work on a farm for three months, cooking, baking bread, doing farm work, healing her sore heart with honest physical labour. It was at this point that she had her epiphany. As her friend Molly Holmes tells it, while May was on the farm she decided to turn her back on her own troubles and throw herself into concert work. She was already in demand as a pianist and vocalist for private social gatherings, but now she would organise more formally. She would devote herself to giving pleasure to others, through music and amateur theatrics. The world had changed, and Perth was suddenly full of young men in uniform, about to take off for that far-off theatre of war. May decided that her contribution to the war effort, and to eventual peace, would be to form an amateur theatre and concert party group specifically to bring pleasure to the departing troops. She wanted to lighten their hearts for a moment, lift their spirits, give them sweet memories of music and laughter and dancing. She would raise funds, too, for charities, for those less fortunate than herself.

The Entertainers, 1920s. May Holman in dark blouse.

On her return to Perth she *organised a galaxy of amateur talent into a popular concert party*,[15] and set about training her troupe, which she called The Amateur Entertainers. Their debut performance was held at McLeod's Hall, Mt Lawley, on 10 July 1916, before an invited audience of about one hundred and fifty friends and family of the company. By all reports it was a huge success.[16] Not content to be the accompanist, May also played the role of soubrette, that saucy, coquettish, intriguing maidservant of the comic opera world. That night her young brother Jack, still only sixteen, embarked on what would become a lifelong career as a comedian. Singers in the company included May's friends Bessie Rockliffe, Alice and Freda Wilson, Jack Myssonski, Chas Gillan, and Harry Kirkby. Ivan Mannion was listed as another comedian. At the end of the evening, May announced that, in addition to performing for soldiers, the company would give their assistance to any patriotic and charitable cause. And with a clever eye to the future, she also told her audience that a social and dance would be held the following week at this same Grosvenor Road hall, to raise funds for travelling and music expenses of the company.

The people of Perth quickly took The Amateur Entertainers to their hearts, and seemed moved by their talent and their generosity. *Never before in the history of Mt. Hawthorn was there held in the Congregational Hall such a fine concert as was given by the Amateur Entertainers (led by Miss May Holman) on Tuesday evening last,* enthused the Perth Prattle writer for *The Sunday Times*:

> *The Amateur Entertainers consist of nine young men and women who have banded together to the end of using their vocal and musical talents for charitable and patriotic purposes. Always ready to assist in any noble cause, they were only too eager, when they heard of the objectives of the Ladies' Patriotic Guild…, to do what they could to assist the funds which go towards providing comforts for our soldiers at the front. Pretty well every household in Mt. Hawthorn was represented at that concert last Tuesday night. Husbands*

who couldn't attend sent their wives, wives who couldn't get there sent their hubbies, and hubbies and wives who couldn't get away from household duties or business engagements sent along their kiddies. The little hall was crammed to the back of the porch entrance ... From start to finish the concert went with a swing, and old and young from the venerable grandma to the very tiny toddler enjoyed themselves immensely.

The article praised *the sweet singing of the Misses Rockliffe and Wilson, and the vivacious ragtime items by Miss May Holman, who accompanied herself and the other members on the piano ... Mt. Hawthorn will look forward with pleasure to the next visit of this talented company who are doing so much "for sweet-charity's sake."*[17]

So began a series of concerts that occupied almost every non-working waking hour of Miss Holman and her troupe for the duration of the war. May kept meticulous records of each performance, with its location, program, list of performers, mode of transport, distance travelled, and audience composition carefully recorded. On Thursday 25 January 1917 they gave their fiftieth concert, this time for the soldiers from Blackboy Hill camp. As an example of the intensity of their performance regime, in the following week they performed on Saturday 3 February at Osborne Park for the Scarborough Relief Fund; on Tuesday at Perth Town Hall for the Painters and Paperhangers Union; on Wednesday 7 February at Gosnells for the local Red Cross branch; and on Saturday 10 February at Kalamunda, under the auspices of the Darling Range Roads Board raising money for the children's hospital.[18]

The responses to Miss Holman and her troupe were as warm and heartfelt as the performances themselves. For example, after a concert for two hundred soldiers from the Belmont Camp on Tuesday 5 September 1916, Captain Ogilvie spoke eloquently and sincerely, with the flourishes of the day, about the pleasure The Entertainers gave to his men. *When men throw in their lot with the forces of the Empire*, he said,

> *they leave behind them everything: they forgo pleasure, the happiness of domestic life, and to a certain extent their liberty, and so they all the more appreciated the entertainments which had from time to time been given by concert parties, of which Miss Holman's was not by any means the least. The visits of the Amateur Entertainers to the various camps were as bright gleams of sunshine in the murky gloom, and hundreds of our lads who are now at the front – some of them alas! – we shall never see again – took away with them pleasurable recollections of the happy hours spent during the programmes provided by the Entertainers. At great personal inconvenience and on wet and dreary nights, had the party come out to cheer the boys, and, because the nights were wet and miserable, the concerts were all the more appreciated.*[19]

The report goes on to say that each guest was given a souvenir of the company.

In early April 1917, less than nine months after the debut performance, The Entertainers gave their eightieth performance. *The West Australian* gave it a splendid write-up, underscoring in its attention to detail the significance of the event and re-creating the pleasure given to its audience:

> *The eightieth performance of Miss May Holman's clever company of entertainers was given in the Church Hall, Queen's Park, on Saturday evening, in aid of the Queen's Park Fire Brigade. The Queen's Park Band, which has been chosen by the executive committee to take part in the annual fire brigades demonstration at Geraldton during Easter week, marched through the streets prior to the concert, and received hearty applause along the route. The hall was crowded and for over two hours the audience enjoyed a succession of songs, concerted pieces, and vaudeville sketches, almost every item being encored. A sprightly opening chorus by the full strength of the company was succeeded by "Jingle Johnny," a lively*

costume selection from "High Jinks," effectively given by Miss Bessie Rockliffe. After its repetition Master Harry Drysdale contributed "Pretty Ladies," and as an encore "The trail that leads to home." Miss. Freda Wilson, the possessor of a well-trained voice, was heard to much advantage in the songs "When you come home" and "I wonder if ever the rose." Miss Alice Wilson sang with much effect "The Valley of Laughter," and as an encore "Just for Me." Mr. Jack Myssouski sang "A little bit of heaven" followed by a highly humorous sketch, "The Fireman," by Mr. Jack Holman. He also contributed "Follow the Sergeant," receiving an encore for each. Mr. Harry Kirkby, another gifted member of the company, gave "Up from Somerset" and "Mother Machree," and took part in a trio with Messrs. Holman and Myssouski. A quaint little Dutch song and dance in national costume with sabots complete was given by Miss Rockliffe and Mr Drysdale, and had to be repeated. Miss May Holman, who acted as accompanist, and never left the platform during the progress of the entertainment, sang charmingly "Home from Tennessee," which received a double encore, in response to which she gave "This is the Life" and "Winter's Night." Concerted numbers were interspersed with good effect, and gave evidence of careful training. They included "Sunshine," "My Orange Girl," "The House that Jack Built," and the "Sunshine Girl." The performance went with a swing from start to finish, and there was not a dull moment, and a desire for another performance in Queen's Park was generally expressed. Mr. R. Coker moved a hearty vote of thanks to the company for the treat they had afforded and, in responding, Miss Holman wished the band a pleasant trip to Geraldton, where she was certain they would obtain an appreciative reception. The National Anthem was sung by the company [and] *the audience, and a social dance concluded the proceedings.*[20]

In engaging so fully with departing soldiers, The Entertainers were both reflecting the intimacy of the war experience for Perth citizens, and helping create an engagement with the war effort that sustained and nourished the isolated community of this south-western corner of the continent.

An indication of the everyday connection that ordinary citizens made with soldiers serving in France is found in this touching letter to *The West Australian*, written under the heading 'Y.M.C.A Military Work', and sharing column space with a short article on the work of The Entertainers. The letter, from Mr B. W. Gibson of Bridgetown, reads:

> *My daughter, aged 10 years, sent a billy along to the boys at the front last Christmas-time, which fell to the lot of Private J. M. L. Brown, No. 22, 28th Battalion, A.I.F., in acknowledgment of which he sent a card and letter, asking to be advised if they were received, which my daughter did, by sending back a card. By the last mail from France, my daughter received a letter from Sergeant Ryan, of Mr. Brown's company, stating that Private Brown had been killed in action. The only things found on him to give any clue as to his relatives were the card sent to him by my daughter and two photos. The conclusion drawn by the sergeant was that probably there was something in common between the photos and card with my daughter's name attached, so he posted them to her, along with a lock of hair. This is the point: [Mr.] Brown was a complete stranger to us. He must have had someone to whom that lock of hair would be precious, and it would be nice if these photos could find their proper owners. I would be glad if the 'West Australian' would assist me by publishing this letter, to place these things.*[21]

Some families were reluctant to let their sons go to war without a formal send-off, and here, too, the services of Miss Holman were requested. Sometimes these events were very close to home. In February 1916, before The Entertainers had been formally established, May was invited to arrange a program of music and dance for a social evening given by Mr and Mrs Shaw Walker in McLeod's Hall, Mt Lawley, in honour of their only son, Signaller Kenneth Shaw Walker, who was about to go to the front. The Shaw Walkers were neighbours of the Holmans in Beaufort Street. There were about ninety guests, and May, with a group of eight performers, provided the entire entertainment. It was a sentimental send-off. *The West Australian* records that on entering the hall, each of the ladies was given a blue and white ribbon with the initial 'K' in gold lettering.[22] The sad end to this tale is that Kenneth Shaw Walker died of wounds and gas poisoning in a hospital in Boulogne, France, on 1 November 1917. *Our brave boy. For Australia.,* read the funeral notice.[23] He was twenty years old.

In mid-1917 May went to Kalgoorlie for a year, to work as a cinema pianist. She returned to Perth in 1918 to take up a position as assistant secretary and confidential clerk to her father, who was again secretary of the Timber Workers' Union, and federal president of the Australian Timber Workers' Union. She stayed in this position until 1925, when the death of her father propelled her headlong into a life in parliament. She did not know it at the time, but the apprenticeship she served with her father during these years was excellent preparation for the history-making public life that lay just around the corner. Crucially, as part of his role with the Timber Workers' Union, John Barkell Holman was also an advocate for the union in the Federal and State Arbitration Courts, and May became experienced as his assistant in the courts, representing him when he was absent. In 1923 they went to Melbourne together for almost nine months, working together to present the Timber Workers' case for a forty-four hour week, increased wages and better conditions to the Federal Arbitration Court.

The Entertainers continued to perform whenever possible

throughout the war years and into the 1920s, with breaks when May was not available. Those who knew her well understood that the war years were crucial years for May, helping her to see that it was possible to offset the pain and grief of a broken heart with lighthearted fun and beautiful melody. Her friend who wrote the article in the *Westralian Worker* after her death in 1939 noted:

> *During those first gay years of her amateur theatrical work, May Holman learned to love the bright vivacious people of the stage, men and women, and all the fantasy and sparkle which hangs round that world of make-believe. When overworked or otherwise fagged, while most of us would go to bed, May went to a show and was always refreshed.*[24]

Crowning Queen Hospital Appeal, c. 1924. May Holman wearing crown.

But with hindsight we can detect a brittle quality in this frenetic pace of life. The schedule of The Entertainers was what we would now call punishing, and May Holman an exacting boss. Not only did she record dates, the venues and the audiences of all their locations, but she also recorded the attendance of her troupe at rehearsals and performances. It's not a big leap to suggest that the control she exerted over her troupe and their schedule echoed the control she exerted on her own unruly emotions. Did she pay a bodily price for this? We already know from our encounter with her eulogies that May Holman was plagued throughout her life, sometimes bedridden for months at a time, by bouts of debilitating illness: asthma, heart trouble, arthritis. Seen from this angle, hers is a sad story. That her response to personal grief is in keeping with the responses of the women and men of her community and her time does not make her story any less intriguing, nor does it remove the pain that sits alongside the joy she creates and expresses throughout her life.

May Holman's love of theatre, music and performance stayed with her for the rest of her life. Throughout her parliamentary career she charmed and cheered the families in her electorate with countless concerts, performances, and singalongs, at weddings, socials, electioneering rallies, family parties. Her friends and younger sisters recall that, long after her siblings had left home to establish families of their own, she loved nothing better than to hark back to their original family life by gathering them all together in the big house in Bassendean for an evening of song and silliness.

As May matured, so too did her understanding of the power of performance. Her friend writing for the *Westralian Worker* observes:

> *Always romantic, this quality, as with us all, took on new phases and methods of expression as her life matured. She*

had always a delicious sense of humour, and reveled in recounting funnyisms at her own expense, in teasing her friends without sarcasm about their weaknesses, and in discovering the comical in all the varied situations in which she found herself.[25]

No doubt these qualities – of courage and resilience in masking her own pain in order to perform and bring joy to others – came at a cost to her own wellbeing. But they also proved to be essential to her success as a politician.

Holman family, 3 Ida Street, Bassendean, early 1920s.
Back row, from left: Bill, Winnie, Ted, John, May, Maude.
Front row: Eileen, John, Sheila, Katherine, Iris.

CHAPTER 6
THE HONOURABLE THE MEMBER FOR FORREST

When May Holman admitted to *feeling terrible* on that history-making afternoon of 30 July 1925 as she entered the parliament for the first time on the arm of her mother before a packed public gallery, her discomfort was surely momentary. In fact she was exceptionally well qualified to take up her role as Member for Forrest. Her years as an entertainer had given her an acute sense of audience and had sharpened her clever wit, which meant she could hold her own on the floor of the House. Her years at Trades Hall under the exacting mentorship of her father had given her a thorough apprenticeship in industrial issues, and her recent experience of advocacy in the industrial courts at State and Federal level gave her a deeper understanding of industrial processes than many of her parliamentary colleagues. This ensured that she felt on certain ground industrially, and when she spoke on these matters she was respected by her parliamentary colleagues as well as by the timber workers in her electorate. Her lifetime of immersion in Labor politics meant that she was philosophically assured, and ideologically committed in ways that were transparent to her colleagues and to her opposition. Crucially, her history as a valued member of an esteemed Labor family meant that to a very large extent her family reputation preceded her, and codes of politeness and loyalty meant she was protected by her Labor colleagues in the House. With her mother she shared a deep interest in finding ways to involve Labor women and their children in working towards the great Labor ideals. Even her position as eldest child in a family of nine meant that she was accustomed to taking responsibility and to attending to the everyday cares of those more vulnerable than she; arguably, this made it possible for her to empathise with the daily lives of the families in her electorate and to willingly undertake to advocate for them wherever possible. And finally, her youthful experience of being for many years the only woman working at Trades Hall meant that she knew how to rub shoulders with trade union men. Members of the House could surely not be much more difficult.

May Holman early in her parliamentary career.

The respect that she was able to command as a result of this unique combination of personal qualities and specific life experiences quickly became apparent. May Holman did not speak often in the House in this first year, nor indeed in any other year, but when she did speak, she was listened to, for the most part, with attention and courtesy. Her colleagues came to understand that she would speak only when she was thoroughly prepared.

Her first engagement with parliamentary debate was in the second parliamentary sitting in September 1925, when she rose to contribute to the discussion of ways to determine the basic wage. She argued that the parliament should set the standard for wage-fixing, rather than the courts doing so. She entered the fray in a manner that became characteristic of her: as a debater she was determined, responsible, and well informed. In response to the argument of Sir James Mitchell, leader of the opposition, that the courts were the only appropriate place where wage-fixing was possible, Miss Holman rose to say, *It is the duty of Parliament, I consider, to set up a standard.* Sir James Mitchell immediately sought to diminish her stature in the House by interjecting, *But then you are new to Parliament*; but Miss Holman was not deterred and stood her ground. Without missing a beat, she launched into a defence of her statement with a speech beginning: *In the past there has not been a standard and the court has not had sufficient ground on which to work.*[1] In the subsequent debate she successfully drew on her experience of the obfuscation and delay being exacted by employers in repeatedly taking challenges to improved wage conditions back to the courts, so causing repeated and unnecessary delays, to the disadvantage of workers.[2] The media reported her performance favourably, impressed by her poise and her articulate capacity to bring her industrial expertise to the floor of the House.[3]

By far the most memorable of her speeches to the House was her introduction to the Timber Industry Regulation Bill that went before parliament in 1926.[4] We know that her two-and-a-half hour speech in support of this bill on 19 October 1926 earned her the respect of the House.[5] We know too that the work she put into researching and framing this bill was widely admired beyond the Western Australian parliamentary sphere, and copies of her work were requested by the International Labor Organisation in Geneva, by several American university libraries, and by legislatures around the world. This work cemented her reputation in the Western Australian parliament for hard work and intelligent preparation.

As a parliamentarian, May Holman was in the happy position of being on the government side of the House for eleven of the fourteen years of her career. Her term of office occurred at a time of great Labor stability, with a Labor government headed by the long-serving premier Philip Collier for two terms (from 1924 until 1930, and 1933 until 1936) and then by premier John Willcock from 1936 until 1945. During these two decades of Labor rule, it was only for three years during the Great Depression, from 1930 until 1933, that Labor relinquished power to a Nationalist–Country Party coalition government led by Sir James Mitchell as premier. Not surprisingly perhaps, May Holman's most impassioned speeches were made during her period in opposition, during the Depression, when her constituents were most vulnerable and most deeply in need of her representation.

The issues she spoke on throughout her career were usually connected either with workers' rights and conditions, or were relevant to the wellbeing of women and children. While her support for the broader suite of Labor ideals was never in doubt, what quickly became clear to her colleagues and to the local media was her intense interest in tracing the impact of parliamentary decisions on the lived experiences of ordinary folk. She saw education as a way out of grinding poverty and powerlessness for the working classes; she saw child rearing as a crucially important activity, and maternal health as central to a satisfying family life; she was aware of the benefits of a good diet and a healthy outdoor physical lifestyle; she understood the need for decent living conditions, good health services, and adequate housing. She knew the dignity of work; and she knew the experience of being valued for her capacities rather than being diminished or limited by her gender. Her own childhood had given her a clear sense of the joys of performance, of music, of a life beyond the everyday drudgery of mere survival. She had loved her life, and was aware, too, of its dark corners: she was driven now by the desire to share the bounty with the working classes, to redistribute not just monetary wealth, but the pleasures of living such as had been available to her. Seen in this light, it's not surprising that among the specific debates with which she engaged during the fourteen year period of her life as a member of parliament, were the debates about raising the school leaving age to sixteen, child endowment, equal pay for men and women, and improving training and working conditions of female domestic servants. Towards the end of her parliamentary career, in 1937, in evidence to the Royal Commission on Youth Employment, she described her work as *convener of a party committee dealing with youth employment problems.*[6] In 1938, at her instigation, a royal commission to inquire into sanitation, slum clearance and health and housing regulations in Perth was set up; Miss Holman was a member.

A thorough reading of Hansard Parliamentary Debates for the period of her parliamentary career indicates that it was characteristic of May Holman's representation of constituents that no issue was too big or too small for her to tackle on their behalf. She was as ready to stand up in parliament to ask the minister for police to consider the question of providing summer uniforms for the police force (*The Minister will readily admit that it is unpleasant for the police to have to stand in the sweltering heat of summer clad in heavy clothing and without shelter*)[7] as she was to tackle the reform of industrial legislation affecting the timber workers in her electorate. She quickly adopted her own style of parliamentary engagement. Rather than using a distanced tone and arguing a point solely on abstract principle, or rather than heckling and inanely ridiculing her opponents, Miss Holman invited her parliamentary colleagues on both sides of the House to imagine the everyday worlds of her constituents through that most ancient of art forms, storytelling. Her purpose seems to have been twofold: she wanted members to empathise with the plight of the constituents under discussion; and she wanted to illustrate to her electorate that she had their interests at heart.[8]

One of the earliest examples of what became her trademark storytelling technique occurred on 6 October 1925, several months into her first sitting of the House, when she supported the amendment to the Primary Products Marketing Bill, permitting growers of fresh fruit and vegetables to sell direct to customers rather than going through a Fruit and Vegetable Board. In the course of her speech she told this story:

> *Down in the Manjimup District an orchardist made arrangements with his mill people to sell them apples at 6s. a case. He kept his contract although he found he could have got 15s. a case in Perth. The selling of those apples led to quite a brisk little trade in fresh vegetables as well, to the advantage of both the producer and the consumers.*

She went on to combine principle with image in the following argument: *There is also the advantage of selling direct in the open markets and selling in the orchards, where fruit such as peaches and apricots can be picked fresh off the tree and the buyer can have it packed and transported.*[9]

When in the October sitting of parliament in 1925, May Holman rose to speak in support of the needs of women about to give birth at King Edward Memorial Hospital in Subiaco, Perth, she once again gave specific glimpses of daily life to illustrate the need to accede to her request for extra funding:

> *Expectant mothers have to be taken into the ward at the King Edward Memorial Hospital where they have to be treated amongst others who are already in labour. While the newly arrived expectant mothers cannot see the other patients, they can hear what is going on. This is unnerving to the expectant*

mothers and is not in their best interests. An ante-natal ward would, therefore, be of great assistance.[10]

Her storytelling on the floor of the House in 1925 initiated several quests that were to persist well beyond her first year in parliament, and indicates a willingness to argue with and make specific requests of ministers on her own side of the House, even while in government. The first concerns child endowment. Her request was directly to the minister for justice, concerning the possibility of having the allowance for children increased from nine shillings per week. The story she told in support of this request indicates her familiarity with specific cases of real lives affected by child endowment anomalies: *The allowance ceases at age 14 but a girl may not go out to work until she is 15 years of age and in the country there is not work at all for girls of that age. So,* she surmised, *I should be glad to hear the Minister say that he thought of increasing the weekly allowance and increasing also the age to which the allowance is given from 14 years to 15 years.*[11]

She followed up this question on 17 November 1925 with participation in the debate about payment to women with dependent children.[12] As a measure of her persistence, two years later, on 27 October 1927 during the first session of the Fourteenth Parliament, we find her requesting an increase from nine shillings per week to 12/6 per week for each child, to be paid to women on whom children were dependent. Her argument was impassioned but rational, and made all the more potent through story:

A mother may have four children and be in receipt of 36s. per week from the department, but if she earns more than a certain amount it is deducted from the 36s. The sum of 36s. is not sufficient to pay for rent and clothing and all the wants of four children, and if by working she could earn a few shillings, she should be encouraged to do so in order that her children might be better clothed and fed. The basic wage for a man, his wife and a family of three or four children is

£4 5s. a week, on which sum they are supposed to be able to live in reasonable comfort. Yet a family that have lost the breadwinner are supposed to be able to live on a much smaller sum. I hope the Minister will increase the allowance to women as soon as possible.[13]

A second quest begun in 1925 concerns maternal health, and relates specifically to conditions for both nurses and patients in the King Edward Memorial Hospital for Women in Subiaco. Early in her parliamentary life May Holman drew the attention of the minister for health to the absurdity of nurses having to pay a premium of fifteen pounds before doing their training at King Edward Memorial Hospital: *I would be glad to hear from him as to whether anything has been done in that direction.*[14]

A third quest begun in 1925 and followed for many years concerns issues of health and sanitation in the timber settlements of the South-West. Miss Holman requested that health inspectors be appointed to oversee the provision of adequate sanitation and water in the timber country. To illustrate the need for this, she told the story of the outbreak of typhoid fever at Nanga Brook and requested that inoculation against typhoid be introduced: *In one small camp of 40 men at Nanga Brook landing there were six deaths.*[15] Her interest in provision of adequate housing was not confined to her electorate; nor was it a passing fancy of hers that such matters were significant. As we have already seen, in 1938, at her instigation, a royal commission to inquire into sanitation, slum clearance and health and housing regulations in Perth was established, and May Holman herself was a member.

It was in defending the lives and rights of her direct constituents, those forest dwellers in the South-West electorate she represented, that May Holman was most practical and persuasive. Throughout her political career she was warmly admired for her devotion to her electorate. It was here that she shone as a politician and as a woman. Simply put, she came to love the families in her electorate, and they came to love her. She spoke effectively in the House about their poor living conditions, poor health services, inadequate schooling, and dangerous work. She listened to the women as well as to the men and came to know their dreams, their small irritations, their heartaches, their joys. Her electorate was spread over a stretch of country about 150 miles long, and was not easily traversed. When describing it for posterity in 1935, she wrote *the area must be travelled by mill train, navvies' trolley, motor car, and in some cases must be tramped. Many timber mills and small settlements are scattered through the electorate. When working full-handed some of the mills employ 300 or 400 men.*[16]

May Holman in her Tin Lizzie.

She brought to her representation the same kind of relentless energy that she had earlier brought to her performances with The Entertainers. At first she made headlines by travelling on the cow-catcher at the front of the mill trains to visit small settlements deep in the forest. Later, almost every weekend she would pack one or two sisters or brothers-in-law into her Tin

Lizzie, and head down south again. She made a point of visiting every family in her electorate, usually entering by the kitchen door and chatting at the kitchen table, in contrast with male parliamentarians who seemed forced by their gender to adopt the more formal practice of visiting families in their electorate in the front room.[17] She loved nothing better than to provide music for these forest dwellers, and was often invited to perform at weddings, or weekend socials. She also put her musical skills to good use during her electioneering campaigns, and in the lead-up to one election she was memorably accused by her political opponents of using *'insidious propaganda'* by entertaining her audiences with political material.[18]

Her intimate knowledge of her constituents and their lives gave her all the fuel she needed for storytelling on the floor of the House. One of her earliest tenacious defences of timber workers and their needs came during the passage of the Timber Workers Bill that she so eloquently supported. On 14 December 1926 there was debate about an amendment to the bill requiring that 'dangerous trees' be cleared from near the train tracks in the timber country. Hansard records the comments of several members of parliament who admit they know little, and who speak in very general terms;[19] but when May Holman spoke, she was clear and practical. At times she played the maternal card:

> *Women and children ride on the front of the engine or on the rakes of timber wherever they can find a seat. We ask that dangerous trees be taken out if they are alongside the line, past which women and children have to be conveyed on the bush lines. Some of the trees are only eight or ten inches away from the rakes as they pass by. Some of the companies have cleared both sides of their lines back to a considerable distance and have taken out even the blackboy trees! Surely it cannot be regarded as a hardship to make the companies take out the dangerous trees growing right alongside the line. I gave an instance of a man whose knee*

> was cut when passing a dangerous tree close to the line. As to the man with the red flag patrolling the line, there is no such thing suggested. All we ask is that on a dark winter morning an engine shall run out to see if the line is clear and thus protect the lives of those who may be aboard the timber rake later on.[20]

If we look closely at the conclusion to this speech we uncover a rhetorical strategy May Holman liked to use. The expression 'All we ask' has two strategic advantages: it makes her request seem modest; and the use of the inclusive pronoun 'we' suggests wide support for her request, either from her constituents or from her fellow members of parliament.

Although it is certainly possible to read May Holman's interventions on behalf of her timber workers and their families with admiration for her tenacity and deep understanding of their lives and conditions, her determination to bring their plight to the attention of her parliamentary colleagues was not always welcomed. An example of the kind of friction generated by her dogged insistence occurs in Hansard in the debates following the introduction of the Timber Workers Bill. The friction that occurred between Miss Holman and Mr J. H. Smith, the conservative member for Nelson, was all the more surprising because the passage of this bill was considered to transcend party loyalties and to be beyond adversarial party-aligned debate. There had already been friction between Miss Holman and Mr Smith: in an earlier discussion of a proposed amendment to the bill, Miss Holman showed that she was ready to defend herself by rising to ask the speaker, *Is the member for Nelson in order in saying that I have endeavoured to hoodwink members? This is the second time he has made that statement, and I ask that it be withdrawn.* Mr Smith replied, *I withdraw the statement, but the inference is there.*[21]

Later that same week, Mr Smith ridiculed all proposals for amendment of the Timber Workers Bill relating to drainage of bush landings, the use of smokescreens in mills, the need for proficiency in the use of the English language of timber workers, the need to clear dangerous trees from bush lines, and the need to ensure adequate housing of workers. After his tirade, Miss Holman rose to say: *I cannot allow the utterances of the member for Nelson to pass unanswered.* She questions his sincerity in supporting the bill. As an example of the ways she could hold her own in debate even at this early stage of her parliamentary career, listen to this exchange:

> Miss HOLMAN: *I do not think the hon. member is conversant with the conditions in his own electorate or in any other part of the timber industry.*
>
> Mr J. H. SMITH: *I shall not go to you to learn them.*
>
> Miss HOLMAN: *It might be better if the hon. member did. At Jarrahdale, which has been established for nearly 40 years, we tried for months to get Millars to improve the conditions, but they refused. Finally the present Minister sent a health inspector there with special instructions and Millars had to come to heel. This, notwithstanding that the men at that centre had offered to pay the rate for the conveniences. The hon. member will not be at all popular when his utterances become known in his electorate. Here is a statement from Pemberton:*
>
> *"In the summer the smoke from the sawdust fires is a curse; in fact you cannot see in the mill at times, which is a danger to men working around the benches, and I trust that you will try to get something done in the shape of a high galvanised iron wall, so that it will lift the smoke clear of the mills, and also relieve the watchman of some of his anxiety at night time when sparks are getting blown about; also that the sawdust dumps be removed more often and burned away from the spots where they are now dumped."*
>
> Hon. G. Taylor: *That is bad for State management.*
>
> Miss HOLMAN: *It is bad that the hon. member should not know the conditions prevailing in his electorate. [...]*

> Miss HOLMAN: ... *The member for Nelson says he supports the Bill. Yet he is raising objections, although he knows this State is so far behind in legislation of this kind. Nothing was done by him or by his party to give the timber workers the protection to which they are entitled. The hon. member raises the same old cry that this measure will place heavy impositions on the industry. Every movement to better the conditions of the workers has met with the cry that the industry could not stand the expense. In New Zealand the regulations for housing accommodation are much stricter than those we ask. The Minister has not asked for any extravagant power. Bushmen work from early morning till late at night, and they cannot be expected to clear their house sites after finishing the day's work. They are working for employers who are getting the profit out of the timber mills, and surely some portion of it should be applied to making the conditions more comfortable for the employees. Members who express such a high opinion of the timber workers and their common sense, might back it up by conceding them a vote for the Legislative Council.* [22]

After this quite personal attack by Miss Holman, Mr J. H. Smith defended his own motives by arguing that he was doing his best *to eliminate the ridiculous regulations which the Minister has based on the claptrap of Members who know little of the industry and have gained their limited knowledge by sitting in an office and listening to trivial complaints.*[23] If this salvo was intended to silence or ridicule May Holman, it backfired. In addition to her retort that *The timber workers will be pleased to hear that*, the spat was directly commented on by Mr Lambert, the Labor member for Coolgardie, who readily made political mileage out of it and who, like West Australians generally, clearly saw May Holman as her father's direct successor. He said:

> *It is somewhat heroic on the part of the member for Nelson to indulge in a kind of family fight with the member for Forrest. The name of the member for Forrest is honourably associated with the industry, and the workers in it confidently look to her to protect their interests. She is the mouthpiece in this Chamber of a big proportion of them. Every local company that has any regard for the safety of its workers would observe the utmost care regarding them, but other companies might not do so. I am sorry the member for Forrest does not possess a louder voice with which to retort to the circus-like display of the member for Nelson, who would have us believe that the timber companies, acting for profit alone, should be allowed to hold cheaply the lives and limbs of the workers. It is time these corporations gave the workers a little of the benefit they themselves have received from the industry.*[24]

If May Holman was driven by a desire to protect her constituents, she was also driven by a desire to protect the timber industry itself, and the forests that supported it. In what is perhaps one of the earliest public expressions of concern about the plundering of native forests in the South-West of Western Australia, May Holman on 31 August 1927 spoke against the wastage of native timber through the sub-contracting of *the steady influx of foreigners* who knew little about the industry, undermined union wages and wasted a precious resource. She was speaking on the motion to require Millar's Timber Company to lay upon the Table of the House a return with information on its activities in the forest, specifically the number and location of concessions, and date granted, expirations, extensions and the royalties per load or the rent being paid in each case.

> *Shortly after my entering this House I spoke on foreigners cutting timber and to a large extent being victimised. I also spoke of the waste of timber caused by these inexperienced*

men. Since then we have been told, and readily believe, that the forests of Western Australia are a public inheritance, and that we should look after them and try to conserve some of them, and also to replace what has been taken, for the coming generations. I think it is really our concern to see that timber is not wasted.

She recommended that *the Forests Department consider some ways and means of controlling the wholesale cutting and waste that are going on in our forests*, and said that *perhaps the motion to require Millar's to present their returns to the House will help us a little*.[25]

Her parliamentary work and advocacy was not always solely for her electorate. Often her interventions had an impact on city dwellers. For example, in 1928 the *Mirror* reported:

Miss May Holman, M.L.A., deserves an enthusiastic pat on the back... for her work in securing the kiddies' playground up in King's Park. This is the sort of practical good that justifies the election of women members of Parliament and makes us wish there were more. There isn't a harder worker in the House than the member for Forrest.[26]

Frequently, too, she stretched the horizons of the children in her electorate and other rural areas by hosting visits to the city. Soon after her election in 1925 the *Daily News* ran an article about a daytrip to Perth of a group of school children from Jarrahdale, who spent the morning in the city visiting the two cathedrals, the museum and the art gallery, and the afternoon at Parliament House learning about their constitutional history and being entertained to afternoon tea in the members' dining room by Miss Holman.[27] The following article records the visit to the city of a group of country girls studying by correspondence:

> *The girls in camp at Claremont in connection with the correspondence branch of the Education Department are having their time fully occupied, and the schedule of amusement and instruction drawn up for them is most comprehensive. Wednesday, for instance, might be taken as a specimen day. In the morning they visited the Houses of Parliament, where they were received by Miss May Holman, Mr. H. Mann, and Mr. Gray, and shown over the building. Afterwards they attended a reception in the Mayoress' rooms at the Council Chambers; from there they were taken in charabancs to the City Beach, where they had races, competitions, and games, the prizes being distributed by the Mayoress. Then, in the evening, they were entertained by a demonstration of the most modern developments in music, more especially in connection with the mechanical wonders, and some orchestral and vocal music in the recital hall of Messrs. Musgrove's, Ltd., by that firm. Meals, of course, were sandwiched in between these various activities, but the girls, all of whom are from the country, must be quite ready for the day's end when it comes.*[28]

May Holman took a genuine interest in the wellbeing of young people. From the time of her entry into the parliament she racked her brains to find ways to prepare young people for service to the great Labor cause. In 1927 she founded a club for young Labor people, which they named the Meanwhile Club. She wanted to be able to instill in young people an understanding of Labor ideals, and a love and respect for the movement itself. She came up with the brilliant idea of training club members in public speaking, elocution, drama, debate and essay writing. She was delighted and proud when club members made a name for themselves by scooping up many of the prizes for speech and drama in the local eisteddfod competitions. Her interest in helping shape productive and satisfying lives for young people never wavered. In 1935, almost a decade after establishing the Meanwhile Club, she worked with another generation of young people to found the Young Labor League. Her work with young people continued until her death, and from 1937 she convened a party committee dealing with youth unemployment problems.

One of the great debates occurring during May Holman's first years in parliament concerned the question of enfranchisement: who was entitled to vote in the Legislative Council? In 1927 the Government introduced a bill to extend the vote for the Legislative Council (Western Australia's Upper House) to all citizens who could currently vote for the Legislative Assembly (the Lower House). May Holman spoke formally on this bill on 27 September. The problem as it related specifically to timber workers was that entitlement to vote in the Legislative Council was means-tested, and, in this case, depended on the amount of rent paid per household. Rents in the timber country were lower than in the city, and of course Miss Holman was not arguing for an increase in rents to entitle timber-working householders to be eligible to vote! Rather, she argued that the present rents in her electorate were an accurate reflection of the poor quality of housing and services, but insisted that *none of* [this] *ought to condemn a timber worker to being disenfranchised.*[29] Once again her speech was thoroughly prepared. She avoided the kind of posturing and slanging indulged in by other members and instead presented solid evidence to back up her argument, this time giving precise numbers of electors in each of the tiny settlements in the timber country, for example, *Dwellingup has 83 dwellings, 152 people on the Assembly roll and 27 on the* [Legislative] *Council roll. We are asking for the vote for the 83 householders. Even that would be only be 50 per cent.* The argument she made about democratic representation, though insistent, was polite and considered:

> We have been told time and time again by members of the Opposition that the timber workers do not want the vote, have never asked for it, and that nothing has been heard of their desire to get it. I should like to ask members of the

> *Opposition what they think we are here for? Do members of the Opposition want our electors, my electors of Forrest, to come to Perth, swarm around the House and shout, "We want the vote!" Is it not the proper thing for the electors to send in their views through their representatives? Are we not supposed to have from our electors a mandate to speak at all on their behalf? Yet when we ask for the vote for our electors, we are told they do not want it and that nothing is ever heard of their desire to get it! ... The timber workers are responsible for much of the prosperity of the State and for much of the railway revenue, and they are assisting to build up the country ... and it is a crying shame that members opposite should stand in their places and say that such men are not entitled to a vote for the Council.*[30]

On 25 July 1929, May Holman had the honour of making the address-in-reply to the governor's speech opening the fifth session of the Thirteenth Parliament. This was the centenary year of British settlement in Western Australia; May Holman's speech provides a snapshot of the cultural, social and political attitudes of the day. She began: *The State has made such progress that our Centenary year finds us all well on the way to a great harvest, and finds the State on the road to greater prosperity.* She praised the agriculture industry and gold mining, harbour works and water supplies:

> *Wonderful water supplies are being constructed throughout the country and I think the Minister controlling agricultural water supplies, as well as his department, is entitled to praise and gratitude for the work being done in the interests of people who live in the back-blocks. I have seen the water carried for miles and I have seen huge reservoirs constructed, and I am informed that more money has been spent on the provision of water supplies for farmers during the regime of the present Government than ever before in the history of the department.*[31]

But there are some issues that still, in her view, needed addressing, and she did not lose the opportunity to remind the House that the question of adult franchise had not been resolved to her satisfaction: she plugged for a better franchise for people in her district, where of the four thousand people, only about one hundred were eligible to vote at Legislative Council elections. She discussed the timber industry and defended the Forest Department's desire to reserve dedicated areas for forestry. And she continued her lament that foreigners working on private land were inexperienced, wasting timber resources, working long hours for below union wages, and producing sleepers at below mill costs, so that contractors were tendering under those conditions.

Another issue dear to her heart, the provision of good health services, had been addressed, and was worth celebrating:

I believe that never in the history of the State has so much been given to the health of the people in the way of constructing hospitals, adding to existing hospitals and providing X-ray plants… When the present Government took office there was one medical officer examining the school children. Now there are three full time and one half time medical officers, and there are also three school dentists.

She lost no chance to remind the minister of his promise to care for the dental health of country children: *I am looking forward to the time when the Minister will be able to provide the two travelling dental clinics he has promised us, so that children in the country will have a better chance of preserving their teeth.*

And she delighted in celebrating the advances in infant health care: *When the Labor Party took office there was only one infant health centre but there are now 16 infant health centres, which means that 60 per cent of the children born in the State are receiving attention at child welfare clinics and consequently there is a considerable decrease of infantile mortality.*[32]

In a very real sense it can be argued that, in this early period of May Holman's parliamentary career, from 1925 to 1930, she had a dream run. She was deeply respected for her work on the Timber Workers Bill; she was admired for her devotion to her electorate; and her commitment to the great Labor ideals of social justice for the working classes, the right to dignified work, and the equitable distribution of resources was never in doubt. Her parliamentary colleagues respected and supported her from the beginning. No doubt it helped that the premier, Philip Collier, was a close family friend.

However, although May Holman was supported by her Labor Party colleagues on the floor of the House, she was never automatically assured of her seat in parliament. For the first seven years of her parliamentary life, every time an election loomed, her position was challenged by men at the party level and she had to undergo the selection ballot process. The selection ballot, which was then a ballot of unaffiliated members of the Labor Party in the particular district, was held before each election to choose the Labor candidate for the relevant constituency. The first ballot process May Holman underwent in 1925 to get selection for her seat of Forrest involved an all-male vote of party members. Eleven men nominated against May as candidates for selection in that ballot. May's strong links to the union movement, in combination with union loyalty to her father whose death necessitated this by-election, ensured that she won pre-selection. No other party nominated a candidate for that by-election, so after being selected as the Labor candidate, she was elected unopposed to her seat on 3 April 1925. In 1926 her second selection process occurred in the lead-up to the 1927 election. This time two men nominated against her as potential candidates. Again she won the selection ballot, and again she was elected unopposed to her seat. In 1929 she won her third selection ballot against three men, and was elected to her seat by a majority of 1057 votes against two male opponents from the National and Country Parties.

A redistribution of electoral boundaries in 1929 changed the composition of her electorate significantly. The seat now included potato growers, orchardists, dairy farmers and railway workers in addition to timber workers. With typical thoroughness, Miss Holman set about getting to know her new constituents and their desires. Nobody challenged her in the 1932 selection process, and once again in the 1933 elections that followed she defeated her single opponent, this time by a majority of 1537 votes. She was re-elected unopposed in 1936, and in 1939 she easily retained her seat against her single conservative opponent.

From the beginning May Holman knew that diligence held the key to her success as a member of parliament. Throughout her parliamentary life she argued that women can be as successful in parliament as men, but women must understand that they are judged by harsher standards. She surely knew that, had she been a man, she would almost certainly have been offered a ministry quite early in her career. Ironically, it was not until the 1939 election that occurred three days before her death that Labor Women took matters into their own hands and, on 9 January 1939, unanimously resolved to write to the Labor Movement as a whole and to the Parliamentary Labor Party in particular, respectfully suggesting that *the inclusion of Miss May Holman in the Cabinet would give the greatest confidence to the Labor women of the State and would strengthen the position of the Movement in respect of Western Australian women generally.* They were clearly determined to make their point, that Miss Holman was well overdue for consideration for the Cabinet; but the tone of their concluding sentence, *Any move in this direction will be deeply appreciated*,[33] suggests that, even though Miss Holman had spent fourteen years as an exemplary member of parliament, they knew they were on uncertain ground.

With this in mind, we turn now to a closer examination of what it meant to be a woman in parliament in this period of Western Australia's history.

CHAPTER 7
THERE'S A WOMAN IN THE HOUSE!

May Holman was the second woman ever to sit in the parliamentary chamber as a member of the Legislative Assembly in Western Australia. Perhaps because of her youth, perhaps because of her deep immersion in the Labor Party, she did not experience the public lampooning that Edith Cowan had experienced in the same parliament only a few years earlier. No sooner had Edith Cowan been elected to the parliament than a cartoon appeared depicting her as a bossy, unattractive, talkative busybody, standing to wash clothes on the floor of the House to the clear discomfort of the stooped and be-suited men seated beside her.

This image was clearly inaccurate as a representation of Australia's first woman parliamentarian: Edith Cowan was nearly sixty years old at the time of her election to the parliament, and, far from being the working-class harridan that Leason imagined, she was dignified, articulate and well-educated. During her term Edith Cowan herself acknowledged that she suffered through not being strongly aligned with a particular political party. Although she had stood for election as a member of the conservative Nationalist party, as soon as she was elected Mrs Cowan made it clear to them and to the House that she would be voting independently and specifically on behalf of women. She used her term in parliament to promote migrant welfare, infant health centres and women's rights, and she argued forcefully for the establishment of a housewives' union. She is best remembered for opening the legal profession to women in 1923 through her introduction of The Women's Legal

Leason's cartoon, 'The New "House" Wife', Bulletin, 31 March 1921.

Status Act as a private member's bill. Her refusal to align politically with the Nationals won Mrs Cowan no favours in the House, nor indeed in the press, and in spite of her intelligent interventions in parliamentary debate, at the end of her first term she lost her seat, and failed again to be re-elected in 1927.[1]

As we have seen, May Holman's experience as a parliamentarian contrasted markedly with that of Edith Cowan. Rather than being treated with disdain, she was apparently welcomed in the House. It probably helped that she actively distanced herself from the feminist label, preferring instead to demonstrate strong allegiance to the Labor movement and to fight for her constituents on the basis of class rather than gender. This position was consistent with the rhetoric within the Party throughout her parliamentary career. A statement of admiration in 1935 from John Curtin, then MHR for Fremantle, in celebration of May Holman's ten years in parliament, spells out this position:

> *A woman who believes in the Labor Movement and its principles is far better equipped to aid mankind in the struggle for justice and social peace than any man who opposes the principles of Labor. But no celebration in honour of Miss Holman must blind us to the fact that a man who stands for the faith and the policy of Labor is infinitely more competent to contribute to the resolving of the difficulties of the time than any woman whose participation in public life is synonymous with support for Capitalism and the maintenance of the existing order.*[2]

Miss Holman herself made her position quite clear in 1937 when interviewed on whether women can be a success in parliament:

> *To go into parliament, and to stay there, one must belong to a party. 'Independent' women will not get anywhere. Some women candidates for parliament take their stand as feminists and state that they will sit in the House – if elected – to represent the women's viewpoint. But to be a success in parliament, one has got to drop the purely feminine point of view and look on things absolutely as a member representing her electors and party.*[3]

Even though she did not actively identify as feminist, Miss Holman did prove time and again that she was prepared to argue with members on her own side of the House on issues relating to the wellbeing of women and children. One such incident happened on 24 November 1927, when she challenged the minister for health and the premier on their lack of support for a motion to appoint a female probation officer to oversee the probation of young women and girls who appeared before the Children's Court. In her frustration, she cried, *I do not know what is wrong with members on this side of the House, who are supposed to stand for sympathy and humanity, that they do not see the necessity for the appointment of a woman probation officer? By what authority would women police* [the alternative to a female probation officer] *keep cases out of the court?*[4]

Although for the most part she enjoyed the respect of her parliamentary colleagues, Miss Holman was aware that her gender elicited responses that continued to set her apart. She was especially aware of the slightly avuncular approach taken towards her by many of the men. She became skilled at the art of parliamentary repartee: her responses to overt sexism were most successful when they were dignified and witty. For example, on one occasion from the floor of the House she invited another member to her parliamentary office to check some information. When some clown interjected, *She will need an escort if you go with her*, Miss Holman's immediate response was to retort: *In this house I am, as had been said on a previous occasion, no lady, but simply a member.*[5]

As an indication of the kinds of sexist attitudes prevalent amongst members of parliament on both sides of the House in 1927, and consequently, as an indication of the persistence and fearlessness of May Holman in arguing the ways she did on this issue, hear this chorus of hecklers that accompanies the debate about child endowment payment to widows:

> Mr. BROWN: ... A family of four is small, and if a woman has only four children she is still young. She has a better chance of re-marrying than a single woman ...
>
> Hon. G. Taylor: What! With four children?
>
> Mr. Angelo: She is generally a merry widow.
>
> Mr. Griffiths: Beware of the widows, said Weller.

> Mr. BROWN: If a woman is left a widow with a number of small children she cannot very well go out to work. The Minister should not confine himself to an allowance of 9s. a week. That is altogether too small. I believe that when a woman becomes a widow she has a better time than when she was a wife. She certainly wears better dresses.
>
> Mr. Angelo: You will be inducing women to become widows.
>
> Mr. BROWN: Indeed, many husbands are an encumbrance upon their wives. People have said to me, "I have never seen Mrs So-and-so, so well dressed. She could not dress like that when her husband was alive."
>
> The Premier: And on 9s. a week!
>
> Mr BROWN: Very often when she becomes the breadwinner she displays more ability to look after herself and the children than was possessed by her husband. On the other hand there are many sad cases...

Hansard records reveal that May Holman retains her dignity and takes no part in this extraordinary attempt at wit. The debate is ultimately summed up by the minister, Mr H. Millington:

> The question has been raised by the member for Forrest and other members, and it will receive sympathetic consideration immediately the opportunity arises... We all regret that it has not been possible to increase the subsidies, but we hope it will be possible to do so in the near future. We are not prepared to argue the question as to whether the amounts are sufficient or not. We merely say that with the money at our disposal we have done our utmost in the cause of charity. Now that our finances have been straightened out to a degree this, among other questions, will certainly receive the earnest consideration of the Government.[6]

Overt sexism was tolerated in the House throughout May Holman's political career, but she did her best to combat it. One occasion on 7 November 1927 demonstrates just how thick-skinned she had to be to survive the slightly patronising, slightly teasing, sometimes openly hostile remarks of her parliamentary colleagues. May Holman had risen to speak in support of a motion to regulate working conditions for domestic servants, and to import domestic labour from England. She responded with dignity and evidence to the frivolous and inane comments of some of the members of parliament. Of the member for Pingelly, she said:

> *He did not seem to think much of the modern girl. He said he had seen girls who appeared to be under 20 in the street, beautifully dressed. I wish to point out to the Honourable Member that the reasons they looked so nice was because of their domestic science training and because of their doing their own dressmaking, sewing, washing and ironing after they returned home from work... Not long ago we had the spectacle in this Parliament of legislators refusing to allow domestic servants to enjoy any protection of the Arbitration Court...*

May Holman went on to argue that domestic servants had to work very hard, and *if they do get £1 a week as the member for Pingelly suggested, they are very lucky.* But her parliamentary colleagues on the opposition benches lost no chance to ridicule her concerns:

> *Hon. Sir James Mitchell [Opposition Leader]: What a rotten world it is! Why not all come into Parliament?*
>
> *Miss* HOLMAN: *Thank God, some of them can enter Parliament nowadays.*
>
> *Mr. Brown: That is the trouble.*

> Miss HOLMAN: *The hon. member wants only a few domestics to come into the country, to work hard and long and get only small wages.*
>
> Mr. Brown: *They make very good wives anyhow.*
>
> Miss HOLMAN: *How many wives does the hon. member want?... The member for Pingelly said they make good wives. They do, but surely they are entitled to an opportunity to work for a living between the time of leaving school and making good wives!*[7]

The attacks on May Holman as a woman surfaced from time to time throughout her parliamentary career, and she defended herself however she could. A version of her usual defence (*In this House I'm a Member, not a lady*) is used again on 11 November 1937 when Mr Thorn accuses her of *cattishness* when she and the only other woman in the House, Mrs Cardell-Oliver, disagreed about how best to supply milk to school children. On this occasion May Holman retorted:

> *In this House there is no distinction between Members, and as therefore there are no women here, there can be no cattishness. Women are supposed to have all the cattishness in the world. I would like the Minister to give further consideration to the request for free milk for all school children.*[8]

Her parliamentary colleagues may have been condescending and sexist from time to time, but the press loved her. It probably helped that she was young, vivacious and charming. She also seemed to know intuitively when to exercise restraint in the public arena, and when to be flamboyant. A woman friend noted that, although *a good looker and well dressed*, May Holman *was never assertive or spectacular, she was a woman of the people.*[9] But even though they loved her, the press did not quite know what to do with her as a young woman in public life. On the one hand there appeared to be genuine admiration of her professional capacities, but on the other hand her appearance was almost always the focus of any report. She emerges as a curiosity rather than a problem. An article in the Adelaide *Advertiser* in 1928, for example, begins with an account of her political views on women's role in public life, but then discusses her hobbies and focuses its gaze admiringly on one particular part of her anatomy:

> *Her chief hobby is dramatic work, and she is deeply interested in music. She has produced several musical comedies for charity, and is also well known as a musical monologue entertainer. It is probable that if she were not in Parliament she would be on the stage. A pair of particularly trim ankles suggest that she might have been just as successful as a dancer.*[10]

Another striking example of this kind of reductive reporting is found in an article titled 'Man of the Week. A Woman Doing a Man's Job', July 1926. It began: *Miss May Holman, member of the West Australian Legislative Assembly, can well come under this heading of the "Man of the Week" because she is, and has been, doing a man's job, and doing it well*... It immediately denies any suggestion of masculinity in her appearance or in her demeanour with this extravagant and lingering gaze upon her person:

> *but the member for the jarrah constituency of Forrest is not a masculine type. Picture a pleasant-featured, medium built young woman, with teeth that would not shame a dentist's ad, modest little ears, brown haired and brown-eyed, and, unlike NSW's lady member, un-shingled hair.*

(This latter reference is to Miss Preston-Stanley of the NSW parliament – clearly an outrageously masculine type, not worthy of the kind of admiration reserved for feminine young women like Miss Holman). At this point the tone becomes overtly patronising: *Miss Holman is a Broken Hillite, but came West with Dad and Mum and the family early in life* ... But then, confusingly, it reverts to acknowledgment and admiration of her political views:

> *Last month she was in NSW and states that Premier Lang treated her wonderfully, making the trip perhaps her life's most pleasant experience. But she did not meet Miss Preston-Stanley, to her infinite regret. The meeting would have been interesting, especially if politics had been gossiped instead of frocking. For, although Miss Holman has excellent taste in her attire, she prides herself most on her stalwart support of Labor's causes.*[11]

If May Holman was admired for her *even teeth*, her *modest little ears* and her *trim ankles*, she was admired even more for her organising ability. She used her parliamentary status to undertake an extraordinary amount of community building within the Labor movement. Not surprisingly, perhaps, in addition to wanting to educate children and young people, she was intent on widening the horizons of Labor women. May had watched as her mother became involved in Labor women's activities before the Great War. She remembered that it was through her mother's influence that she had been appointed scribe at the first Labor Women's Conference in Perth in 1911, when Mrs Rapley succeeded Mrs Henshaw as secretary of the Women's Social Club and formed the Perth Labor Women's Organisation. She remembered, too, the flurry of activity amongst her mother and friends when in 1914 the Labor women made a great effort to support the Labor daily paper that her father had initiated. The women raised £1100 and purchased shares in the People's Printing and Publishing Company. May herself went to work there in 1914 after her job as her father's clerk finished.

May knew that the objectives of the women's branches included the return of Labor candidates to state and federal parliaments and the education of women politically and industrially. Labor leaders in WA at the time acknowledged the substantial role played by these women's branches. In many ways they provided an organised and organising forum for women committed to the Labor movement but who did not belong to trade unions. John Curtin showed great interest in the women's section of the party and once expressed the view that a Labor Women's Organisation was the logical counterpart of the trade unions, linking men and women in the Labor cause. 'Milestones on the Way to Progress' was how Prime Minister Curtin saw the development of the Labor Women in Western Australia.

But conditions for women were changing in this post-war period, and May wanted the women she knew to feel entitled to take their place in the new world that was emerging. An article that appeared in the *Kalgoorlie Miner* of 8 June 1927 gives a clear insight into the changing roles of women, and the ways that a Labor thinker might reconcile these changes with women's traditional roles as helpmeet to her husband and moral compass for her family. The article is titled 'The Influence of Women'. It is cited here in its entirety to allow the twenty-first century reader full access to the nuance of its argument. It also provides fascinating insight into the world of the readership of a working class publication like the *Kalgoorlie Miner* in the late 1920s. Clearly, belonging to the working class did not mean being unintelligent, or unthoughtful. Indeed, as archival records demonstrate again and again, the labor movement of this period in the early twentieth century in Australia was peopled by philosophers, ideologues, political activists and social commentators, whose tasks became to ensure the kinds of social change that led to fair representation and dignified lives for workers and their families.[12]

Its opening quotation from Thackeray cleverly positions the article in the wider literary sphere and invites readers to think more broadly than their everyday worlds permit:

"All men who avoid female society have dull perceptions and are stupid, or have gross tastes and revolt against what is pure," wrote Thackeray; and what man who has read the inimitable "Book of Snobs" will deny that Thackeray possessed an insight into human nature that entitled him to speak with some authority? If Thackeray's belief be right, men are now less stupid and have less gross tastes than of an previous stage of the twentieth century. Within that period there have never before been so many dances and other social functions designed to give men and women the opportunity of enjoying each other's company. Far from commencing to pall, such events are gaining rapidly in popularity, and many staid young men who have long been regarded as misogynists are being lured from their books and pipes by the pleasures of female society. Even in our great public schools – strongholds of masculinity – it has become the practice to teach the graces of the ballroom and to hold periodical dances for the purpose of "rounding off the rough corners" acquired by the young gentlemen in the boisterous atmosphere of the playing field. No longer does the college boy blush awkwardly in an unequal contest of wits when introduced to his sister's charming friends; and 'tis well that he has acquired this new poise. It saves him much mental anguish and adds to his self-esteem – a quality with which the female of the species is generously endowed by Nature.

In public life, women now enjoy a higher status that at any time in history – English history, at any rate. Powerful women's organisations, such as the National Council of Women, the Housewives' Association, and the Women's section of the Labour Movement, exert an important influence in the politics of the nation, and, indeed, in the affairs of the League of Nations. Our own State Parliament can claim only one woman member, Miss May Holman; but she is able to meet her fellow members on equal terms, and is a living contradiction of the libel that woman is unable to resist the temptation to talk all the time instead of only when she has something worth saying. Miss Holman has filled fewer pages of "Hansard" than many men who, unlike her, are afflicted with the "cacoethes loquendi" and to whom little knowledge of the subject is seldom a deterrent to their engaging the attention of Mr. Speaker. In commerce, too, women have firmly entrenched themselves, and their sphere of activities is rapidly expanding. The law and medicine, two professions long held sacred to the male, have been opened to them, and the latter, in particular, has proved extraordinarily attractive. When the State Government recently decided to engage a psychologist, the choice fell upon a woman, Miss Stoneman. A quiet, but extremely cheerful, little lady, she has embarked upon the duties of her office with a thoroughness and enthusiasm rarely displayed by a male member of the army of Government officials. It is reported that she even went to the length of having an anaesthetic administered to herself in order that she might gain first-hand knowledge of the sensations experienced "going under" and "coming out." In her leisure hours, Miss Stoneman is an amateur aviatrix; but whether she goes aloft for the sheer joy of flying or in pursuance of her study of "sensations" is a question which only she can answer.

This higher status of women in public, professional and commercial life, combined with the greater freedom of social life, has undoubtedly contributed to the modern idea that a wife should be a comrade as well as a dutiful housekeeper and mother; that she should share her husband's recreations and join him in the occasional dissipation of a "night out" with a few kindred couples. Behind this ultra-modern notion of the proprieties of married life is man's recognition of women's claim to equality or near-equality. Sentimentally, the idea may be commendable, but it is doubtful whether it *is justified by experience. When the former restraining hand becomes a marcher in the extravagance which is an innate vice of most males, there remains but little inducement to be thrifty; and there is even a danger that in the long run the children may be the losers. Again, there is the suggestion that the extraordinary activity of the divorce courts is due to the loosening of family ties by the craze for dances and parties at which mild impropriety is regarded as "smart." In these criticisms of the trend of society there is a considerable amount of truth, but it is also true that the individual is usually as blameworthy as the system. Men and women may be divided into those who will go right in any circumstances, those who will go wrong in any circumstances, and those who remain on the balance until circumstance influences them one way or the other. It is from this last class that the victims of the modern social system are culled. The number may appear large, but it is small in comparison with that of the men who have been uplifted and inspired by the society of women. In the home, woman fulfills the most exalted duties of her sex; but the purists who would confine her entirely to that sphere would deprive man of his most powerful influence for decency and right living.*[13]

For the twenty-first century reader, this treatise is riddled with sexisms and essentialisms; but the tussles it gives voice to – between confining women to the home and encouraging them to experience life beyond it – are clearly articulated, and are surely the tussles that the women in May Holman's sphere were experiencing in their own lives. Miss Holman, as politician, daughter, aunt and friend, genuinely wanted to find ways to broaden and deepen women's experiences. And so she decided to revive the Labor Women's Organisation that her mother had been involved in before the Great War. Her first act, in 1927, was to convene a Conference of Labor Women in Perth – the first since 1911 – as a way of alerting women to the changing times. This conference was such a success that it became an annual event to which Labor women looked forward. Later, in 1933, May hit upon the idea of bringing the combination of information and pleasure to women in an even more focused way, and organised the first of many summer schools, which combined lectures on interesting subjects with more conventional pleasures like dinners, picnics, games nights, concerts and socials.

Throughout her parliamentary life Miss Holman was admired for the leadership role she played in Labor Women's Organisations. She was credited with reviving interest in Labor women's activities in Western Australia in the late 1920s, and with helping to establish the Western Australian Labor Women's Central Executive body and the Labor Women's Interstate Australian Executive body. She was widely hailed as a natural leader, and it's easy to imagine that her experience throughout her life, of successes in organising her smaller brothers and sisters, and her concert troupe, and now her electorate, reinforced in her the desire to take the lead.

But sometimes, it seems, May Holman's feeling of entitlement to be the leader meant that she stood on the toes of erstwhile colleagues. The revival of interest in the Labor Women's Organisation was consequently not without conflict. In the late 1920s a struggle over the leadership of Labor women emerged between a group of women in Fremantle and a group in Perth. The story of this struggle provides a glimpse of May Holman that we rarely see. In 1924 the Fremantle Labor Women's Organisation had been formed, with Mrs Clarke as its president. The following year May Holman was elected to the seat of Forrest, and thereafter became interested in reviving the Perth Labor Women's group to which her mother had belonged more than a decade ago. She worked hard to ensure that Labor women were taken seriously by the party administration, and, for example, lobbied successfully to have them invited by the party secretary to nominate a woman to join three men in a deputation to the premier about the basic wage and family endowment. In 1926 Miss E. Hooton (May's close friend Harriet Hooton, known as Ettie,[14] and a member of the Perth

Labor Women's group) became the Labor Women's representative on the *Westralian Worker*. No doubt this provided Perth Labor Women with excellent publicity. In that year the Perth Trades Hall furnished a room which they put at the disposal of Labor women as a club and meeting room.

It was at this time that a struggle for power occurred openly between the Fremantle Labor Women and Perth Labor Women. Mrs Jane Ryan, the Fremantle Branch secretary, urged her group to request a name change, presumably to indicate that they represented Labor women in Western Australia. A correspondence between the Fremantle group and state executive of the ALP started in March 1927 and continued almost all that year. In July, Mr Barker, the state secretary of the ALP, issued a circular to all district councils and unions:

> *Owing to the existence of two women's organisations in Perth claiming to represent Labor Women, I have been instructed by the State Executive to draw your attention to the fact that there is only one organisation* [an alteration was made here in pencil for the copy which went to Fremantle unions to delete the words 'in Perth'] *which is within the Labor Movement, that being the Perth Labor Women's Organisation of which Miss M. Holman MLA is secretary and their headquarters are at the Trades Hall, Perth.*
>
> *Should there be any women known to your members who are desirous of communicating with this organisation, you might impress upon them the necessity of making sure that they send all communications to, and make all enquiries from Miss Holman, as the other women's organisation referred to has been expelled from the Labor Movement and has no connection whatever with it.*[15]

This circular invoked Mrs Ryan's fury. She claimed in a letter to Mr Barker that the circular was resented by the members, all seventy of them. But the wheels of the Labor machine had begun to grind, and Fremantle's bid for power was doomed. On 19 August 1927, the Midland District Council wrote to May Holman to recommend some branch stacking to rid Labor Women in Perth of the thorn the Fremantle branch had become:

> *This Council endorsed the Bassendean branch's view that your organisation should be written to respectfully suggesting that a determined effort be made to swamp the bogus organisation with members for the purpose of transferring the assets to your organisation and carrying a resolution to the effect that we close up the bogus organisation.*
>
> *I was directed to say that this Council would be pleased to assist in any way to get possession of the assets and to effectively rid the movement of this so called Labor Women's Organisation.*[16]

It is difficult not to think that some prior arrangement had been made between May, whose home ALP branch by this time was Bassendean, and the officers of the Midland District Council. May seemed not to know what to do with the branch-stacking letter from the Midland District Council, and apparently sat on it for two months. She eventually sent a copy to the ALP State Secretary, Mr Barker, on 19 October 1927. In her covering letter to Mr Barker she suggested that it would be appropriate to refer the Midland District Council's letter to the state executive for its advice.

Meanwhile, no doubt at least in part in response to the struggle for power that was disrupting the harmony of Labor women's interactions, May and the Perth group decided to take charge. They held a Labor Women's Conference – only the second in WA in more than two decades, the sequel to the 1911 conference where the nineteen year old May Holman had been scribe – and at that conference they resolved to establish a peak body of Labor Women, called the Labor Women's Central Executive. May and her group were aware of the significance of this new body. The ALP Congress had agreed that a representative of the Labor Women's

Central Executive should attend the state executive meetings of the ALP. For the first time in the history of the party in WA, women would have direct access to the decision-making of the central party room.

The second Labor Women's Conference was held on 25, 26 and 27 October 1927. That conference resolved to create a Western Australian Labor Women's Central Executive. At the first meeting of the central executive body on 1 December 1927, May Holman was elected president, Mrs Beadle vice-president, and Miss Ettie Hooton secretary. Committee members came from Midland Junction, Guildford, Jarrahdale, Mornington (all, it can be noted, from May's territory) as well as from Kalgoorlie. The valiant Mrs Ryan with Mrs Laidlaw from Fremantle must have acquiesced to the Party's demands, because they too became committee members of the central executive body. It had taken some fancy footwork, but May's ascendency in this arena was now assured.

As we might expect, Miss Holman became an enthusiastic leader of Labor Women, and the membership increased dramatically in the city and in the rural areas. Branches were formed in other states. In 1929 she initiated an interstate organisation of Labor Women. It should come as no surprise that May herself was president of this interstate organisation, and her friend Miss Ettie Hooton was secretary. These women were not simply flirting with power. They knew the potential impact of collective action, and they knew how crucial it was to steer it in the right direction.

In 1930 Miss Holman and colleagues organised the second Annual Interstate Conference of Labor Women in Canberra. This was a significant gathering of Labor women nationally, and the agenda dealt with sixty-eight items including international relations, economics, health and unemployment. *The Canberra Times* took the conference very seriously and on 22 May 1930 carried a detailed report of the conference's concern with the specific impacts of the worldwide economic depression on Australian citizens.[17] In particular, it noted that a committee had been formed to make recommendations to the federal government following discussion of a suite of related matters including the establishment of an emergency relief fund pending the introduction of a national insurance scheme; a maximum forty-four hours working week for women in industry; reduction of the basic wage through *the pernicious system* of part-time work; the question of married women in industry; raising the school leaving age and increasing bursaries for school students; and the employment positions of men less than sixty-five years of age and women less than sixty. That same edition of *The Canberra Times* noted that the conference was presided over by Miss May Holman MLA, and reported that proposed changes to divorce laws and other items on the legal agenda had sparked the genuine interest of the Victorian attorney-general, Mr W. Slater, whose attendance was marked with a vote of acclamation.[18] In her own report of this conference, May Holman wrote of the *cause for gratification, that in spite of the turmoil and stress in economic and social life, the foundation of the federal organisation of Labor Women had been successfully laid.*[19]

‡

As the first Labor woman elected to any Australian parliament, May Holman was already of interest to the Australian public. Her more frequent visits to the Eastern States on Labor women's business meant more press coverage. By 1930 May Holman was a household name across the nation. She was more than ready to embark on the international stage. Her family, colleagues and the wider public were delighted but not surprised when, in 1930, she was nominated to be part of the Australian delegation to attend the prestigious League of Nations Assembly in Geneva.

CHAPTER 8
LEAGUE OF NATIONS

When May Holman set out on her journey to Europe aboard the SS *Oronsay* at the end of July 1930 to attend the League of Nations Assembly in Geneva, she was aware that, as a member of the Australian delegation, she was one in a long line of Australian women to have made this journey. She knew that the primary goals of the League of Nations were the maintenance of world peace and disarmament as an international reaction to the horrors of the Great War; but she knew too that the League was centrally concerned with issues of equity in all spheres, and at the time of its establishment in 1919, international feminist organisations had ensured that the Covenant of the League of Nations carried a clause stipulating that it would be open to men and women alike. Strategic lobbying of Australian prime minister Billy Hughes by members of the Australian Federation of Women Voters to implement the equality clause of the Covenant meant that a woman was to be included in every Australian delegation to the League of Nations Assembly as a substitute or associate delegate. May Holman was included in the 1930 Australian contingent as a substitute delegate. She had been nominated for this position by the women's executive of the Labor Party and by the Western Australian Women's Service Guilds.

By 1930, at thirty-seven years of age, May Holman was a much-admired public figure, and the local and national press followed her preparations with intense interest. *The West Australian* of 25 July 1930 reported that Miss Holman said she felt a great responsibility in going to Geneva:

"Perhaps because I am a Member of Parliament... I feel that more will be looked for from me than from an ordinary woman citizen. I can only hope that I will come up to expectations. I have the lead of fine women in previous substitute delegates to follow. The aims and ideals of the League of Nations are a fascinating study and inspire one to energy in becoming familiar with every phase, and possession of information likely to be useful at the Assembly. The fifth Commission, to which I shall be attached, deals with various points of national responsibility for the welfare of women and children. This necessitates the collection of facts concerning Commonwealth conditions."

The article added that *It was her intention... to study Labour conditions in every country she visited, as they affected women and their families.*[1] No doubt she went about her political preparations with characteristic thoroughness and attention to detail.

It is clear that local expectations of the success of her trip were high. Soon after her departure, *The West Australian* reported that:

In Miss Holman, Australian women have a representative qualified by training and observation, not only to study conditions in other countries through contact with delegates from many nations, but to analyse differences and advise procedure likely to make for industrial and international peace so far as the Commonwealth of Australia is concerned.[2]

‡

Miss Holman took her responsibilities in attending the month of sittings in Geneva very seriously indeed, and readers were doubtless reassured to hear that she was well equipped to do so. But of far more interest to the reading public before her departure, it seems, was her wardrobe. *The West Australian* reported delightedly to its readers:

[O]ne of Miss Holman's first resolves, on receiving news of her appointment to represent the women of the Commonwealth at Geneva, was to take advantage of the opportunity to advertise Australian products and textile industries by purchasing such goods only, when selecting wardrobe requirements for the tour. Miss Holman has a tailored costume of Australian twist in a brown shade with a suggestion of blue in its weave, and a smart skirt of tweed. Her thick, warm travelling rug is Australian and she will use a presentation hand bag of sharkskin, processed, dyed and made up in the Commonwealth. Miss Holman went to great trouble in getting gloves specially made from Australian calf, with rabbit fur lining the gauntlet tops. Her leather coat is made of Australian cow-hide. Her frocks, including several handsome evening dresses and reception gowns, have been made in one or other of the leading State capitals. Miss Holman's "trousseau" as she laughingly terms it, does not contain one imported manufactured garment. Her shoes are Melbourne made and of the three felt hats she is taking, one was made in Kalgoorlie and the other two in Perth. Miss Holman's travelling outfit includes sets of dainty underwear in fine silk and wool, stockings, corsets and fabric gloves, all bearing well-known Australian factory brands.[3]

Preparations were certainly festive. In the weeks prior to her departure May Holman was given a rousing send-off. The *Westralian Worker* of 25 July 1930 reported on a long series of socials, luncheons and parties, which began in Melbourne in mid-June with a farewell function organised by the ALP and the Labor Women of Victoria, continued with functions in Adelaide and Kalgoorlie, and ended in Perth in late July with a round of events hosted by the Labor Women, the Perth Hospital Board, and the Women's Services Guild. In typical fashion, she made time to visit her electorate in these last weeks to be farewelled by her constituents in many of the little timber settlements, including Holyoake, Dwellingup, Railway Mill, Nanga Brook, Brunswick Junction and Donnybrook.[4] The sense of fun that seemed to surround May Holman and her close friends was captured in this report of a party at her home ten days before she sailed: *On Saturday night last, a hilarious party, promoted by Misses Freda Wilson and Mollie Holmes, was held at the Holman home in Bassendean. Over fifty people of all ages were present. Musical items, dancing, games, and a delightful supper made the evening pass on wings.*[5] The *West Australian* advised that Miss Holman hosted a reception for her travelling party of distinguished Australians on their way through Perth.[6] The party comprised the Honourable Mr Frank Brennan (Commonwealth attorney-general) who was leader of the Australian delegation to Geneva, his wife and daughter, Sir Robert Garron (Commonwealth solicitor-general) and Lady Garron, and Mr Brennan's secretary, Mr Cameron.

There is no masking the relish with which the preparations were undertaken. Fortunately for those of us interested in history, this entire journey is well documented. Before she left, May Holman was commissioned by the Melbourne *Herald* group to write a series of articles of her experiences as traveller and as delegate to the League of Nations Assembly. This was her first and only journey overseas. Her collection of nineteen articles, written specifically as entertaining travelogue for an audience for whom overseas travel was glamorous and largely unattainable, provides fascinating lighthearted insights into her experiences and into her own world view. In addition to these articles, a series of letters home allows us to glimpse behind the public figure into the world of the sometimes homesick, sometimes overwhelmed, often adventurously curious traveller.[7] It is testament to her personality that, in undertaking this journey to represent Australia at the League of Nations, May Holman was able to take such girlish delight in the preparations for her journey, in the journey itself, and in the entire experience of being part of an international gathering in Geneva, while still giving serious attention to her political role at the Assembly.

Her first letter home, dated 12 August 1930, is written to an intimate audience about her arrival in Ceylon. Her descriptions of this sensuous and colourful world are vivid and immediate. She appreciates the beauty and strangeness of the tropical scene, and writes of the betelnut, the flowers, the rickshaws, the clothing, and the singsong speech of the locals. She admits her puzzlement about the patterns of growing rice: *there did not seem to be any rule or rhyme about it*. She describes their visit to the city of Kandy, which is *like every other native village only on a larger scale. Small shop fronts, tiny houses ... and coloured people everywhere.* She includes juicy bits for her sisters, like her account of her visit to a fortune teller, who told her that she would *get a husband in October next year*, and that she had had *much trouble in 1914* (the year of her twenty-first birthday and her marriage) and *also in 1928–30*. She does not comment on these pronouncements, but presumably there is a coded message for either her sisters or her friends to unravel. In this letter she tells her sisters and women friends about the *beautiful sets of undies* that she might buy on her way home for them if they send the money and their specifications and, surprisingly perhaps, she schemes and plots about how to avoid customs duty: to avoid looking like purchases other than for personal use [they] *will have to come home in my dirty linen bag or rumpled a bit*.[8]

Her second letter is dated 22 August 1930, almost a month after she set out on her journey, and is written from Rome. She recounts their trip through the Suez Canal and on to Italy. One gets the sense in this letter of the normalising of shipboard life, and the consequent exaggeration of the strangeness of the places they visited. On returning to the ship from their Egyptian sortie they *began to get anxious about the cricket test – the ship, of course, being divided – English people on one side and us on the other.* And we get sense that May herself was finding her feet in this company: *On Sunday night we had a concert ... I performed and surprised the ship – I had been so quiet until then ...*

May Holman, MLA, bound for Geneva aboard the SS Oronsay, 1930.

In this letter May's tone is conversational and relaxed. We glimpse the little party landing at Suez, haggling over prices for a car journey to Cairo and the pyramids, paying for an Egyptian man to climb the highest pyramid *(he went to the top and back in the boiling sun in six and a half minutes)*, visiting a museum and a bazaar. We glimpse them, too, sailing through the Straits of Messina past Sicily to arrive at the bustling port of Naples, and on to the *magnificent* Royal Hotel Grande with its *marble floors, beautiful furniture and private balconies*. We see them travel by funicular railway to marvel at the erupting crater of Vesuvius, and then to Pompeii where she *went round in a chair carried by two men*. She was clearly thrilled: *I can't explain it or describe it all in a letter. It was too wonderful.*

She was delighted to be in Italy, and almost overwhelmed: *Gee you can't imagine what I have seen already, and now we are in Rome, the Eternal City...*[9] Her visit to St Peter's left her stuck for words again: *It's a huge place with wonderful paintings and statuary. I cannot describe it*; but her reflections on her visit to Rome just a week later are warm and insightful:

> *Rome left a wonderful impression on me – the old old things still standing in defiance of time – the Colosseum with the animal cages built in rock, the seats where the people sat and watched the Christians torn to pieces, the Churches, the fountain, the old walls... every stone in the cobbled streets could tell a story...*[10]

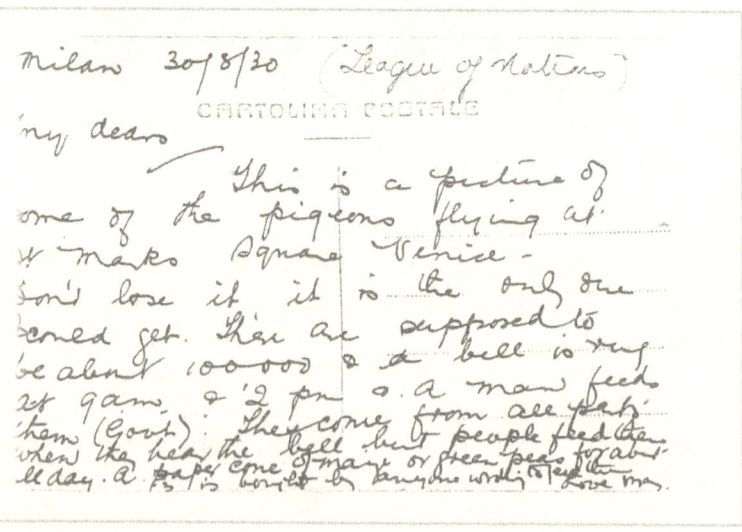

A postcard from Venice, 30 August 1930.

She and her party travelled to Florence and then on via Milan to Venice. Sometimes she was excited: on an afternoon in Venice *we went to the fashionable Lido, in a motor boat to the Excelsior Hotel and walked in like duchesses ... I saw a movie picture man taking us – hope it gets to Australia. I looked nice if I do say so myself*; and sometimes she was shocked: *On all the beaches* [at the Lido] *the men walk about in trunks only – just like big, hairy gorillas, most of them.*[11]

We know that she spent the month of September in Geneva attending the League of Nations Assembly. Afterwards Miss Holman travelled again in Italy and then on to Britain. By October she had relaxed into revealing more of her inner world. On arriving at Monte Generoso, in the mountains beyond Lugano, she wrote:

Sat and watched the sunset from my windows and seemed to be alone with the mountain tops. The valleys and spaces were seas of mist although occasionally I could get sight of the lakes below ... The clouds seemed to me as I looked down on them like big packs of wool and one almost thought one could rest gently on them and not fall through.[12]

She laughed at her ridiculous layers of clothing to fend off the cold after an early morning mountain climb to see the sunrise: *Gee I was a sight for sore eyes. I put on all my day clothes and then my blue satin pyjamas, then my dress, then my dressing gown, and a black velvet bridge coat that was lent to me. And still it was cold.*

Running through this series of letters is her concern for her family and her desire to feel connected with them throughout her journey. Only two of her eight siblings – Winnie, aged twenty-eight, and Ted, aged twenty-six – had married and left home. Of the other six, Maude, Jack and Bill were independent adults, but May felt responsible for her mother in the big old house in Bassendean and worried for the three youngest girls, Iris, aged nineteen, Eileen, aged sixteen, and Sheila, aged fourteen. Her early letters acknowledge that she is homesick, and she knew that she could not expect mail from home until she reached Geneva in early September. However, when the mail arrived she was bitterly disappointed with what she viewed as the dearth of letters: only thirteen letters were sent in the first three weeks. She listed them and then wrote indignantly, *Now, you blighters, this was all up to the 17th August – three weeks after I left Western Australia. What have the rest of you been doing? None from Mum, none from Ted or Bill, none from Charlie, none from Freda, Mollie or Bessie and none from Miss Hooton. Well look out or I'll treat you the same way and then see how you will like it.*[13] In her next letter she apologised and recorded with relief that another thirteen letters arrived in the very next mail. However, although her sisters and close friends had written, her mother had not. *Hope Mum will write to me some day,* she wrote plaintively.[14]

Her preoccupation with family connection and responsibility is further revealed when she was writing about her experiences at Monte Generoso in the letter of 1 October. After writing about the cold she confessed: *When I went back to bed I dreamt of you all and that I had a number of letters and two telegrams. I read the letters in my dreams, but was greatly worried because I awakened before I could read the telegrams ...*

Although her letters end with this fifth one on 1 October, 1930, the nineteen articles she wrote for the Melbourne *Herald* group document her entire journey. The articles are keenly observed and concern themselves with everything from fashion to idealism to politics to travelogue. In their formality they provide a fascinating contrast to the direct intimacy of her letters. They also occasionally allow us to glimpse the woman behind the public persona. For example, everyone knew that May Holman was from a large Catholic family and there's no doubt that she was thrilled to be in Rome. But when describing her audience with the Pope, *an elderly man of medium height with a clever, intelligent and kindly face ... [who] looked ... as if he had the peace of the world at heart and the peace of heaven in his soul,*[15] we become aware from her clichéd remarks that spirituality is not a topic she's especially comfortable with. Her Catholicism seems conventional and her capacity to give expression to matters of the spirit to be slight. This reticence to plumb spiritual depths is consistent with her reluctance to speak or write of personal matters that troubled her deeply, like her illnesses or her family frustrations and disappointments.

In an early article, which she titles 'Remarks of an Inexperienced Traveller Abroad', she expresses her loyalty to Australian everyday conventions with an amusing but telling paragraph about the sound of car hooters:

> *One of the things that made a very great impression on me during my time in various towns after leaving Australia was the sound of the rubber hooters which are attached to every car. The drivers in Colombo – where I first heard the continual blah, blah – seem to wish to press the rubber bulb on every and all occasions. To an Australian used to the softer hooter attached to the various cars, the noise is nerve-racking, and the small boys who tell a car by the sound of its hooter at home would be utterly at a loss. Not only are these infernal machines attached to the cars but also to the little motor boats that ply for hire around the harbours. I think my most unpleasant memory will be the continual, sudden spurt of sound in all the places I visited – Colombo, Egypt, Italy and Switzerland. In Geneva it was quite soothing to hear the hooters of the British Foreign Office cars ... brought over for the Assembly.*[16]

The League of Nations Assembly was held in Geneva during September. May was aware that this was the first Assembly of the League of Nations at which women could be present as full delegates. She was one of fourteen women who attended this Assembly as either full delegates or substitute delegates for their nations. The other women came from Britain, Bulgaria,

Canada, Denmark, Finland, Germany, Hungary, Lithuania, Norway, Rumania, Sweden, and the Netherlands.

Interestingly, there are few political observations in the articles she wrote about her journey to Geneva. Presumably she thought her audience would not be interested in her political observations. In one article she does comment on the status of women in Italy: *Italian women have not yet the franchise and there does not seem much likelihood of their getting it. I was told that Mussolini's ideals for the country of Italy are home women with families of 12 children or more.* She seems most comfortable when writing about fashion. Of the Lido in Venice she wrote:

> *I was very disappointed ... The beach itself is very much like one of our Australian mudbanks ... The nicest costume I saw was on one of the youthful, slim girls and was only a pair of white duck shorts and a cream woollen sweater. Another striking costume was of red crepe-de-chine with large white spots, very wide trousers, blouse with little white front and no sleeves, coat and Panama hat with scarf of the red and white.*[17]

Indeed, her first article on the League of Nations was concerned only with people's appearance and not at all with their policies. She did note that although the official languages of the League of Nations were English and French (no doubt in deference to the victors of the Great War) the German minister for foreign affairs, Dr Julius Curtis, *spoke always in his native German* when addressing the Assembly and brought along his own French translator. However, this is the closest her account gets to observations of power struggles or political plays among Assembly delegates.[18]

Another article muses positively on the processes of disarmament and begins with her acknowledgment of the feelings of *wonder, thankfulness and enthusiasm* that rushed over her when she saw the representatives of so many countries sitting around the Council table in friendship *proving by their very presence that their countries would try arbitration before guns...* She notes with gratitude that France could tell the Assembly that it had *reduced their compulsory training term by half, and England and Australia had abolished compulsory military training,* and that *the ruling princes of India spoke in the strongest terms of disarmament,* and concludes (naively, to twenty-first century eyes) that because the *Foreign Office Department of each country must have knowledge of each other's difficulties, the personal touch must surely count for something.*[19]

But her greatest gift is for acute observation of people, and this, combined with her theatrical sense of humour, is what ensures that her articles will be welcomed by an Australian reading public. She writes of *the crowds of people who stood outside the Assembly every day to see celebrities arrive, and says that she was told there were many spies and Secret Service men in Geneva. In fact,* she writes, *one English paper printed a scare sensation of proposed murder and assassination based on the fact that Italy's leading delegate had returned to his country and that there were picturesque policemen in three-cornered hats and rope barriers...* Her article concludes with the wry observation that *The League of Nations and its headquarters in Geneva has given one thing to the world – blessing or otherwise: a framework for dozens of best-sellers.*[20]

May Holman was clearly fascinated by the women she met in Geneva. In an article on Geneva during the League of Nations Assembly, she writes with pleasure about:

> *the intense degree of interest taken by the women of the world in the League of Nations, so much so that eight international women's organisations have a permanent Joint Standing Committee on Women's Issues. These women's organisations – The International Council of Women; the Universal Temperance Association of Women; The International Council of Nurses; the International Alliance for Suffrage and Civic and Political Action; the International Council of Young Women's Christian Association; the*

International League of Women for Peace and Freedom; the Union of Women for International Concord; and the International Federation of University women – are given a great deal of consideration by the League and no doubt, do a great deal of work.

She writes then of the special officers whose task it was to liaise between the League and the women's organisations, one of whom, the *efficient and gracious Princess Radziwill*, May Holman met in the lobby of the League quarters – *a lobby which might with truth be termed the meeting place of people from all over the world* – and declared her to be *well informed on a great number of subjects dealt with by the League*. One gets the sense in this article that the experience of being in such esteemed company was at first intimidating, but *this lady afterwards gave an afternoon party so that delegates, officers of organisations, members of the staff and residents could meet each other and get some of the shyness off*.[21]

She recalls the dinner given by this joint standing committee for the delegates and women members of the delegations to the assembly: *this year's dinner was a most brilliant function attended by nearly two hundred guests*. Once again it's the personalities she recalls with admiration: the capable chair, Mme Avril de Saint-Croix, and the intelligent, passionate and witty speakers: the Canadian Irene Parlby (who rapidly became one of May Holman's favourites among the women she met) who spoke of the need for cooperation amongst the different nationalities of Canada; Madame Ciurlionis of Lithuania who told an old legend of her country in poetry; and Mary Hamilton from Britain, who *was called on unexpectedly and proved herself an orator of the first order*. For a young woman accustomed to fashioning her entertainment crews from amongst her small circle of friends and family in Western Australia, these occasions must have been thrilling indeed.

She was particularly drawn to observe and comment on eccentricities of manner or style. For example, she writes vividly of the British MP Susan Lawrence who, as parliamentary secretary to the Ministry of Health, was appointed rapporteur of the Health Section in the Second Commission of this League of Nations Assembly:

> *She gives one the idea of great efficiency but great reserve. She is middle aged and nicely plump. Her hair is cut short and combed back from the face in an almost masculine fashion and she is a keen smoker of cigarettes. Her voice is a deep contralto and she speaks in rather a jerky manner which is emphasised by the movements of her body and head... She is rather reserved and avoids, rather than seeks, women's organisations outside the Labour Party.*[22]

May Holman writes also of British Labour MP Mary Hamilton who was thoroughly at home, this being her second League Assembly. She generously swept May Holman into her sphere at the dinner given by the British delegation and the two women soon became friends. *She is a fine speaker with a good contralto voice which charms more and more ... She is a novelist of repute ... and a student of ancient history...* She and May shared an interest in employment issues and industrial conditions.

> *Personally, she is a woman of great charm, quite young, dark, good features, wears tortoise shell rimmed glasses, small hats, and, more often than not, black dresses. But, whatever the colour of her dress, Mrs Hamilton always has a touch of red on it or, if that is not possible, then she carries a red umbrella or handbag.*

She made a big impression on the young Australian: *Mrs Mary Hamilton MP was, I confess, one of my favourites at the Assembly.*[23]

We read of the Bulgarian delegate who *seemed unable to speak English*, and of the German woman with the *rich, round, very loud voice who made two impassioned speeches*, and of Lithuanian

MP Mme Ciurlionis whose voice was *sweet, though, to my mind, a little too high-pitched*. Disappointingly, there's absolutely no comment on the intellectual or political work of the League of Nations Assembly in these articles, nor of the political or intellectual contributions made by any of these brilliant women.

However, she does write of the community work of the Canadian delegate and of the political work addressing the trafficking of women and children undertaken at the first meeting of the League of Nations in 1920 by the Danish delegate Miss Forchhammer. She tells her readers, too, of the social work of Finnish linguist Tilma Hainari, whose activist interests included temperance, moral work and child welfare, and who had entered parliament in 1906 as a foremost feminist in the Finnish women's fight for franchise.

As the Australian substitute delegate, May Holman was attached to the Fifth Commission of the Assembly which dealt with social and humanitarian issues. During the month of sittings she did much committee work and was required to give two speeches. Although enchanted by the experience of being there, it's clear too that she found the demands of the month in Geneva to be very taxing. She reported on numerous invitations she had been unable to accept, both in Geneva and later during her travel in Britain, because of ill-health. Her letters home indicate that while in Geneva she felt alternately that she was drowning or that she was under siege: she complained that there was not enough time to read all the reports that began to *pour in* as soon as a delegate arrived; and she wrote of the criticisms and pamphlets that begin to *rain on one*; and of the invitations by the dozen that *attack one from all quarters*.[24] She observes that

> *the Assembly and Commission sittings take up a great deal of time and any delegate who tries to attend all the sittings and all the receptions and dinners given by the various countries, must have an iron constitution. The receptions and dinners are most elaborate and are sometimes attended*

by hundreds of people; for instance the reception of the British delegation at which it was reported that there were about seven hundred guests.

It is a pity, she lamented, *that the Assembly could not be finished before the entertainments commenced.*[25]

The first of the two speeches May Holman gave to the Fifth Commission of the Assembly reported on Australia's response to the dangerous drugs conventions,[26] and the second concerned the trafficking of women and children. It was her second speech that drew attention in the Australian press. *The Brisbane Courier* ran with the headline 'Miss Holman's Forcible Speech',[27] and the Hobart Mercury with 'White Slave Traffic. League Taken to Task. Australian Delegate's View'.[28] In her speech Miss Holman said she was not satisfied that forcible enough steps were being taken to stamp out commercialised vice, and that despite the League's thorough inquiry, *many people were incredulous and still denied the existence of the traffic, except in novels and cinema films.* She argued that the system of licensed houses *should be stopped*, and claimed that *Hitherto the reports of the League on the subject had resulted only in resolutions which were mere pious hopes.* She urged the League to convene a conference to adopt a tightly drawn-up convention on the subject.

In a letter home she expressed relief that her two speeches were over, but in an article written for her Australian readers it was not the content of the speeches she discussed, but rather the thrilling experience of sharing the platform with an all-woman executive when she addressed the Fifth Commission. She explained that during commission hearings and debates, three people sit on a platform facing the assembled delegates: the chair, the rapporteur, and the speaker. Because so few women were sent to the League of Nations Assembly as delegates, the three figures on the platform in commission hearings were usually men. On this occasion, though, in yet another history-making moment, when May Holman spoke to the commission she found herself as one of three women sitting on the platform: for the first time ever, a woman, Madam the Countess Apponyi of Hungary, was appointed to chair a commission's hearings in the League of Nations Assembly; and on this occasion the rapporteur was also a woman, Kirsten Hesselgren from Sweden. May Holman was delighted to be part of this moment, and wrote of it glowingly to her Australian readers: *Our chairman (or should I say chairwoman) acquitted herself very creditably and received many compliments and congratulations from delegates who were pleased to sit on the Commission having the first woman chairman.* She then went on, in typical fashion, to provide a vivid description of the distinguished countess for her readers to imagine: *The Countess* [who is president of the Hungarian National Council of Women] *is a dainty little lady with grey hair – I do not recollect having seen her without a hat – and a very pleasant voice and charming manner.*[29]

There's no doubt that the experience of travelling to the League of Nations Assembly was a hugely significant one for May Holman, not least because it allowed her to put her own experience as Australia's first Labor woman parliamentarian into international perspective. Weaving its way through this series of articles is an incisive interrogation of what it means to be a woman in this period of history, especially a woman in public life. Time and again we see in her writing an intense interest in the ways women comport themselves, dress, move, and interact in the public sphere. She clearly views herself as independent and capable when she writes briefly of the experience of travelling alone as a woman: *On the whole a woman traveller meets with great courtesy and every assistance when travelling alone on trains or boats abroad;*[30] but it's in her humorous stories of mistaken identities that we find an undercurrent of protest at the persistent assumption that women attempting to gain access to a privileged parliamentary location must be lost and in need of re-direction. These stories all appear in an article written about her experiences in London in November 1930.[31]

The first such story is set immediately after the Empire Parliamentary Luncheon held to mark the opening of the British Houses of Parliament in November 1930. May Holman was there as a distinguished parliamentarian from the Dominions, and consequently held a privileged pass in to the Dominion Gallery from where she could watch the opening ceremony and debates. In a scene reminiscent of the arm-flapping consternation of Virginia Woolf's famous Beadle who insists that only Fellows of the College can walk on the grass, May Holman found her way up a staircase to the Gallery blocked by a policeman and an attendant, who advised that *only members of Dominion Parliaments were allowed in that particular gallery*. Unlike the narrator in *A Room of One's Own*, Miss Holman gained her privileged entry, but it took some persuading: only *after some explanation were* [they] *willing to believe that I was one who would come under that denomination.* She recounts with distanced restraint that *A large book had to be signed and then I was told I was the third woman member to sit in the Gallery* and comments, presumably with a little irony, *I felt highly honoured…*

The next occasion when her entry to a privileged location was barred on the assumption that she was in the wrong place, was a few nights later, again at Parliament House in London. On that occasion she had been invited to a dinner given for the Dominion prime ministers and ministers and for other members of the Parliamentary Association from the Dominion parliaments and from India. On that same evening a second dinner was being given by the speaker of the House of Commons for the wives of parliamentarians and their visitors. *On this occasion also*, she writes, *the police officers at the entrance tried to persuade me that I was at the wrong door,* [telling me that] *the door for wives and non-members was further along.* She allows their response to speak for itself, but recalls immediately two previous cases of attempted exclusion on the grounds of her sex that had occurred during earlier travels in Australia:

> *It all reminded me of the time when I dined at Canberra Parliament House with Senator Rae and the manager of the dining room came to the Senator and said "Ladies are not allowed in this dining room, Senator," and the Senator replied, "She is not a lady, she is a Member"; and again when a conductor on the Sydney train locked me in the carriage at Spencer Street* [in Melbourne] *so that he could get me identified before the train left.*

She concludes this story with a slightly mocking observation: *a female with a gold pass is unexpected in some places.*

Clearly, stories of exclusion on the grounds of one's sex were on the menu that night. In this same article she recounts a conversation with one of the agents-general she met before the dinner, who told her that when he visited the House some years before with his daughter *she was not allowed in. It was during the time of the suffragette riots and the lady had to sit and wait for her father in the hall with a policeman on either side of her. Nothing her father or she herself could say would disabuse their minds of the suspicion that she might be a suffragette.*[32]

May Holman's solution to this kind of discrimination was to argue strongly for the inclusion of capable women at every level of public life. In an article outlining the operations of the International Labor Office (ILO), an autonomous organisation within the League of Nations which, like the League of Nations Assembly held an annual conference in Geneva, she argued that Australia ought to follow the lead of Canada, South Africa, India and Ireland and send women as delegates or technical advisors to the annual ILO conference. As a parliamentarian with a particular interest in the industrial conditions of workers in the timber industry, and with her recent experience of successfully researching and framing the legislation to ensure better safety conditions for workers in that industry, she was aware of her own expertise and knew that she herself would have been ideal as a delegate to this conference. Her article ends with a relatively uncharacteristic demand:

> *Australia should mend its ways in this direction. Surely a country where so many women are employed in industry should send a woman adviser to the delegation at least, or should send a woman as one of the Government Delegates. There are plenty of women in Australia who have the knowledge of industry that would enable them to carry out the work, and, that it is necessary is proved by the fact that many of the questions considered deal with women and children.*[33]

Her final article records her attendance at the British Labour Conference, held at Llandudno, North Wales, and chaired in a history-making gesture by the British MP Miss Susan Lawrence. On her eventual return to Australia May Holman spoke glowingly about the experience of attending this conference on behalf of Australian Labor women.

When she set out for Geneva, Miss Holman planned to be away for seven months or longer, returning via America, but the ill-health that persistently dogged her, in combination with her deep concern about the dramatic changes to Australian social and living conditions that had occurred during her absence, wrought by the onset of the Depression, ensured her earlier return home. In her letter of 1 October 1930 she wrote *I am very sorry to know that things are so bad over there – of course the shearers being out and the mills closing and the railway men being sacked must make a terrific difference.* She clearly feels a personal responsibility to return as soon as possible: *I felt like flying home when I read all about it...*[34] Although she was reluctant to dwell on the state of her health, it's clear from her letters and articles that the combination of asthma and arthritis had caught up with her, and she was often exhausted by travel. Her articles reveal that while in Britain after the Assembly, she became so ill that she had to cancel many pre-arranged meetings, political excursions and social events.

No doubt May Holman was immeasurably enriched by her experiences of travelling to and attending the League of Nations

Assembly. But the intensities of these experiences took their toll, and it was an exhausted and seriously ill woman who returned to Australia directly from London in early December 1930. She arrived on the wharf at Fremantle walking with two sticks, and although she then attended a round of welcome-home events, she was soon admitted to hospital, and was unable to return to her parliamentary work for the best part of a year.

May Holman, on her return from Geneva, 1930s.

CHAPTER 9
LET HER STORY, THEN, BE WOVEN ...

May Holman's prolonged illness on her return home from Europe gave her plenty of time to mull. In Geneva and in London she had come into contact with women who were fearless, intelligent, articulate, and determined to create a new world order. Some, like her new English friend Mary Hamilton, were aligned specifically with the left, and fought their fight from within Labor Party ranks; others, like the much-admired Princess Radziwill, drew on their family's historical status to operate on behalf of their nations, outside a party political arena. Although she never travelled overseas again, from this point onwards May became a committed internationalist. Her views had broadened. For the first time in her life she truly identified with other women. She stayed in close contact with women from the International Labour Organisation and the League of Nations, and drew inspiration from her membership of a select company of inspiring women, each breaking new ground. For the rest of her life she maintained her commitment to the great peace ideal that underpinned the League of Nations, and openly opposed conscription when, towards the end of the 1930s, many of her Labor colleagues were calling once again for its introduction. And her focus, during the 1930s, was more and more strongly upon working with women.

At home in Bassendean, her own struggle to regain good health and her mother's battle with alcoholism and depression echoed the social conditions of the world around her, and developed in her a renewed compassion and empathy with people whose lives are dark. Her support for the vulnerable became noticeably impassioned. Soon after her return from Europe, on 16 December 1930, before she took to her bed for the best part of a year, she participated in the huge parliamentary debate about the right of State Sawmills to continue to operate. There had been a change of government, and the conservatives were in power under Nationalist premier Sir James Mitchell. May Holman had her first taste of defending her constituents as a member of the opposition when she moved an amendment to the proposal to sell off state trading enterprises by excising State Sawmills. Her amendment was lost twenty-two to twenty-three.[1]

By 1932 when May was well enough to return to parliament, it was clear that the Depression was hitting hard. In parliamentary debates it was acknowledged that some men had been out of work for two and three years. May Holman argued fervently for the need for more efficient systems in delivering support to those experiencing the horrors of genuine poverty. On 18 August 1932, for example, she made an impassioned plea to the employment minister to answer the queries of a deputation of six members of parliament, a union organiser and a foreign consul, concerning sustenance payment for single men, delays in getting sustenance approvals for workers in the country, and conditions of a workers' camp which was boggy, flooded, and leaking sewage. As usual she backed up her plea with actual evidence. She invited her parliamentary colleagues to imagine their way into the lives of particular people: the woman who sought prenatal allowance and whose case was finally attended to when the baby was several months old; the family with three children whose baby needed medicines that cost that family one third of their income each week. Her sincerity in making these speeches was never in doubt. She spoke with authority and conviction when she said, *A lot more could be done than is being done. We do not wish to criticise unfairly. All that we want is justice, and if it will do any good I am prepared to talk until we get it.*[2]

A fortnight later, on 31 August 1932, Miss Holman sought justice for people on sustenance relief in the timber country, pointing out how devastating it was for people who had to prove total destitution before qualifying for sustenance relief. She cited

May Holman, 1930s.

case after case where the regulations discriminate in nonsensical ways: she told of the beekeeper who had been refused sustenance payments because he still had hives that might earn him an income; the young nurse who could receive no sustenance relief because she had a parent who was in part-time work; the families who had to wait till their few pounds in the bank were spent before seeking sustenance. *People who have taken up blocks of land should be encouraged to remain upon them, to grow their own vegetables, and otherwise help themselves. They should not be forced to come to town and go on to sustenance… We want relief to be applied generally in the South-West.* She argued for reforestation projects to pay one pound per week above the sustenance level. *We do not want to be unreasonable. The timber workers are not loafers. All they want is work.*[3]

Again on 13 October 1932 May Holman argued alongside her colleague Philip Collier, now leader of the opposition, in support of a bill to allow the Agricultural Bank to support farm mortgages. In a debate about the role of the Agricultural Bank, she told the story of a farmer and his wife and grown-up family who had secured title to their little farm but who had no work; they applied for assistance to the Unemployment Relief Department, but their application was referred to the Agricultural Bank who offered an advance of twelve pounds in exchange for a caveat on their land. They were so desperate that they agreed, and on 12 September they were told that their twelve pounds was coming. However, Miss Holman told the parliament that she had visited the family on 1 October and found no money had been paid. This specific matter was referred to the premier. On the matter of principle she argued, *If people have to mortgage their land for an advance of £12, it would be better for them to raise something approaching the value of their land.*[4]

An insight into her anxiety and her compassion for people hit hardest by the Depression is found in her contribution to the debate about the imposition of a financial emergency relief tax. The Government's plan was to impose a tax of four-pence-halfpenny in the pound on everyone, including sustenance workers, in order to raise £300,000 for the government. This proposal was ridiculed by the opposition as taxing the unemployed to provide sustenance for the unemployed. Miss Holman called this an imposition on sustenance workers, and was backed by Mr Heagney, who said, *When we realise the conditions of the sustenance workers, especially those with large families, we see it is monstrous to ask them to contribute to this special taxation for the needs of the Government.*[5]

Again on 27 October 1932 in the Second Reading Speech debate for this bill, May Holman opposed it.

The Government are taking a very indifferent view when they show themselves willing to tax sustenance workers 4½d. in the pound and take from those on higher incomes only the same amount of tax. I would sooner pay 2s. in the pound myself than have any one of my constituents who is on sustenance taxed 4½d. in the pound. We have tried to get these men exempted from this tax, but without success.[6]

In a later sitting of parliament, in November 1932, Miss Holman brought the plight of specific sustenance workers to the attention of the House.

Many complaints have been made as to the manner in which operations are carried out at the irrigation works ... Men on sustenance are not at all satisfied with the way in which they are being treated. Men have to dig thick wet clay with shovels, which they have to scrape every time they use them. They have no forks, and are not receiving a fair rate of pay for the work they do. They cannot make sustenance or relief wages. I feel that the Minister is pressing these workers down as far as they can be pressed. If they complain about it they are given the sack, and are put off sustenance.

Once again she had specific examples to back up her claims and to illustrate that she was in close contact with her electorate: *One man could earn only £4 in two weeks.*[7]

‡

It was not only sustenance workers who caught her attention during the Depression years. Miss Holman was only too aware that timber workers who had managed to avoid having to go onto sustenance were also doing it tough. On 28 September 1932 she delivered a Second Reading Speech on a Private Member's Bill to protect the rights of sleeper hewers. Her speech gives an insight into the lives of vulnerable forest workers at this time of desperate poverty and hardship. The bill, designed to give protection to the sleeper hewers, had become necessary when a court ruling found that they were not covered by the provisions of the Master and Servants Act, nor by the Industrial Arbitration Act. Hence they were unable to sue employers for failure to pay wages. In her speech Miss Holman explained that unscrupulous contractors sometimes made a practice of taking out a contract to supply sleepers, with no capital and no land behind them, and would go broke or bankrupt, leaving sleeper cutters and storemen without any payment for goods supplied or sleepers cut. Foreign sleeper cutters were often tricked into signing worthless contracts and then hoodwinked.

> *I ask the House carefully to consider the Bill. I believe the sleeper cutters are entitled to the same protection as any other workers have. They work hard and they have to carry out their work to a fraction of an inch. If the sleeper is not cut to the exact liking of the person who has ordered it, it is condemned and the work is not paid for. There are about 400 sleeper cutters now employed on various works, and in normal times the number would be much greater. So there is quite a large section of the community suffering under*

> an injustice, because they cannot sue for their money in the courts. The sleeper cutter is under great expense, for he has to have certain tools ...

She drew parallels between the piece work of sleeper cutters and that done by shearers, wheat lumpers and woodworkers on the goldfields, all of whom were covered by industrial awards. She reminded the House of the similarity between this bill and a much earlier one introduced by the current premier Sir James Mitchell in 1923, to allow sleeper cutters to be entitled to workers compensation. She concluded her speech with an understated plea for justice: *I feel confident that I may leave it to Members to see that justice is done to a large section of the community working in the timber industry.*[8]

Members of both sides of the House may well have been sympathetic to the plight of the sleeper cutters, but the wheels of parliament turn slowly and Miss Holman was frustrated by the repeated deferral of her Bill. On 8 December 1932 she made an uncharacteristically desperate speech to the parliament, deploring the fact that the Private Members Bill seeking justice for timber workers had been delayed. She cited the dates of its first and second readings – 7 September and 28 September – and reminded the House that on 16 November she especially requested that Private Members Bills would be scheduled for consideration before the pre-Christmas rush to pass legislation, to no avail. *As time goes on*, she said, *I feel more and more hopeless about getting any help for the timber workers. The pastoralist leases have 16 years to run before they expire, but the timber workers have been waiting ever so long to get justice. They have failed to get it from the court and now desire to appeal for it to Parliament ...* The desperation in her language is unlikely to be mere theatrics: it was unusual for her to appear to be so desperate and vulnerable in the chamber.

> Hope deferred maketh the heart sick. Our hopes have been deferred so long that out hearts are very sick.

> *Justice is being withheld from the timber workers, and the Government do not seem anxious to allow them to get it. I protest strongly against new legislation being put ahead of private members' business.*[9]

The bill was finally brought before the House again on 14 December 1932, and after debate in which the conservative attorney-general opposed the bill on the grounds that it falsely implied a master-and-servant relationship rather than a vendor-buyer relationship, the bill was passed and referred to the Legislative Council for ratification.

It was defeated in the Legislative Council on 21 December 1932.

A second attempt to establish appropriate industrial protection for sleeper hewers was made two years later in 1934, via a similar bill introduced by the Labor minister for works, Mr McCallum, on 26 September, but it too suffered a similar fate to Miss Holman's Private Members Bill, and was defeated in the Legislative Council on its Second Reading.

‡

Although May Holman was admired for her tenacious representation of her electorate, sometimes her persistence provoked exasperation in her parliamentary colleagues. On 2 November 1932 when she rose to say she wanted to put a few requests to the minister for health about hospitals in her electorate, the minister replied, *You can have* [no requests] *left!* She then asked for an X-ray plant, a drainage system, a water supply, painting of the building and a little more for the nurses' quarters at Dwellingup Hospital. This latter request for more furnishings provoked the following hilarious exchange:

> *The Minister for Health: We furnished the place.*
>
> Miss HOLMAN: *I was not going to mention the furniture. I have seen it. When the Minister promised it I was very*

> *jubilant, but when I saw it I felt sure the Minister had not seen it before it was sent down. I will tell the Minister what was forwarded. There was one table for the sitting room in the nurses' quarters, two fairly decent cane chairs, and one very ordinary cane chair such as could be purchased for 7s. 6d. at a sale. They have to be well padded before anyone can sit on them.*
>
> *The Minister for Health: That is a summer chair.*
>
> *Miss* HOLMAN: *Well, there are two winter chairs and one summer chair.*

She went on to discuss the stuff sent for curtains:

> *Miss* HOLMAN: *… beautiful soft silk poplin of a beige colour with blue trimming which would have done beautifully for a partition across the room, but not as curtains. As I have said, I did not intend to bring up this question of furniture; the Minister himself did it.*

With characteristic fancy footwork she then put amusement aside and segued from this exchange into the more serious portion of her request, using her speaking opportunity to reinforce her central message: *We want a good drainage system at this hospital. The Minister promised to send a man down to look at it, but the man has not turned up yet. The building requires painting, if only to preserve it. Then a water supply is required.*

She then read a report from the hospital outlining the generous donations from the community of fresh eggs and fruit and vegetables, butter and edible dainties. Money for bed linen and general equipment had been raised by the hospital auxiliary committee. She reported that the Dwellingup Hospital had fourteen beds and two cots, took two hundred patients per annum, had a seven-bed average occupancy, and in the previous year had ten deaths from disease and accident, but none from maternity cases. Once again we see May Holman as well informed, fiercely protective of her constituents, admiring of the community spirit of her electorate, fearless in exchanging repartee with the minister, unafraid of appearing to be droll or tart, but never aggressive or losing her dignity. She concluded with her usual composure, *I feel sure the Health Department will give these requests every consideration.*[10]

✧

In 1933 the Labor Government was returned to power, again under Premier Philip Collier, in a landslide victory. By 1934 the worst of the Depression had passed, and Miss Holman expressed her gratitude to her government for its successful reduction of unemployment during their new term of office: *On this subject I can speak from my heart, because at the time of the last general election there were hundreds of sustenance workers in the electorate of Forrest, and now there are comparatively few. Almost all the mills are working again, and the sleeper cutters also are at work.*[11]

Underpinning much of her idealism about the creation of a new social order was her conviction, heightened by her visit to Geneva, *that the future of mankind … this greater, nobler era, is dependent upon what is done for children.* The League of Nations Declaration on children –

> *that the child must be given the means for its normal development, both materially and spiritually; the child that is hungry must be fed; the child that is sick must be nursed; the child that is backward must be helped; the delinquent child must be reclaimed; and the orphan and the waif must be sheltered and succored. … The child must be brought up in the consciousness that its talent must be devoted to the service of its fellow men.*[12]

– fuelled her long-term engagement with the Parents and Citizens' Association, and spurred her ongoing commitments to providing excellent education for children, and bringing young people into the Labor movement.

When in government, May Holman seems to have had the happy knack of praising the government for the good work it is doing, but drawing attention to problems by regretting something specific. For example, on 6 October 1936, on the increased expenditure on education she was full of praise, but:

> *I am sorry, however, that a greater increase has not been made for the provision of material and furniture ... It is time the Government took heed of the fact that the provision for manual and sewing materials is inadequate ... We are almost back to pre-depression expenditure and that being so, we should revert to pre-depression conditions regarding these matters.*[13]

Similarly, she congratulated the government on building the new school for girls in East Perth, but complained that it had no grounds; she requested that *beautiful schools for boys and girls* should be established in country areas too; she asked for a city hostel for country kids; and, *at the risk of being parochial in meeting matters affecting my district,* she asked for a new school at Treesville in her electorate but *as I do not trouble members much I shall continue being parochial for the time being*. Here again she demonstrated an intimate, hands-on knowledge of the lives of her constituents: *At the present time the hall used for school purposes is situated between four railway lines and is dangerous. The lighting is bad and there are not the conveniences that should be available.*[14]

‡

May Holman openly acknowledged her desire to bring pleasure and happiness to difficult lives, and after the worst of the

Depression had passed, when she herself was well again in body and spirit, she set about organising Labor women to within an inch of their lives, with annual summer schools and conferences, and, from 1936 onwards, a choral union that she conducted and administered. To outside observers her life was gay and busy and full of laughter and good cheer, but close friends and family knew that even in good times she was shadowed by misery.

One of the troubling personal issues she had to contend with during the 1930s concerned the family. Ever since she could remember, her younger siblings had been scooped into her life. As they all grew up, May had been the leader of this merry band, the big sister to whom the others looked up. We have already watched as she whisked her brothers Jack and Ted, and her sisters Maude and Winnie, and even, at times, the much younger Cis, Eileen and Sheila into The Entertainers during and after the years of the Great War.

From the moment she was first elected to parliament in 1925, May's political life became a family affair, and family activities were arranged around it. At first Winnie kept house and Maude, by then a schoolteacher of more than a decade, helped with secretarial activities. During the 1930s the role of secretary was passed on to the much younger sister, Sheila. At weekends May would pile one or two of her siblings into her Tin Lizzie and take off for the timber country to visit her electorate. Of her activities in 1929 she was able to boast that she spent forty-two weekends visiting constituents in her electorate – always, it seems, with at least one family member in tow. At election times everyone was roped in to help campaign. Somehow, May made these activities fun.[15] And in the late 1930s, when the incomparable Miss Holman organised a Christmas party for underprivileged guests, it was her sisters who willingly toiled to provide the sandwiches for lunch. As historian Marian Sawer has noted, her sisters were, in effect, her wives.[16] That is, she was supported as much by her sisters as a male politician would have been supported by his dutiful wife.

May repaid them with a generous attention to creating pleasure in their lives. Photographic records show us that her younger sisters made their debuts at Labor Party balls organised to coincide with Labor Women's summer camps at Yanchep during the 1930s, and that her brothers were frequent escorts to debutantes. Family legend has it that May loved nothing better than to gather her siblings together at weekends at the lovely old family home at 3 Ida Street, Bassendean, for meals, parties and singalongs.[17]

We know that May had willingly taken on the guardianship of her four youngest siblings in 1925 when her father died; together with her sister Maude she had supported them financially and emotionally as they grew into adulthood. But few could have anticipated the extent of May's heartbreak and sense of loss as each of her younger siblings found life partners and left the family home to marry. Her sister Winnie and brother Ted each married within days of the other in 1928, two years before May set out for her League of Nations adventure in Geneva; and her sister Maude, by then a mature thirty-three years old, married the year after May's return, in 1931. Their mother died in 1934; and as each of her younger sisters married – Eileen in 1937, Iris in 1938 – May's responses seemed to become more extreme. She made no secret of her own feelings, and lamented the disintegration of family life as they had known it.[18] We don't know whether their marriages recalled her own disastrous liaison with Joe Gardiner. Perhaps it was inevitable that this intensely family-focused, determinedly single older sister should feel displaced, irrelevant even, as life changed around her. The extent of her distress, though, seems to have taken even May herself by surprise, and gives us, in retrospect, insight into the intensities of her emotional landscape.

‡

No doubt her increasing freedom from family affairs gave her more time to devote to public life. Throughout the decade of the 1930s she continued to hold executive positions in party and public organisations. She had stepped down as president of the Labor Women's Central Executive of WA in 1930, but became its secretary from 1932 to 33, and she remained president of the Labor Women's Interstate Executive and of Perth Labor Women's Organisation. In 1933 she was prestigiously appointed secretary to the Parliamentary Labor Party. She was a director of the *Westralian Worker* newspaper, and was general president of the WA Federation of Parents and Citizens' Associations.

1937 Labor procession, Perth. May Holman in decorated car in front.

LET HER STORY, THEN, BE WOVEN ...

Labor Women's Camp, Yanchep, 1930s.
May (in blazer) with Miss Hooton and Mrs Laidlaw.

Labor Women's Organisation Summer Camp, 1935.

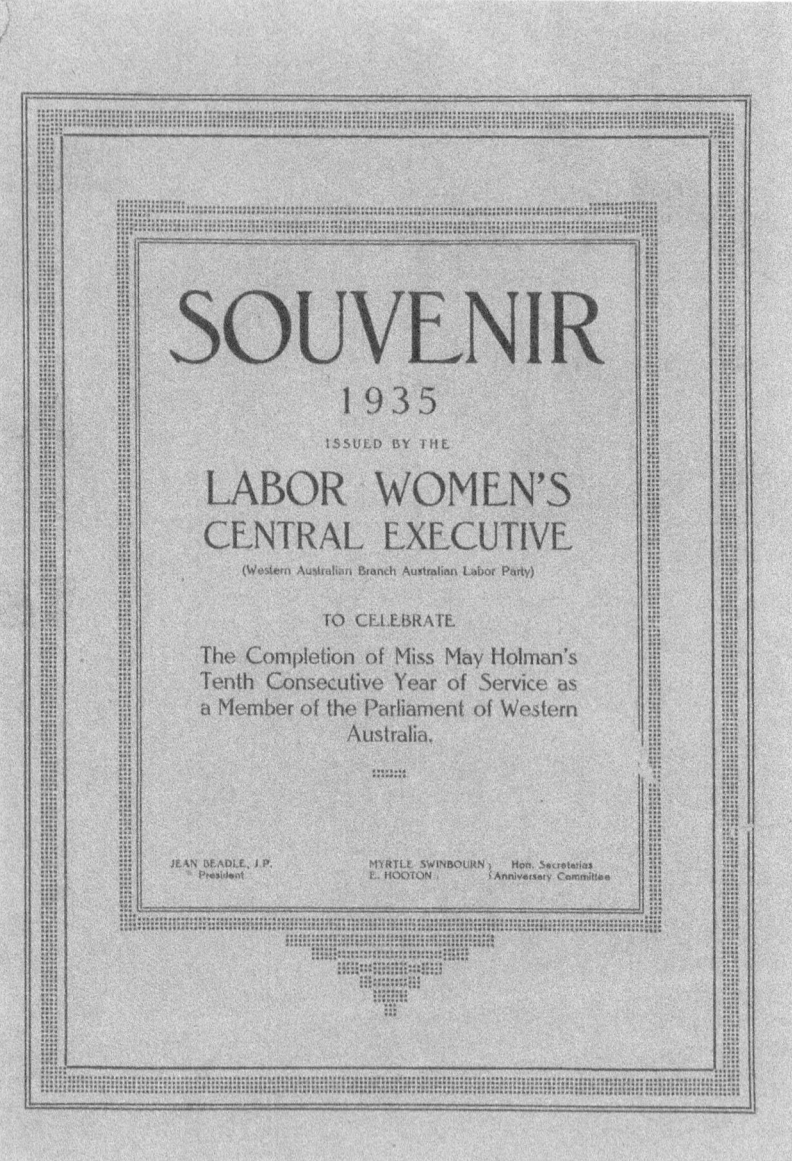

Souvenir, May Holman tenth anniversary edition.

LET HER STORY, THEN, BE WOVEN ...

MISS MAY HOLMAN, M.L.A.
Probably the Only Woman in the World who has held a Labor
Seat in any Parliament for Ten Years

In 1935 the Labor Women's Central Executive compiled a booklet titled *Souvenir*, published to *Celebrate the Completion of Miss May Holman's Tenth Consecutive Year of Service as a Member of the Parliament of Western Australia.* This document opens with a beautiful photograph captioned *Miss May Holman MLA, Probably the Only Woman in the World who has held a Labor Seat in any Parliament for Ten Years.* In an introductory biographical statement, Ettie Hooton wrote of her good friend with insight and accuracy:

> *[May Holman] is now a woman in middle life, youthful in outlook and appearance, highly emotional and impulsive, quick to sense and resent an injury, and quick to forgive and forget. She combines a certain refinement with a personal knowledge of the struggle to live, knows nothing of snobbishness, and so gets along happily with most people.*[19]

May's own introductory article, called 'My Stewardship', reads exactly as one might imagine, reflecting simultaneously the pride she took in her life of service to the community, and the humility with which she carried out her duties. *Surely there is nothing in this life that thrills and appalls so much,* she writes,

> *as the knowledge that one has been deliberately selected from a group ... of one's fellows, for the express purpose, not only of improving by legislative action the conditions under which all live at the moment, but also that a hand might be stretched across the years into the long future of humanity, thus helping to shape the destiny of millions unborn.*

She writes of *the splendid faith of a people who trust an individual to be just and fair to all; and of the big vision of achievement and responsibility that parliamentary responsibilities open up.* She writes, too, of one's own *distracting limitations ... so that, however brilliant or commonplace, we are never able to do all that we would wish*; and of the *bigger life* that emerged through study and investigation.

Her piece ends with a blessing on her readers which, ironically, desires a radically positive change in world conditions in the next decade: *May the next ten years see the dawn of a new and happier day*... Its final flourish carries all the hyperbole that the period demands: *Nothing would give me greater joy than to be numbered among those who will greet that glorious sunrise.*[20]

Tributes to May's parliamentary career are warm in their praise. The WA Timber Workers' Union writes:

> *Ten years of service as Parliamentary Representative in an industrial electorate is surely something unique for a woman, and speaks eloquently of the confidence reposed in this popular member by her constituents. Devoted service and interest in those whom she represents, combine with close knowledge of the nature and requirements of her electorate, form the reasons for continued expressions of confidence and satisfaction... Miss Holman has become... not only a member for the district but one of its institutions.*[21]

The premier, Hon. P. Collier, describes her *conspicuous success* and invites more women to stand for parliament:

> *I am confident that the Movement possesses an abundance of women of the highest character and ability who for various reasons are not taking the prominent part in the affairs of the country for which they are fitted. He urges women to assist in the magnificent work she is doing for the people generally and for women in particular.*[22]

James Scullin, leader of the Federal Parliamentary Labor Party, writes of her *notable success* and urges women to *continue to exert their beneficial influence;*[23] Jean Beadle, state executive of WA Labor Women, writes of her *unlimited ability, capacity, grit and unselfish work*[24]; and Mrs Mannion of Fremantle Labor Women writes *We* *feel that her position is a tribute to all women who have worked and battled since adult franchise was first mooted.*²⁵ Others acknowledge that *her efforts are of utmost value to Labor;*²⁶ admire her *worthy record;*²⁷ and wish her *many, many happy returns.*²⁸ Jean Daley, of the Labor Women's Interstate Executive, writes indignantly:

> Looking around the world today at the frightful waste of human life and human effort everywhere apparent, I wonder that any man dares say or think that women are unsuited for public life. If women had ruled or governed for hundreds of years as men have done, and if they had involved the special aid of the Prince of Darkness, they could hardly have produced more chaos, or more cruelty than is evidenced in world affairs today.²⁹

Mary Sutherland of the British Labour Party acknowledges that:

> these ten years have coincided with a very difficult period in the economic life of Australia, with an unprecedented worldwide depression, with a period of unparalleled difficulty for the Labor and Socialist movement in many countries, difficulties which for the time being have defeated it in certain countries. The Labor Movement in Western Australia deserves admiration for the way in which it has come through these years, and it is not too much to claim that the work of the women has been a big factor in consolidating the party. And in the women's movement the drive and the leadership of women like Miss Holman is of tremendous importance.³⁰

John Curtin, then the member for Fremantle in the Commonwealth parliament, waxes lyrical:

> If the task of civilisation be to raise the whole body politic and to uplift and irradiate the life of the many, rather than to increase the culture and wealth of the few, then Miss Holman

has laboured magnificently in the greatest of tasks. She has set an example; she has shown inspiration; she has proved that the Labor Movement can not only be served magnificently by a woman, but that Labor is capable of giving to a woman a magnificent opportunity.[31]

Mr J. J. Keneally, minister for employment and industry, calls her an outstanding figure in the public life of the Commonwealth.[32] The South Australian Labor Women acknowledge her *magnificent record* and assert that *all Australians must appreciate the value of women in social reform*.[33] Percy Trainer, secretary of the state executive, takes the opportunity to express Labor ideals:

The Labor Woman visionary sees the possibility of getting away from the drab, colourless monotony and commonplace of a capitalist world. She sees the possibility of a new era where, through the agency of science and power, laughter may become enthroned in place of today's tears. Happiness will take the place of sorrow, and hunger and rags will be no more. The peace of the world also has its place in the Labor Women's propaganda. She can plainly visualise the time when greater importance will be attached to solving the problems of life rather than giving concentrated attention to the problems of war and death.[34]

Lewis McDonald, secretary to the Queensland Central Executive, writes:

Miss Holman's many outstanding and excellent qualities: her personal charm and accomplishments; her ability, tact, earnestness, and indefatigable energy on behalf of the Cause which she espouses, have endeared her to many thousands of admirers throughout Australia.

He asserts that *her record is an inspiration to women*.[35]

‡

As we have seen, throughout her parliamentary career May Holman distanced herself from women whose agenda was specifically feminist, preferring instead to subsume gender issues to issues of class. The media relished this stance. *The Australian Women's Weekly* was insistent that, in spite of her success as a woman politician, May Holman should not be considered a feminist – or at least, not *the feminist of tradition*, whoever she may be. *She dressed well, in attractive clothes, and wore her hair softly waved, and she had a fresh, vivid complexion.*[36]

Interestingly, the view that emerges here, of a womanly woman doing her political work more effectively than a manly man could do is in sharp contrast to the view of possibilities for women in public life taken in an article in the *Sydney Morning Herald's Women's Supplement* of 27 March 1939, shortly after May Holman had died. The article is titled 'Feminine Influence in National Life'. It laments that the death of May Holman *removes a prominent member from the ranks of influential women in the Commonwealth* at a time when women ought to be more influential than they are permitted to be: *though the era of so-called equal opportunity for the sexes opened long years ago, the acceptance of the principle has been a matter of slow progress and not of sharp revolution.*[37]

Instead of calling herself a feminist, May Holman aligned herself strongly with Labor women and their ideals of equal opportunity for all. The line she trod was a fine one. On the issue of wages justice, she strongly supported the full participation of women in public life, and, during the early part of the 1930s, frequently argued for equal pay for equal work. She strongly supported the views that single women were as likely as single men to have dependent parents or siblings to support, and ought on those grounds be offered equal wages for equal work. She became impatient with the argument that women were the cause of men's unemployment, and argued that if women and men were given equal pay for equal work, the grounds for employment would shift from salary to ability, and the focus of legislators could then shift to addressing the real causes of unemployment instead of discriminating for superficial reasons against women as a group.[38] By 1936 her views on the equal pay for equal work issue had changed, and she argued strongly, against her own party, for equal pay for the sexes. Her views were reflected by the fourth Interstate Conference of Labor Women held in Hobart in February 1937, which *resolved to do everything in its power to have the principle recognized and adopted.*[39] Several months later, in May 1937, May Holman was able to report to the *Kalgoorlie Miner* that the federal Labor Party had adopted the principle of equal pay for the sexes as part of its policy platform for the upcoming elections.[40]

This was clearly one instance where May Holman's alignment with women overrode her loyalty to Labor Party policy. If we look closely at her participation in a parliamentary debate on 28 October 1936 about the employment of youth in Western Australia, we see how she walked the tightrope between her wholehearted support of Labor ideals, and her increasingly overt championing of women's issues within that Labor framework. On that day a motion was moved by the Labor Member for Yilgarn-Coolgardie, Mr Lambert:

> *That, in the opinion of this House, a Board ... should be appointed to inquire into and investigate generally the question of employment of the male youth of the State, having regard to the social and economic conditions which are likely to result by their non-employment, and in view of the increasing number of young females engaged in clerical and other occupations which could be filled by males, and, further, with a view of rationalising employment on an equitable quota basis of all juvenile workers.*[41]

May Holman voted with Mrs Cardell-Oliver and other conservatives in support of an amendment to this motion which would ensure that the wages of junior male workers in shops, factories and warehouses apply also to junior female workers. She argued that Mr Lambert's motion intended to displace female labour, and argued that attention needed to be focused on the employment of all youth (boys and girls). She said, *It is time we set an example by asking, not for equal pay for equal work – with which I do not agree – but for equal pay for the sexes. The principle of equal pay for equal work ... pre-supposes some means of measuring the work, which is entirely impossible ...*[42]

There was discussion in this debate about the difficulty of obtaining reliable census figures about employment rates of young people; and of the need to raise the school leaving age to fifteen; and of the need to dignify housework by introducing domestic science training and monitoring the conditions of housemaids so more young women would be willing to work in households. Miss Holman argued that housework for girls should be made a profession, that they be given decent wages and living conditions, and that whilst they do their work on the same footing as men, they be given equal pay. Her speech ranged across the employment of young people to the employment of women: she noted that the *so-called emancipation under which women are suffering to-day is that they are given a vote and are told they have all the social and civic opportunities granted to men,* and yet the motion under discussion would have them sent out of industry altogether.[43] She cited conditions for housemaids in many countries – Switzerland, Austria, Denmark, Iceland, Germany, Soviet Russia and Mexico, and argued,

> *It is interesting to learn that we who think ourselves such leaders in social progress, who consider ourselves the salt of the earth with regard to industrial conditions, are absolutely only a little fullstop at the end of the line, not even the last letter, when conditions here are compared with conditions obtaining in other countries.*[44]

She also likened the thrust of the motion (to exclude women from industrial positions to make way for men) to the situation in Hitler's Germany, where equality of opportunity for women in education, the professions and public life cannot be endured in the man's state.[45] Her amendment was passed, so empowering the board in question to enquire into every phase of youth employment that could be elucidated, including whether young women are displacing young men in the workplace. It is a measure of the esteem in which by then she was held in the House that, at the conclusion of this debate, following the successful passing of her amendment, her erstwhile adversary, Mr Lambert, acknowledged that her contribution to the debate was eloquent and informative.[46] Although it's clear that her attention was increasingly on the ways women were affected by legislation and public policies, a skirmish on the floor of the House in October 1938 with the conservative Mrs Cardell-Oliver about which women should be entitled to sit on juries clearly demonstrates May Holman's sensitivity to issues of class and status, bred of her long immersion in Labor ideals. Mrs Cardell-Oliver had introduced a bill providing that women with fifty pounds be allowed to sit on juries. May Holman attacked her assumptions about the connection between monetary wealth and human worth:

> *No member has any right to come to this House and state that lack of money or possessions means lack of education and ability and I am surprised at the Member's pretending to speak on behalf of equality of the sexes. She is doing nothing of the kind. She is pleading for equality of the sexes if they have equality of money and property.*

On this occasion Miss Holman was rebuked by the eloquent but restrained conservative Mr Keenan for the heated nature of the debate.[47]

May Holman frequently argued that women must stand shoulder to shoulder in support of each other. Many of her views on issues centrally important to women – their social status and sense of self-worth, their reception and participation in the public sphere, and their role in establishing and maintaining world peace – are outlined in a speech she gave in Brisbane to members of the Queensland Citizenship League in January 1934. She began with the provocative assertion that *Most women prefer to go to a man doctor rather than to a woman doctor – and that is only one instance of woman's belief that a man can do a job better than one of her own sex*, and argued that women must be educated into accepting their own sex as being equal to men. She said that women *should secure full citizenship rights for themselves. She did not believe that women should be limited to work dealing only with women and children*, for it was her conviction that *if a woman really studied any work, she could do that work as well as a man. But*, she continued, no doubt drawing on her own experiences in the parliament, *I believe that no woman can maintain her status unless she works harder than a man to prove that she can work equally well*. She told her audience that *when she was elected, in 1925, one of the arguments raised against her was that she would not be able to travel about among her people, but she went right out in the country among the timber-getters, and disproved the statement*. She boasted that she had *drafted one of the most technical Bills dealing with the timber industry, and in getting it through Parliament spoke for 2½ hours on practically every type of machinery connected with the timber industry, and was proud to say that she had not made one mistake*. Urging the need for women to stand together, Miss Holman said that:

> *there were many points on which women could meet, despite any differences in their politics. First of all, there were all the points pertaining to the welfare of women and children. So many women had to work for their living now that they ought to demand a say in the conditions under which they would work. One of the biggest works in which all women could unite, however, was the work dealing with the peace of the world. And that peace of the world, she said, cannot be attained until women teach it to their children from infancy. At school children learn poems about war, all their*

> *history is of war, at home the boys play with toy soldiers and drums, and little girls want to be war nurses when they grow up – everywhere, war is presented to them as a glory. Women must teach their children not to have anything to do with war. That is the only way to bring about the peace of the world.*[48]

Although there can be no doubt that her experiences in Europe broadened her horizons and drew her attention to the need to work explicitly with women to help change the conditions of their lives, her solutions to the ills facing women – workplace discriminations, negative personal status, war – seem to be that women themselves must work harder to change attitudes and practices. Her life's work was to get privileged men to move over to make space for women and others disadvantaged by class. She did not seek to re-educate the men of her acquaintance beyond a challenge to their overtly sexist behaviours on the floor of the House.

Although Australian feminists like Bessie Reischbeth and others had been calling for women to join feminist groups to lobby politically for the kinds of changes necessary for women to take their place as full human beings in the society, May Holman was unrepentant about turning her back on such groups and placing her faith in the Labor Party and its social agenda. In terms of her personal psychology, one could well argue that her place in the family, as favourite eldest daughter equally aligned with mother and father, and oldest child responsible for the wellbeing of a string of small brothers as well as sisters, kept her focus firmly on families as units, rather than on gendered subgroups within them. One could also argue that throughout her parliamentary career she was aware of a great range of analyses and tactics being adopted in the women's movement in Western Australia and indeed throughout the nation. These included the practical but socially conservative approaches of the Women's Service Guilds and the Karrakatta Club women at one end of the political spectrum, through to the radical approaches of extreme-left women like Katharine Susannah Prichard at the other. Labor Women sat somewhere firmly left-of-centre on this spectrum, and May Holman took utmost advantage of this relatively comfortable position. Her location within the Labor movement gave her all the protection and the bolstering necessary to pursue her goals of creating a better world for everyone who suffered disadvantage.

But it's in her daily working and living practices that perhaps the most intriguing legacies can be found. We have seen time and again her attention to the everyday matters of people's lives: her electorate work meant that she was always available to listen to people, to understand the small joys and upsets of their daily lives. Her emphasis on creating pleasure through music, dance, amateur theatre, silliness and song was born of her conviction that *hearts starve as well as bodies*[49] and attests to her belief that spirits need uplifting, and that small gestures of kindness and generosity are the stuff of robust and healthy communities. It would be churlish to argue that May Holman, in attending to the interpersonal and small gestures of daily life, was merely fulfilling her feminine role and therefore guilty of maintaining the status quo rather than challenging it. Rather, I would argue that her intelligent and careful attention to interpersonal exchange and to the processes of ensuring that people's spirits were uplifted, along with their wages, is a fine example of best practice twenty-first century community development process. Rather than denigrating those qualities of attentiveness to the nuance of interpersonal encounter as being merely feminine and therefore unworthy of notice in the public arena, if we shine the light differently we can view these qualities, as contemporary community development workers do, as crucial in establishing and maintaining community connection at all levels, from the most secretly intrapersonal to the most overtly public arena. We have much to learn from the life of May Holman.

LET HER STORY, THEN, BE WOVEN ...

Let her story, then, be woven into the tasks we will endeavor to do and in the lives we each have yet to live. Let us take up the work that has been left yet unfinished, preserve the good that has been done, and in that way give fullness and completion to the glorified life of Miss Holman.[50]

‡

It is deeply ironic that May Homan met her end while intent on fulfilling just one more obligation to her beloved electorate.

Imagine how exhausted they both are.

Iris – Cis – sits at the wheel. She's already six months gone and tired. This has been the most exhausting campaign ever. Sheila's out for the count, tossed into hospital with appendicitis after only two weeks of campaigning. Eileen, so busy at this time, is nowhere to be seen. So Cis, who had planned to spend much of this last fortnight safely tucked up at home in bed, finds herself on the road with May, driving, driving, driving, 'Just one more, Cis, just one more event tonight, then it's over.' May herself is exhausted. She has just enough reserve to lay it on thick tonight for the good residents of Brookhampton. It's going to be a loud and triumphant affair. The whole hamlet will be there: all fifteen families, kids in 'jamas, mums and dads dressed in their party gear, all celebrating not just the end of the week, but the end of this campaign, the end of so much hard slog, so many miles of driving, so many meetings, singalongs, speeches ... May settles back into her seat. Her neck relaxes. She closes her eyes, opens them again, sees the trees rushing past. Shadows whoosh overhead like wind. Closes. Opens a fraction. Closes again. Nods off. Cis, driving, glances sideways, thinks, *Good. She needs a rest. Bit of shut-eye. She pushes herself too hard. All of us. She pushes all of us too hard. So glad when this is over. So glad.* Trees, shadows, wind ...

There's a bump, a clatter, a jolt. The steering wheel leaps about, alive. Cis grabs it tighter, wrestles. But it's disconnected, broken. Doesn't respond. The car hurtles straight ahead. Misses the bend. Brake. Too late. Ditch. Bump. Jolt. Leap. May wakes, gasps, leans in to grab the wheel. Useless. Cis wrestles. A rushing of air, a hurtle through space. A crash. A thud. A crushing weight. Dark. Out. Gone.

EPILOGUE

John Curtin's exhortation *to take up the work that has been left yet unfinished, preserve the good that has been done, and in that way give fullness and completion to the glorified life of Miss Holman* seems to have been taken seriously by those who were inspired by her leadership.

At the time of her death, in addition to carrying out her parliamentary duties, May Holman was deeply involved in a range of political and community organisations. She was secretary of the Parliamentary Labor Party; a member of the State Executive Australian Labor Party; president and former secretary of Perth Labor Women's Organisation; secretary of the Labor Women's Central Executive; conductor and secretary of the Labor Choral Union; president of the Interstate Labor Women's Executive; a representative of Labor Women in the Labor Economic Council; a member of the committee on women's work of the International Labor Organisation; director of the *Westralian Worker*; a delegate to the South-West District and Metropolitan Councils; president of the Parents and Citizens' Association; Labor representative on the Adult Education Board; a member of the Board of Management of Perth General Hospital; and president of the Sacred Heart Old Girls' Association.[1]

Miss Holman's official positions within the party were filled in the weeks after her death. But it was the response of Labor women in her choir which is recorded as being heartfelt and tender. An article in the *Westralian Worker* of Friday 31 March 1939, titled

'Labor Women Meet', recorded an open discussion that was held regarding the best way to honour Miss Holman's memory:

> *A large gathering of very sad women met at the Trades Hall on Friday night last, the time at which the weekly classes in physical culture and singing are held, but nobody thought of these things that evening. All were overwhelmed because of the tragic happening which had removed from them a great leader, and all seemed to be seeking some convincing way of expressing their sorrow. After discussing the matter informally for over an hour, all were agreed that this could only be done by carrying on the work which she loved so well, and eager as they have been in the past to co-operate, there was never more enthusiasm and determination shown than marked the proceedings when they realised that this difficult task would have to be done now without her inspiring influence. There was no shirking the work, and it was decided to try and get a conductor for the choir who had helped Miss Holman in times past, and to keep everything going just as they knew she would wish them to do.*[2]

But less than six months after her death, war was declared on 1 September 1939, and once again life as everyone knew it was turned on its head. In the circles in which May Holman had moved, pacifists were shunned,[3] Communists were outlawed,[4] young people in their thousands signed up to defend their country, and public and private energies were once again directed specifically towards sustaining the war effort.

Within the parliament, with May Holman's death, Labor women lost their chance to put a woman into Cabinet. The honour of being the first woman minister in a Western Australian parliament went to the conservative Nationalist Florence Cardell-Oliver, who became minister for health, supply and shipping on 7 October 1949. And, in spite of Miss Holman's own excellent record of parliamentary service, it was fifteen years before another Labor woman, Ruby Hutchinson, was elected to parliament in Western Australia, this time to the Legislative Council. In 1983, forty-four years after May Holman died, there was a relative deluge of Labor women in parliament in WA when four women (Pam Beggs, Pam Buchanan, Yvonne Henderson and Jackie Watkins) were elected to the Legislative Assembly and one (Kay Hallahan) to the Legislative Council. By the time more Labor women began to enter both houses of the Western Australian parliament in the late 1980s and early 1990s (including Carmen Lawrence, Judyth Watson, Judy Edwards and Diana Warnock in the Legislative Assembly, and Beryl Jones, Cheryl Davenport, Val Ferguson and Alannah MacTiernan in the Legislative Council) few electors knew directly of May Holman's life or legacy.[5]

Within the Holman family, May's sister Cis – Iris Demasson – gave birth on 6 May 1939 to the baby girl she was carrying at the time of the accident, naming her in honour of her beloved eldest sister, May Holman Demasson. And on 15 July 1939, May's youngest sister Sheila married Tom Moiler, her football star suitor, in St Joseph's church, Bassendean – the fifth Holman family wedding to take place there. But the wedding was a quiet one because the family was still in turmoil. The abruptness of May's death caused a deep and lasting grief, traces of which were still apparent when Judyth Watson interviewed an eighty-one year old Sheila Moiler for this biography project in 1997. Sheila and her sister Eileen Thomson were the only siblings still living at the time. Sheila died in 2003.

Within the wider community, in the decades following May Holman's death, the art of challenging patriarchal follies (war, violence, sexism, elitism) to claim full human status for women and others who are marginalised – and that had been practised in such exemplary fashion by those determined women activists of the first wave of feminism and by May Holman and friends in the Labor movement in the 1920s and 1930s – was refined even further in Western Australia by far-sighted, hard-working, creative activist women like Bessie Rischbieth, Katharine Susannah Prichard, Irene

Greenwood, Joan Williams, Elsie Gare, and Bernice Ranford. Arguably, the impulse to change, sparked in the 1920s and 1930s, lay latent in the conservative postwar 1950s and 1960s, to reignite through the interventions of some of those same women – Irene Greenwood, Joan Williams, Elsie Gare – in the early 1970s through the pacifism of the anti-Vietnam moratorium movement and the formation of Western Australian branches of the Women's Liberation Movement, and the Women's Electoral Lobby.[6]

‡

What can we learn from May Holman's life and its aftermath? Here was a woman in full flight, living, loving, working, playing to the limit of her capacities. In her story we find courage and frailty, joy and misery, passion and pain. Certainly she charted new territory for women, and demonstrated how possible it is for a woman to be an excellent parliamentarian, a fine friend, a compassionate soul. But her story also holds its warnings for women, that masculine privilege is invisible to those who continue to enjoy it, and remains an almost impenetrable impediment to those who would seek to challenge it.

Let her story, then, laden with warnings and in all its fullness, be woven into the tasks we have yet to do and the lives we have yet to live.

Labor Women's Silver Anniversary Souvenir

Message from Miss MAY HOLMAN, M.L.A., J.P.

President of the Labor Women's Interstate Executive and Secretary of the Labor Women's Central Executive

I am delighted to add my congratulations to those of other Laborites on the occasion of the Silver Jubilee Anniversary of the First Labor Women's Conference.

In 1912 I had the honor of being the "Official Recorder" at the First Conference, and in 1927 assisted in organising the Labor Women's Central Executive of W.A. and was elected first President.

To-day I have the honor to be Secretary of the Central Executive and to-day my faith in the ideals of the Labor Movement is as steadfast as ever.

Labor women have done much to help their brother comrades in the movement during the past 25 years (and for many years before) and I believe that work will be continued and at last our ideals will be achieved. The Message of Labor is a message of hope, of faith and brotherly love, and I believe this ideal will be realised if we "Stand all as one till right is done: Believe and Dare and Do."

May Holman

Miss May Holman, M.L.A., J.P.

Message from May Holman, MLA, JP, Souvenir 1937.

ENDNOTES

NOTES

Quotations of primary sources throughout have been reproduced verbatim. Inconsistent spelling and variations reflect original source material.

The spelling of 'Labour' in 'Australian Labour Party' changed to 'Labor' in 1912. However, the two spellings remained interchangeable for some decades.

All newspaper articles have been retrieved from <http://trove.nla.gov.au> unless otherwise specified.

All references to Hansard refer to the Hansard of the Western Australian Legislative Assembly.

PROLOGUE

[1] LABOR LEADER'S MAGNIFICENT TRIBUTE TO A GREAT LABOR WOMAN. (1939, March 31). *Westralian Worker* (Perth, WA: 1900–1951), p. 1.

CHAPTER 1 Here she is

[1] STATE POLITICS. (1925, March 10). *The West Australian* (Perth, WA: 1879–1954), p. 7.
[2] May Holman was the second Australian woman parliamentarian. Edith Cowan was the first. Cowan was elected to the WA Legislative Assembly on 12 March 1921, aged fifty-nine, and lost her seat in the following election on 22 March 1924. May Holman was elected to the seat of Forrest in that same parliament in a by-election held on 3 April 1925, following the unexpected death of her father, John Barkell Holman, whose parliamentary career began in 1901 and who had held the seat of Forrest since himself winning it in a by-election on 8 December 1923 occasioned by the death of Peter O'Loghlen. May Holman's reign as the only woman in an Australian parliament ended on 30 May 1925 when Millicent Preston-Stanley was elected to the NSW Legislative Assembly. Like Edith Cowan, Millicent Preston-Stanley was defeated after her first term in office. May Holman remained in parliament through five successive elections in 1927, 1930, 1933, 1936 and 1939. At the time of her death by accident in 1939, after fourteen years in parliament, she was the longest serving woman politician in the British Empire.

ENDNOTES

3. CITY NOTES. (1925, August 7). *The Midlands Advertiser* (Moora, WA: 1907–1930), p. 1.
4. LOOKING DOWN. (1925, July 31). *The Daily News* (Perth, WA: 1882–1950), p. 7.
5. CITY NOTES. (1925, August 7). *The Midlands Advertiser* (Moora, WA: 1907–1930), p. 1.
6. ADELAIDE VISITOR WHO BECAME MP WHEN 30. (1930, 23 June). *The Register News Pictorial* (Adelaide, SA: 1929–1931) p. 27.
7. As above.
8. IN THE ASSEMBLY. MISS HOLMAN'S MAIDEN SPEECH. TIMBER EMPLOYEES. THEIR CAUSE ESPOUSED. (1925, July 31). *The Daily News* (Perth, WA: 1882–1950), p. 5.
9. LOOKING DOWN. (1925, July 31). *The Daily News* (Perth, WA: 1882–1950), p. 7.
10. WOMAN'S WAYS. WOMAN LABOR MEMBER. (1925, August 13). *Worker* (Brisbane, Qld: 1890–1955), p. 19.
11. Jean Beadle was a Labor Party activist. She was a founder of Labor Women's Organisations in Fremantle and the Eastern Goldfields; one of the first women justices of the peace in WA, a voluntary Children's Court magistrate and a keen writer and orator. See Bobbie Oliver (2007). *Jean Beadle: A life of Labor activism*. Perth: UWA Press.
12. Ettie Hooton was a Labor women's activist and good friend to May Holman. She was foundation member of the Women's Service Guild, the National Council of Women of WA, the Perth branch of the Australian Labor Federation and the WA Parents and Citizens' Association. She edited the monthly *Parents and Citizens' Broadcaster* from 1926 for fifteen years; she was women's editor on the *Westralian Worker* for two decades from 1927. During the Depression she was secretary to Bessie Rischbieth. See Michael Bosworth (1996). 'Hooton, Harriet (Ettie) (1875–1960)'. *Australian Dictionary of Biography*, vol. 14, Melbourne: MUP.
13. Oliver, Bobbie. '"In the Thick of Every Battle for the Cause of Labor": The Voluntary Work of the Labor Women's Organisations in Western Australia, 1900–70', *Labour History*, vol. 81, November 2001, pp. 93–108.
14. Spearritt, Katie (1992). 'New Dawns: First Wave Feminism 1890–1914', in Saunders and Evans (eds). *Gender Relations in Australia*. St Lucia: UQP.
15. The Women's Christian Temperance Union lobbied strongly throughout the 1890s to give women the vote, and held that it was largely due to the efforts of its leader Christina Clark that franchise was achieved for WA women.
16. The Karrakatta Club, founded in 1894, was the first women's club in Australia. Its members were well educated and well connected socially and politically to men of influence in the administration and government of the colony. It aimed to *bring into one body the women of the community for mutual improvement and social engagement*. <www.karrakattaclub.org.au>
17. The Women's Franchise League was established expressly to fight for women's suffrage. It drew women from both the WCTU and the Karrakatta Club. It aimed, additionally, to attract women who were neither temperance supporters, nor privileged Karrakatta Club members.
18. Western Australian women were the second in Australia to get the vote, preceded by South Australian women in 1895.

19 Founding members included Lady Madeleine Onslow, whose husband was the chief justice; Lady Margaret Forrest, whose husband was the first premier of WA, 1890–1901; Edith Cowan, whose husband was a magistrate; Lady Eleanora James, whose husband was a prominent lawyer and premier from 1902–1904. Not all members supported the fight for women's franchise, e.g. Lady Margaret Forrest sided with her husband in opposing it.
20 Karrakatta Club Incorporated: History 1894–1954. <www.karrakattaclub.org.au>
21 The Women's Service Guilds were established in 1909 to form a core feminist connection for the exchange of feminist ideas and strategies. *This group of irrepressible and politically diverse women networked, lobbied and struggled towards gender equality. Perth, the most isolated State capital in the country, was described by a visiting Victorian feminist as 'the Mecca of the Women's Movement in Australia.* Davidson, Dianne (1997). *Women on the Warpath: Feminists of the first wave.* Nedlands, WA: UWA Press.
22 Bessie Rischbieth was born in Adelaide and lived in Perth from 1899 until her death in 1967. She was a theosophist and a prominent Australian feminist. She was actively involved in the Women's Service Guilds, the Australian Federation of Women Voters, the Children's Protection Society and in conservation groups, and was well connected to international feminist groups. See her entry in the *Australian Dictionary of Biography* <http://adb.anu.edu.au/biography/rischbieth-bessie-mabel-8214>
23 Dr Roberta Jull was the first woman in WA to establish a medical practice and was a founding member of the WA branch of the British Medical Association. She was active in campaigns to improve women's reproductive health and was an authority on venereal diseases and prostitution. See her entry in the *Australian Dictionary of Biography* <http://adb.anu.edu.au/biography/jull-roberta-henrietta-margaritta-6892>
24 Throughout her parliamentary life May Holman demonstrated her allegiance to the Labor cause. At her death P. J. Trainer, general secretary to the WA Executive of the ALP, spoke of her as *a Laborite whose loyalty to the movement was never in doubt.* TRAGIC DEATH OF MISS HOLMAN, M.L.A. (1939, March 24). *Westralian Worker* (Perth, WA: 1900–1951), p. 1.
25 LABOR LEADER'S MAGNIFICENT TRIBUTE TO A GREAT LABOR WOMAN. (1939, March 31). *Westralian Worker* (Perth, WA: 1900–1951), p. 1.
26 Brown, Margaret (1981). 'Edith Dirksey Cowan (1861–1932)'. *Australian Dictionary of Biography,* vol. 8, Melbourne: MUP.
27 Sawer, Marian (1992). 'Housekeeping the State: Women and parliamentary politics in Australia', *Trust the Women: Women in the Federal Parliament,* Papers on Parliament 17, September. Canberra: Department of the Senate.
28 BY WIRE AND WIRELESS. (1925, July 3). *Westralian Worker* (Perth, WA: 1900–1951), p. 12.
29 MEN AND OTHER THINGS. (1925, June 24). *The Australian Worker* (Sydney, NSW: 1913–1950), p. 1.
30 THREE WOMEN. (1925, September 16). *The Australian Worker* (Sydney, NSW: 1913–1950), p. 5.
31 WOMEN'S SPHERE. (1925, April 10). *Westralian Worker* (Perth, WA: 1900–1951), p. 12.

ENDNOTES

32 PEEPS AT PEOPLE. (1925, April 5). *Sunday Times* (Perth, WA: 1902–1954), p. 10.
33 TIMBER TOILERS' TOPICS. (1925, May 1). *Westralian Worker* (Perth, WA: 1900–1951), p. 10.
34 COTTELSOE'S NEW OVAL. (1925, May 3). *Sunday Times* (Perth, WA: 1902–1954), p. 1.
35 A THOUSAND ON THE ESPLANADE. (1925, May 15). *Westralian Worker* (Perth, WA: 1900–1951), p. 5.
36 LADY LEGISLATOR. (1925, April 11). *Toodyay Herald* (WA: 1912–1954), p. 1; FORREST ELECTORATE. (1925, April 2). *The Daily News* (Perth, WA: 1882–1950), p. 10.
37 Throughout her parliamentary life, May Holman was seen as her father's legitimate successor. A eulogy following her death in 1939 observed: It was *only natural* that the timber workers should see in his daughter a fitting successor to his seat and she had little difficulty in gaining it in 1925. MISS HOLMAN'S DEATH. (1939, March 21). *The West Australian* (Perth, WA: 1879–1954), p. 15.
38 PEOPLE IN THE NEWS. (1925, April 17). *Westralian Worker* (Perth, WA: 1900–1951), p. 11.
39 Throssel, Ric (2012). *Wild Weeds and Windflowers: The life and letters of Katharine Susannah Prichard.* Sydney: Allen & Unwin.
40 Nile, Richard (1990). 'The Making of a Really Modern Witch: Katharine Susannah Prichard 1919-1969'. *Working Papers in Australian Studies,* University of London, Working Paper no. 56. London: Sir Robert Menzies Centre for Australian Studies, University of London.
41 Elsie Gare (1987). Interview with Lekkie Hopkins for *An Oral History of Women and the Peace Movement Project.* Tape 11. Battye Library, Perth, Western Australia.
42 Hopkins, Lekkie (1999-2001). 'Katharine Susannah Prichard: A biography', in Anne Commire and Deborah Klezmer, *Women in World History: A biographical encyclopaedia.* Waterford: Yorkin Publications.
43 Perth's population in the mid-1920s was approximately 200,000.
44 Dixon, R. (2009). 'Australian Fiction and the World Republic of Letters, 1890–1950', Peter Pierce et al. (eds), *The Cambridge History of Australian Literature,* (pp. 223–254). Australia: CUP.
45 Modjeska, Drusilla. *Exiles at Home. Australian Women Writers 1925-1945.* Sydney: Angus and Robertson, 1981, p. 6.
46 As above, p. 8.
47 Palmer, Nettie. *Nettie Palmer: Her private journal,* Fourteen Years, *poems, reviews and literary essays.* Vivian Smith (ed.). St Lucia: UQP, 1988, p. 24.
48 WOMAN MEMBER FOR FORREST. (1930, June 13). *The Herald,* found in a photocopied newspaper cutting in Judyth Watson's archive, sent to her by one of MH's relatives. Handwritten *The Herald* with date 13 June 1930. Not available from Trove.
49 Hansard, vol. 74, 19 October 1926, p. 1485.
50 As above, p. 1486.
51 Prichard, Katharine Susannah. *Child of the Hurricane: An autobiography.* Sydney: Angus and Robertson, 1963.

52. In 1896 J. B. Holman led a strike against a proposed reduction of 5/- per week for miners in the Murchison. The strikers won and Holman was jubilant.
53. ALLEGED LIBEL. (1923, October 16). *The Daily News* (Perth, WA: 1882–1950), p. 8.
54. ALLEGED LIBEL. (1923, October 17). *The Register* (Adelaide, SA: 1901–1929), p. 12.
55. UNION OFFICIAL SUES NEWSPAPER. (1923, October 18). *The Argus* (Melbourne, Vic), p. 4.
56. LIBEL ACTION. ELECTION SEQUEL. UNION SECRETARY SUES NEWSPAPER. *The Brisbane Courier* (Qld: 1864–1933), p. 7.
57. HOLMAN LIBEL CLAIM. THIRD DAY'S HEARING. (1923, October 19). *The West Australian* (Perth, WA, 1879–1954), p. 8.
58. The minutes of the Perth Labor Women's Organisation recorded *that regret was expressed at the sad death of the late Hugo Throssell, VC, and it was moved that a letter of sympathy be sent to Mrs Throssell*, in WOMEN'S SPHERE. (1933, December 8). *Westralian Worker* (Perth, WA: 1900–1951), p. 6. The item PERTH LABOR WOMEN'S ORGANISATION in WOMEN'S SPHERE (1934, August 3) records that *Mrs Hugo Throssell is coming to speak at the next meeting of the Perth Labor Women's Organisation. Westralian Worker* (Perth, WA: 1900–1951), p. 7.
59. FEDERATED MOTHERS' CLUBS. (1934, November 21). *The Argus* (Melbourne, Vic.: 1848–1957), p. 15. WOMEN'S SPHERE. (1933, December 8). *Westralian Worker* (Perth, WA: 1900–1951), p. 6.
60. Hansard WA Legislative Assembly, vol. 88, 21 August 1932, p. 321.
61. *The West Australian* (1938, May 3) (Perth, WA: 1879–1954), p. 12. The Modern Women's Club was billed as a non-political, non-sectarian club *where women and girls working in the city could rest, have a social life and take part in discussions.*
62. Ettie Hooton, 'Miss May Holman, MLA' in *Souvenir 1935*. Perth: Westralian Worker.

CHAPTER 2 'I can only say that her life was magnificent ...'

1. MISS MAY HOLMAN'S LIFE IN DANGER. SHOCKING INJURY IN CAR ACCIDENT. (1939, March 20). *Recorder* (Port Pirie, SA: 1919–1954), p. 1.
2. MISS HOLMAN INJURED. CAR LEAVES ROAD. (1939, March 18). *The West Australian* (Perth, WA: 1879–1954), p. 21.
3. e.g. *The West Australian* (1939, March 18, p.21); *The Daily News* (1939, March 18, p. 37); *The Sunday Times* (1939, March 19, p.12); *The Canberra Times* (1939, March 21, p.2); *Recorder*, Port Pirie (1939, March 20, p.1); *The Worker*, Brisbane, (1939, March 21, p. 6); *The Argus*, Melbourne (1939, March 21, p. 1).
4. MISS HOLMAN STILL ON DANGER LIST. (1939, March 18). *The Daily News* (Perth, WA: 1882–1950), p. 37.
5. MISS HOLMAN'S NAME STILL ON DANGER LIST. (1939, March 19). *Sunday Times* (Perth, WA: 1902–1954), p. 12
6. MAY HOLMAN WEAKER. (1939, March 20). *The Daily News* (Perth, WA: 1882–1950), p. 1.
7. MISS HOLMAN, M.L.A. CONDITION CONTINUES GRAVE. (1939, March 21). *The Canberra Times* (ACT: 1926–1995), p. 2.

ENDNOTES

8. MISS HOLMAN KNEW OF WIN. (1939, March 21). *The Daily News* (Perth, WA: 1882–1950), p. 1.
9. "LABOUR WAS PROUD OF HER". MR. CURTIN'S WARM TRIBUTE. (1939, March 21). *The West Australian* (Perth, WA: 1879–1954), p. 15.
10. DEATH OF MISS MAY HOLMAN, M.L.A. (1939, March 21). *The Worker* (Brisbane, Qld: 1890–1955), p. 6.
11. PREMIER'S TRIBUTE. (1939, March 21). *The Daily News* (Perth, WA: 1882–1950), p. 1.
12. MAY HOLMAN'S DEATH. (1939, March 22). *The West Australian* (Perth, WA: 1879–1954), p. 19.
13. As above.
14. MAY HOLMAN. (1939, March 24). *Westralian Worker* (Perth, WA: 1900–1951), p. 8.
15. MISS HOLMAN'S DEATH. CAR SMASH PROVES FATAL. (1939, March 21). *The West Australian* (Perth, WA: 1879–1954), p. 15.
16. LATE MISS HOLMAN. (1939, March 23). *Albany Advertiser* (WA: 1897–1950), p. 1; FUNERAL NOTICES. LARGE CROWD AT FUNERAL. (1939, March 23). *Geraldton Guardian and Express* (WA: 1929–1947), p. 5.
17. WOMEN'S SPHERE. MAY HOLMAN. AN ABIDING MEMORY. (1939, March 31). *Westralian Worker* (Perth, WA: 1900–1951), p. 10.
18. FAMILY NOTICES. (1939, March 21), p. 1. Undertakers Bowra and O'Dea advised that *Friends wishing to attend the Funeral may proceed by the 3.45 o'clock train leaving Perth*. FUNERAL NOTICES. *The Daily News* (Perth, WA: 1882–1950), p. 21.
19. WOMEN'S SPHERE. MAY HOLMAN. AN ABIDING MEMORY. (1939, March 31). *Westralian Worker* (Perth, WA: 1900–1951), p. 10.
20. As above.
21. THE LATE MISS HOLMAN. LARGE ATTENDANCE AT FUNERAL. (1939, March 23). *The West Australian* (Perth, WA: 1879–1954), p. 20.
22. Letter from Kathleen Haines (nee Corboy) to Judyth Watson dated 10 October 2000. Judyth Watson private collection.
23. 'Miss May Holman, MLA, JP', Sacred Heart High School newsletter, March 1939, in May Holman Family Papers (1893–1951), Battye Library: Private Archives Collection.
24. A COURAGEOUS FIGHTER. A STAUNCH FRIEND. (1939, March 25). *Mirror* (Perth, WA: 1921–1956), p. 15.
25. LAST RESPECTS. (1939, March 30). *Western Mail* (Perth, WA: 1885–1954), p. 3.
26. TWO PERTH ITEMS IN NEWSREEL. (1939, April 6). *The West Australian* (Perth, WA: 1879–1954), p. 18.
27. FUNERAL NOTICES. (1939, March 21). *The Daily News* (Perth, WA: 1882–1950), p. 21.
28. STATE'S LAST TRIBUTE TO MISS HOLMAN. (1939, March 22). *The Daily News* (Perth, WA: 1882–1950), p. 13.
29. THE LATE MISS HOLMAN. (1939, March 23). *The West Australian* (Perth, WA: 1879–1954), p. 2.
30. WOMEN'S SPHERE. MAY HOLMAN. AN ABIDING MEMORY. (1939, March 31). *Westralian Worker* (Perth, WA: 1900–1951), p. 10.

31 THE LATE MISS HOLMAN. (1939, March 26). *Sunday Times* (Perth, WA: 1902–1954), p. 13.
32 WOMEN'S SPHERE. MAY HOLMAN. AN ABIDING MEMORY. (1939, March 31). *Westralian Worker* (Perth, WA: 1900–1951), p. 10.
33 Arthritis is thought to have been caused by *an accident in 1905 that caused her much suffering: only her intimates know how much. To the world she presents a charming manner and winning smile, but close observers notice signs that betray pain. However, she always answers, "'Tis nothing. It will soon pass.: And it does – for she makes it.* In AUSTRALIAN'S PREMIER WOMAN LEGISLATOR. THE STORY OF MISS MAY HOLMAN'S CLIMB TO FAME. Success story no. VII, by Emswin, in *The Australian Woman's Mirror*. (1936, March 3).
34 Elsie Gare (1987). Interview with Lekkie Hopkins for *An Oral History of Women and the Peace Movement Project*. Tape 11. Battye Library, Perth, Western Australia.
35 Irene Greenwood (1899–1992) – journalist, peace activist, campaigner on women's issues – was one of the key figures in the women's movement in Western Australia during the twentieth century
36 Joan Williams (1914–2008) – journalist, poet, peace activist, Communist – played an activist role in the women's movement and in social justice politics from the 1930s until her death in 2007. She was one of a few crucial figures who played a central role in establishing the fledgling Women's Liberation Movement and the Women's Electoral Lobby in Perth in the 1970s.
37 Elsie Gare – Quaker, peace activist, women's advocate, social justice campaigner – was active in grassroots politics throughout the twentieth century. She worked alongside her husband Cyril Gare to establish the Vietnam Moritorium movement in Perth in 1970.
38 LATE MISS HOLMAN. (1939, March 22). *The Argus* (Melbourne, Vic.: 1848–1957), p. 2.
39 S.A. LABOR REGRET AT MISS HOLMAN'S DEATH. (1939, March 22). *The Advertiser* (Adelaide, 1931–1954), p. 14.
40 DEATH OF MISS MAY HOLMAN, M.L.A. (1939, March 21). *Border Watch* (Mount Gambier: 1861–1954), p. 7.
41 LATE MISS HOLMAN. MOTION OF SYMPATHY. (1939, March 23). *Advocate* (Burnie, Tas.: 1890–1954), p. 2.
42 FIRST WOMAN MEMBER. MISS MAY HOLMAN'S DEATH. (1939, March 21). *Examiner* (Launceston, Tas.: 1900–1954), p. 6.
43 MISS MAY HOLMAN, M.L.A. DEAD. (1939, March 21). *Barrier Miner* (Broken Hill, NSW: 1888–1954), p. 1.
44 WOMAN M.L.A. DEAD. MISS MAY HOLMAN. (1939, March 21). *The Sydney Morning Herald* (NSW: 1842–1954), p. 11.
45 MISS MAY HOLMAN. SUCCUMBS TO INJURIES. (1939, March 21). *Geraldton Guardian and Express* (WA: 1929–1947), p. 1.
46 STOP PRESS NEWS. MISS MAY HOLMAN DEAD. (1939, March 21). *The Mercury* (Hobart, Tas.: 1860–1954), p. 8.
47 DIED ON DAY OF RE-ELECTION. W.A. WOMAN M.L.A. (1939, March 21). *The Courier-Mail* (Brisbane, Qld: 1933–1954), p. 3.
48 MISS HOLMAN DEAD. VICTIM OF ACCIDENT. (1939, March 21). *The Townsville Daily Bulletin* (Qld: 1885–1954), p. 7.

ENDNOTES

49. MISS HOLMAN, M.L.A. DIES FROM HER INJURIES. (1939, March 21). *Kalgoorlie Miner* (WA: 1895-1950), p. 4.
50. MISS MAY HOLMAN DEAD. FIRST WOMAN LABOUR M.L.A. IN AUSTRALIA. (1939, March 21). *Northern Star* (Lismore, NSW: 1876-1954), p. 7.
51. 'Miss May Holman, MLA, JP', Sacred Heart High School newsletter, March 1939, in May Holman Family Papers (1893-1951), Battye Library: Private Archives Collection.
52. MAY HOLMAN'S TRIUMPH AT HOUR OF DEATH. (1939, April 1). *The Australian Women's Weekly* (1933-1982), p. 22.
53. As above.
54. LATE MISS MAY HOLMAN. TRIBUTE FROM GENEVA. (1939, May 29). *Recorder* (Port Pirie, SA: 1919-1954), p. 3.
55. STATE PARLIAMENT. (1939, August 4). *The West Australian* (Perth, WA: 1879-1954), p. 18.
56. MISS HOLMAN'S DEATH. EXPRESSIONS OF REGRET IN ASSEMBLY. (1939, August 9). *The West Australian* (Perth, WA: 1879-1954), p. 14.
57. HEPZIBAH. FOOTBALLER'S WEDDING. (1939, July 1). *The Daily News* (Perth, WA: 1882-1950), p. 23.
58. OLD GIRLS MEET. (1939, April 21). *The West Australian* (Perth, WA: 1879-1954), p. 10.
59. LABOUR WOMEN. (1939, September 28). *The West Australian* (Perth, WA: 1879-1954), p. 5.
60. BRIDGE AND RUMMY PARTY. (1939, November 1). *The West Australian* (Perth, WA: 1879-1954), p. 5.
61. WHAT WOMEN ARE DOING. (1939, December 2). *The West Australian* (Perth, WA: 1879-1954), p. 11.

CHAPTER 3 Honour thy father ...

1. Sheila Moiler, in conversation with Judyth Watson, 19 May 1997.
2. Letters held in May Holman Family Papers (1893-1951), Battye Library: Private Archives Collection.
3. SOCIAL NOTES. (1914, January 9). *The West Australian* (Perth, WA: 1879-1954), p. 8.
4. Marriage Certificate 351/1914, Perth Registry Office.
5. Divorce 102/1919 Matrimonial Causes Supreme Court WA. Gardiner v. Gardiner.
6. A SECRET MARRIAGE. (1919, December 4). *The West Australian* (Perth, WA: 1879-1954), p. 9.
7. Letters held in May Holman Family Papers (1893-1951), Battye Library: Private Archives Collection.
8. Letter from Joe Gardiner to May Holman, 15 May 1914.
9. Letter from Joe Gardiner to May Holman, 24 June 1914.
10. Letter from Joe Gardiner to May Holman, 24 June 1914.
11. Letter from Joe Gardiner to May Holman, 12 July 1914.
12. Letter from Joe Gardiner to May Holman, 12 July 1914.
13. Letter from Joe Gardiner to May Holman, 18 July 1914.

[14] Letter from Joe Gardiner to John Barkell Holman, 19 August 1919.
[15] Magarey, Susan, *Passions of the First Wave Feminists*. Sydney: UNSW Press, 2001, back cover blurb.
[16] Eileen Thompson in conversation with Judyth Watson, 27 November 1997.
[17] Evelyn Cloverley in conversation with Judyth Watson, 10 September 1997.
[18] PEOPLE IN THE NEWS. (1925, April 17). *Westralian Worker* (Perth, WA: 1900–1951), p. 11.
[19] Sheila Moiler in conversation with Judyth Watson, 19 May, 1997.
[20] Sandra Bloodworth (1998) *Militant Spirits. The Rebel Women of Broken Hill*, ch. 1, pp 21–38 in Sandra Bloodworth and Tom O'Lincoln (eds), *Rebel Women in Australian Working Class History*. Richmond East: Interventions.
[21] LABOR MOVEMENT'S GRIEVOUS LOSS: DEATH OF MR. JOHN B. HOLMAN. (1925, February 27). *Westralian Worker* (Perth, WA: 1900–1951), p. 4.
[22] Sheila Moiler, in conversation with Judyth Watson on 19 May 1997, reported that family legend has it that the young Jack Holman was *driven out of town*. Strike leaders were sentenced to imprisonment by the court at Deniliquin following a *Guilty* decision by the jury on 29 October 1892; Jack Holman left Broken Hill for Nannine nine months later. VALEDICTORY. (1893, July 29). *Barrier Miner* (Broken Hill, NSW: 1888–1954), p. 2.
[23] ALLEGED LIBEL. (923, October 16). *The Daily News* (Perth, WA: 1882–1950), p. 8.
[24] Frances Shea in conversation with Judyth Watson, 16 November 1997.
[25] STATE POLITICS. WESTERN AUSTRALIA. February 27 (1917, March 10). *The Capricornian* (Rockhampton, Qld: 1875–1929), p. 23.
[26] Sheila Moiler in conversation with Judyth Watson, 19 May 1997.
[27] DEATH OF MR. J. B. HOLMAN, M.L.A. (1925, February 23). *The Daily News* (Perth, WA: 1882–1950), p. 8 Edition: THIRD EDITION.
[28] DEATH OF MR. J. B. HOLMAN. STUBBORN POLITICAL FIGHTER. (1925, February 24). *The West Australian* (Perth, WA: 1879–1954), p. 8.
[29] THE LATE MR. J. B. HOLMAN. LARGELY ATTENDED FUNERAL. (1925, February 27). *The West Australian* (Perth, WA: 1879–1954), p. 10.

CHAPTER 4 ... And thy mother

[1] May Holman Family Papers (1893–1951), Battye Library: Private Archives Collection.
[2] Windsors: Victoria Mary of Teck <http://www.britroyals.com>
[3] Solomon, R.J. (1988). *The Richest Lode: Broken Hill 1883–1988*. Sydney: Hale & Iremonger.
[4] VALEDICTORY. (1893, July 29). *Barrier Miner* (Broken Hill, NSW: 1888–1954), p. 2.
[5] May Holman Family Papers (1893–1951), Battye Library: Private Archives Collection.
[6] Mary Alice (May) born 18 July 1893; a boy, stillborn, 1895; Kathleen Maude (Maude) born 6 August 1897; John Barkell Jnr (Jack) born 17 June 1900; Winifred Lillian (Winnie) born 18 May 1902; Edward Frederick Joseph (Ted) born 9 August 1904 ; William Thomas (Bill) born 16 August 1908. Iris Monica (Cis) born 6 April 1911; Eileen Veronica born 22 August 1914; Sheila Josephine born 22 July 1916; Richard born 8 March 1918.

ENDNOTES

7. Two baby boys died: Katherine's second child was stillborn in 1895; her eleventh child, Richard, was born on 8 March 1918 and died in November, aged ten months.
8. CRICKET. (1891, September 14). *Barrier Miner* (Broken Hill, NSW: 1888–1954), p. 2.
9. SPORTING. (1893, March 27). *Barrier Miner* (Broken Hill, NSW: 1888–1954), p. 2.
10. VICTORIA V. SOUTH AUSTRALIA. (1893, July 1). *Barrier Miner* (Broken Hill, NSW: 1888–1954), p. 4.
11. SATURDAY'S FOOTBALL MATCH. (1893, July 3). *Barrier Miner* (Broken Hill, NSW: 1888–1954), p. 3.
12. FOOTBALL ASSOCIATION. THE VICTORIAN SCANDAL. (1893, July 12). *Barrier Miner* (Broken Hill, NSW: 1888–1954), p. 2.
13. VICTORIAN FOOTBALL CLUB. THE RECENT SCANDAL. (1893, July 21). *Barrier Miner* (Broken Hill, NSW: 1888–1954), p. 2.
14. VALEDICTORY. (1893, July 29). *Barrier Miner* (Broken Hill, NSW: 1888–1954), p. 2.
15. Sheila Moiler in conversation with Judyth Watson, 19 May 1997.
16. As above.
17. CUE. (1902, September 19). *The West Australian* (Perth, WA: 1879–1954), p. 5.
18. PERTH HOSPITAL. THE NEW BOARD. (1913, January 13). *The Daily News* (Perth, WA: 1882–1950), p. 6.
19. May Holman Family Papers (1893–1951), Battye Library: Private Archives Collection.
20. Letter 5, 1 October 1930, in Judyth Watson (ed.) (1995). *Remarks of an Inexperienced Traveller Abroad. May Holman*, (Perth, WA: J. Watson, 1995), pp. 62–67.
21. NEWS AND NOTES. A POLITICIAN'S WILL. (1926. January 16). *The West Australian* (Perth, WA: 1879–1954), p. 10.
22. LABOUR MEMBER'S WILL. WIDOW UNPROVIDED FOR. (1926, January 18) *Brisbane Courier* (Qld: 1864–1933), p. 9.
23. PAYMENTS UNDER A WILL. (1926, January 16). *The Advertiser* (Adelaide, SA: 1889–1931), p. 17.
24. LATE MR J. B. HOLMAN'S WILL. (1926, January 16). *The Register* (Adelaide, SA: 1901–1929), p. 13.
25. NOTHING FOR WIDOW. (1926, January 18). *Queensland Times* (Ipswich, Qld: 1909–1954), p. 7.
26. MR J. B. HOLMAN'S WILL (1926, January 18). *The Argus* (Melbourne, Vic.: 1848–1957), p. 15.
27. LATE MR J. B. HOLMAN'S WILL. (1926, January 19). *Western Argus* (Kalgoorlie, WA: 1916–1938), p. 20.
28. NEWS AND NOTES. (1926, January 16). *The West Australian* (Perth, WA: 1879–1954), p. 10.
29. Roy Thompson in conversation with Eileen Thompson and Judyth Watson, 27 November 1997.

CHAPTER 5 The Entertainers

1. Daphne Popham (ed.)(1978). 'May Holman', *Reflections: Profiles of 150 women who helped make Western Australia's history*. Perth: Carroll's.
2. WOMAN POLITICIAN'S HOBBY. MISS MAY HOLMAN'S CHOICE. (1928, July 24). *The Advertiser* (Adelaide, SA: 1889–1931), p. 15.
3. THE LADIES SECTION. WHO'S WHERE. (1920, September 26). *The Sunday Mirror* (Perth, WA: 1920–1921), p. 3.
4. WOMEN'S SPHERE. MAY HOLMAN. AN ABIDING MEMORY. (1939, March 31). *Westralian Worker* (Perth, WA: 1900–1951), p. 10.
5. As above.
6. GREAT DISORDER IN PARLIAMENT. (1911, January 13). *The West Australian* (Perth, WA: 1879–1954), p. 7; POLITICIANS AND THE PRESS. AN INCIDENT IN THE HOUSE. (1911, January 15). *Sunday Times* (Perth, WA: 1902–1954), p. 7.
7. TIMBER WORKERS' UNION. (1911, April 15), Letter from 'A mere paying machine', Nannup, April 5. *The West Australian* (Perth, WA: 1879–1954), p. 10; THE TIMBER INDUSTRY. THE EMPLOYEE'S UNION. (1911, February 23). *The West Australian* (Perth, WA: 1879–1954), p. 2.
8. THE TIMBER INDUSTRY. (1911, February 23). As above.
9. As above.
10. As above.
11. Letter from 'A mere paying machine', Nannup, April 5. *The West Australian* (Perth, WA: 1879–1954), p. 10.
12. THE TIMBER INDUSTRY. WORKERS' ANNUAL CONFERENCE. (1911, November 18). *Western Mail* (Perth, WA: 1885–1954), p. 20.
13. SOCIAL NOTES. (1914, June 23). *The West Australian* (Perth, WA: 1879–1954), p. 5.
14. SOCIAL NOTES. (1914, January 9). *The West Australian* (Perth, WA: 1879–1954), p. 8; SOCIAL NOTES. (1914, January 16). *Western Mail* (Perth, WA: 1885–1954), p. 15.
15. WOMEN'S SPHERE. MAY HOLMAN. AN ABIDING MEMORY. (1939, March 31). *Westralian Worker* (Perth, WA: 1900–1951), p. 10.
16. AMATEUR ENTERTAINERS. (1916, July 15). *The Daily News* (Perth, WA: 1882–1950), p. 6; PERTH PRATTLE CONTINUED. (1916, July 16). *Sunday Times* (Perth, WA: 1902–1954), p. 7.
17. PERTH PRATTLE CONTINUED. (1916, August 6). *Sunday Times* (Perth, WA: 1902–1954), p. 7.
18. May Holman 1917 Diary. Personal possession of Sheila Moiler.
19. PERTH PRATTLE. (1916, September 10). *Sunday Times* (Perth, WA: 1902–1954), p. 6.
20. ENTERTAINMENTS. "THE ENTERTAINERS" AT QUEEN'S PARK. (1917, April 3). *The West Australian* (Perth, WA: 1879–1954), p. 8.
21. MISCELLANEOUS. (1916, August 21). *The West Australian* (Perth, WA: 1879–1954), pp. 5–6.
22. SOCIAL NOTES. (1916, March 14). *The West Australian* (Perth, WA: 1879–1954), p. 8.
23. FAMILY NOTICES. KILLED IN ACTION. (1917, December 6). *The West Australian* (Perth, WA: 1879–1954), p. 1.
24. WOMEN'S SPHERE. MAY HOLMAN. AN ABIDING MEMORY. (1939, March 31). *Westralian Worker* (Perth, WA: 1900–1951), p. 10.
25. As above.

ENDNOTES

CHAPTER 6 The Honourable the Member for Forrest

1. Hansard, vol. 72. 16 September 1925, p. 923.
2. As above.
3. TIMBER WORKERS AND ARBITRATION. MISS HOLMAN'S REVIEW. (1925, September 3). *The Daily News* (Perth, WA: 1882–1950), p. 4.
4. Hansard, vol. 74. 19 October 1926, pp. 1469–93.
5. As above, p. 1486 ff.
6. Margaret Brown. Holman, Mary Alice (May) (1893–1939). *Australian Dictionary of Biography*, vol. 9, 1983. Melbourne: MUP.
7. Hansard, vol. 75. 28 October 1926, p. 1776.
8. Hansard, vol. 74. 19 October 1926.
9. Hansard, vol. 72. 6 October 1925, p. 1195.
10. Hansard, vol. 73. 18 November 1925, p. 2014.
11. Hansard, vol. 73, 17 November 1925, p. 1938.
12. As above, p. 1946.
13. Hansard, vol. 77, 27 October 1927, p. 1478.
14. Hansard, vol. 73, 18 November 1925, p. 2013.
15. As above.
16. May Holman autobiographical notes. Typed by Sheila Holman, 1935, in May Holman Family Papers (1893–1951), Battye Library: Private Archives Collection.
17. ARE WOMEN REALLY A SUCCESS IN PARLIAMENT? (1937, December 30). *Advocate* (Burnie, Tas.: 1890–1954), p. 4.
18. NOTES AND COMMENTS. ON MATTERS TOPICAL. (1926, June 29). *The Daily News* (Perth, WA: 1882–1950), p. 4.
19. Hansard, vol. 75. 14 December 1926, pp. 3000–3002.
20. As above, p. 3001.
21. As above.
22. Hansard, vol. 75. 20 October 1926, pp. 1525–1526.
23. As above, p. 1526.
24. Hansard, vol. 75. 20 October 1926, p. 1527.
25. Hansard, vol. 76, 31 August 1927, p. 655.
26. PERTINENT PARAGRAPHS. (1928, January 28). *Mirror* (Perth, WA: 1921–1956), p. 9.
27. MAINLY ABOUT PEOPLE. (1925, July 10). *The Daily News* (Perth, WA: 1882–1950), p. 9.
28. WOMAN'S WORLD. (1928, March 9). *The Daily News* (Perth, WA: 1882–1950), p. 2.
29. Hansard, vol. 76. 27 September 1927, p. 943.
30. Hansard, vol. 75. 20 October 1926, p. 944.
31. Hansard, vol. 82. 25 July 1929, p. 9.
32. As above.
33. WOMEN'S SPHERE. PERTH LABOR WOMEN (1939, January 13). *Westralian Worker* (Perth, WA: 1900–1951), p. 8.

CHAPTER 7 There's a woman in the House!

1. Margaret Brown (1981). Cowan, Edith Dircksey (1861–1932). *Australian Dictionary of Biography*, vol. 8. Melbourne: MUP.
2. John Curtin, 'Miss May Holman has Served Labor Magnificently', in *Souvenir 1935*. Perth: Westralian Worker.
3. ARE WOMEN REALLY A SUCCESS IN PARLIAMENT? (1937, December 1930). *Advocate* (Burnie, Tas.: 1890–1954), p. 4.
4. Hansard, vol. 77. 24 November 1927, p. 2157.
5. Hansard, vol. 88. 31 August 1932, p. 317.
6. Hansard, vol. 77. 27 October 1927, pp. 1480–1481.
7. Hansard, vol. 83. 7 November 1929, p. 1438.
8. Hansard, vol. 100. 11 November 1937, p. 1746.
9. Margaret Brown (1983). 'Holman, Mary Alice (May) (1893–1939)', *Australian Dictionary of Biography*, vol. 9. Melbourne: MUP.
10. WOMAN POLITICIAN'S HOBBY. MISS MAY HOLMAN'S CHOICE. (1928, July 24). *The Advertiser* (Adelaide, SA: 1889–1931), p. 15.
11. THE MAN OF THE WEEK. A WOMAN DOING A MAN'S JOB. (1926, July). Provenance unknown. May Holman Family Papers (1893–1951), Battye Library: Private Archives Collection.
12. See, for example, *Westralian Worker*, vol. 1, no. 1 (1900, September 7) through to edition no. 2219 (1951, June 22).
13. THE INFLUENCE OF WOMEN. (1927, June 8). *Kalgoorlie Miner* (WA: 1895–1950), p. 4.
14. Bosworth, Michael (1996). 'Hooton, Harriet (Ettie) 1875–1960'. *Australian Dictionary of Biography*, vol. 14. Melbourne: MUP.
15. Labor Women's Organisation papers, Battye Library 1688A/340.
16. As above.
17. LABOUR WOMEN. (1930, May 22). *The Canberra Times* (ACT: 1926–1995), p. 5.
18. As above.
19. LABOUR WOMEN. (1930, May 21). *The Telgraph* (Brisbane, Qld: 1872–1947), p. 8.

CHAPTER 8 League of Nations

1. WOMAN'S INTERESTS. GENEVA DELEGATE. (1930, July 25). *The West Australian* (Perth, WA: 1879–1954), p. 6.
2. WOMAN'S INTERESTS. LEAGUE OF NATIONS. (1930, August 1). *The West Australian* (Perth, WA: 1879–1954), p. 4.
3. WOMAN'S INTERESTS. GENEVA DELEGATE. (1930, July 25). *The West Australian* (Perth, WA: 1879–1954), p. 6.
4. LABOR WOMEN OF WESTERN AUSTRALIA. MISS MAY HOLMAN M.L.A. FOR GENEVA. (1930, July 25). *Westralian Worker*, p. 13.
5. As above.
6. SOCIAL EVENTS. (1930, July 26). *The West Australian* (Perth, WA: 1879–1954), p. 12.
7. A complete collection of May Holman's articles and letters written during this trip has been edited and published by Judyth Watson as *Remarks of an Inexperienced Traveller Abroad* (1995).
8. Letter 1, 12 August 1930 in *Remarks*, pp. 44–48.
9. Letter 2, 2 August 1930 in *Remarks*, pp. 49–51.

ENDNOTES

[10] Letter 3, 26 August 1930 in *Remarks*, pp. 52-56.
[11] Letter 4, 14 September 1930 in *Remarks*, pp. 57-61.
[12] Letter 5, 1 October 1930 in *Remarks*, pp. 62-67.
[13] Letter 4, 14 September 1930 in *Remarks*, pp. 57-61.
[14] Letter 5, 1 October 1930 in *Remarks*, pp. 62-67.
[15] Article 2, 'Miss Dora Ohlafson and His Holiness, Pope Pius xi', in *Remarks*, pp. 9-10.
[16] Article 3, 'Remarks of an Inexperienced Traveller Abroad' in *Remarks*, pp. 11-12.
[17] Article 3, in *Remarks*, pp. 11-12.
[18] Article 6, 'The Council of The League of Nations', in *Remarks*, pp. 16-17.
[19] Article 7, 'The League of Nations', in *Remarks*, pp. 18-19.
[20] Article 7, in *Remarks*, pp. 18-19.
[21] Article 12, 'Geneva during the Assembly of the League of Nations' in *Remarks*, pp. 28-29.
[22] Article 9. 'Women at the 1930 League of Nations Assembly' in *Remarks*, pp. 22-23.
[23] As above.
[24] Article 12. 'Geneva during the Assembly of the League of Nations' in *Remarks*, pp. 28-29.
[25] As above.
[26] DRUG TRAFFIC. MISS HOLMAN SPEAKS AT GENEVA. (1930, September 26). *The West Australian* (Perth, WA: 1879-1954), p. 15.
[27] TRAFFIC IN WOMEN. MISS HOLMAN'S FORCIBLE SPEECH. (1930, October 2). *The Brisbane Courier* (Qld: 1864-1933), p. 13.
[28] WHITE SLAVE TRAFFIC. LEAGUE TAKEN TO TASK. AUSTRALIAN DELEGATE'S VIEW. (1930, October 2). *The Mercury* (Hobart, Tas.: 1860-1954), p. 7.
[29] Article 10. 'Women at the 1930 League of Nations Assembly' in *Remarks of an Inexperienced Traveller Abroad*, p. 34.
[30] Article 15. 'More Remarks of an Inexperienced Traveller Abroad' in *Remarks*, p. 34.
[31] Article 18. 'The British Parliament and the Houses of Parliament' in *Remarks*, pp. 40-41.
[32] As above.
[33] Article 14. 'The International Labour Office' in *Remarks*, pp. 32-33.
[34] Letter 5, 1 October 1930, in *Remarks*, pp. 62-67.

CHAPTER 9 Let her story then be woven ...

[1] Hansard, vol. 85. 16 December 1930, pp. 1691-1697.
[2] Hansard, vol. 88. 18 August 1932, p. 123.
[3] Hansard, vol. 88. 31 August 1932. p. 326.
[4] Hansard, vol. 88. 13 October 1932, p. 1193.
[5] Hansard, vol. 89. 20 October 1932, p. 1341.
[6] Hansard, vol. 89. 27 October 1932, p. 1442.
[7] Hansard, vol. 89. 8 November 1932, pp. 1635-1636.
[8] Hansard, vol. 88. 28 September 1932, p. 890.
[9] Hansard, vol. 89. 8 December 1932, p. 2318.
[10] Hansard, vol. 88. 2 November 1932, pp. 1528-1530.
[11] Hansard, vol. 93. 21 August 1934, p. 195.

12. Geneva declaration on the Rights of the Child. Adopted 26 September 1924, League of Nations.
13. Hansard, vol. 97. 6 October 1936, p. 1024.
14. As above, p. 1026.
15. Eileen Thompson in conversation with Judyth Watson, 27 November 1997
16. Sawer, Marian & Marian Simms (1993). *A Woman's Place. Women and politics in Australia*. Sydney: Allen & Unwin, p. 94.
17. Sheila Moiler, in conversation with Judyth Watson, 19 May 1997.
18. WOMEN'S SPHERE. MAY HOLMAN. AN ABIDING MEMORY. (1939, March 31). *Westralian Worker* (Perth, WA: 1900–1951), p. 10.
19. Ettie Hooton, 'Miss May Holman, MLA' in *Souvenir 1935*. Perth: Westralian Worker.
20. May Holman, 'My Stewardship' in *Souvenir 1935*.
21. H. M. Sweeney and G. Foley, 'A Tribute from the WA Timber Workers' Union' in *Souvenir 1935*.
22. Philip Collier, 'A Message from the Premier of Western Australia' in *Souvenir 1935*.
23. James Scullin, 'Miss May Holman's Notable Success as a Legislator' in *Souvenir 1935*.
24. Jean Beadle, 'Congratulations from Mrs Jean Beadle J.P.' in *Souvenir 1935*.
25. E. Mannion and N. Rankin, 'Miss Holman's Position is a Tribute to all Women' in *Souvenir 1935*.
26. T. Tunnecliffe, 'Miss Holman's Efforts are of Utmost Value to Labor' in *Souvenir 1935*.
27. A. E. Ogilvie, 'Greetings from the Hon. A. E. Ogilvie, M.H.A' in *Souvenir 1935*.
28. M. Wilson and M. Vincent, 'Congratulations from the Goldfields Labor Women' in *Souvenir 1935*.
29. Jean Daley, 'They say the first ten years is the hardest ...' in *Souvenir 1935*.
30. Mary E. Sutherland, 'Greetings from the British Labor Party' in *Souvenir 1935*.
31. John Curtin, 'Miss May Holman has Served Labor Magnificently' in *Souvenir 1935*.
32. J. J. Kenneally, 'Outstanding Figure in Public Life of Australia' in *Souvenir 1935*.
33. H. M. Briggs and M. McCarthy, 'Australians Must Appreciate Women in Social Reform' in *Souvenir 1935*.
34. Percy J. Trainer, 'Our Women Can Popularise the Ideals of Labor' in *Souvenir 1935*.
35. Lewis McDonald, 'Miss Holman's Record is an Inspiration to Women' in *Souvenir 1935*.
36. MAY HOLMAN'S TRIUMPH AT HOUR OF DEATH. (1939, April 1). *The Australian Women's Weekly* (1933–1982), p. 22.
37. FEMININE INFLUENCE IN NATIONAL LIFE. (1939, March 27). *Sydney Morning Herald* (NSW: 1842–1954), p. 2.
38. EQUAL PAY FOR SEXES WILL BE ELECTION ISSUE. (1937, May 14). *The Daily News* (Perth, WA: 1882–1950), p. 3. Edition: CITY FINAL.
39. LABOUR WILL PRESS FOR EQUAL PAY FOR WOMEN AT NEXT ELECTION, SAYS WOMAN M.L.A. (1937, May 15). *Kalgoorlie Miner* (WA: 1895–1950), p. 8.
40. As above.

[41] Hansard, vol. 98. 28 October 1936, p. 1429.
[42] As above, p. 1434.
[43] As above, p. 1435.
[44] As above, pp. 1435–1436.
[45] As above, pp. 1436–1437.
[46] As above, pp. 1429–1438.
[47] Hansard, vol. 101. 19 October 1938, p. 1479.
[48] SHOULDER TO SHOULDER – WOMEN MUST SUPPORT ONE ANOTHER. (1934, January 26). *The Courier-Mail* (Brisbane, Qld: 1933–1954), p. 20.
[49] *Hearts starve as well as bodies/ give us bread but give us roses* is from the chorus of a women workers' protest song of the early twentieth century in the USA, 'Bread and Roses.' The original poem was by James Oppenheim and was first published in *The American Magazine* in 1911.
[50] LABOR LEADER'S MAGNIFICENT TRIBUTE TO A GREAT LABOR WOMAN. (1939, March 31). *Westralian Worker* (Perth, WA: 1900–1951), p. 1.

EPILOGUE

[1] In 1935, May Holman wrote a curriculum vitae which Sheila Holman typed up for her. After May's death in 1939 her friend Molly Holmes added several pages, from which this information is taken. The document is in the private collections of Sheila Moiler and Judyth Watson.
[2] WOMEN'S SPHERE. LABOR WOMEN MEET. (1939, March 31). *Westralian Worker* (Perth, WA: 1900–1951), p. 10.
[3] Elsie Gare (1987). Interview with Lekkie Hopkins for *An Oral History of Women and the Peace Movement Project*. Tape 11. Battye Library, Perth, WA.
[4] Joan Williams (1987). Interview with Lekkie Hopkins for *An Oral History of Women and the Peace Movement Project*. Tape 22. Battye Library, Perth, WA.
[5] Judyth Watson (ed.) (1994). *We Hold Up Half the Sky: The voices of Western Australian ALP women in Parliament*. Perth: Australian Labor Party.
[6] See Lekkie Hopkins and Lynn Roarty (2010). 'Up Close and Personal: WEL and Women's Lib in Perth in the 1970s', in *Among the Chosen. The life story of Pat Giles*, pp. 84–109. Fremantle: Fremantle Press.

BIBLIOGRAPHY

Archives

J. S. Battye Library of West Australia History, State Library of Western Australia:
  May Holman Family Papers (1893–1951)
  Interview with Sheila Moiler (nee Holman) interviewed by Jenny Carter (1916–2003)
  Labor Women's Organisation papers (1927–1929)
Private collections:
  Kathleen Haines
  Sheila Moiler
  Judyth Watson

Interviews

Evelyn Cloverley in conversation with Judyth Watson, 10 September 1997, in Judyth Watson private collection.
Elsie Gare (1987). Interview with Lekkie Hopkins for *An Oral History of Women and the Peace Movement Project*. Tape 11. Battye Library, Perth, WA.
Sheila Moiler in conversation with Judyth Watson, 19 May 1997, in Judyth Watson Private Collection.
Eileen Thompson in conversation with Judyth Watson, 27 November 1997.
Roy Thompson in conversation with Judyth Watson, 27 November 1997.
Joan Williams (1987). Interview with Lekkie Hopkins for *An Oral History of Women and the Peace Movement Project*. Tape 22. Battye Library, Perth, WA.

Newspapers

The Advertiser (Adelaide: 1931–1954)
Advocate (Burnie, Tas.: 1890–1954)
Albany Advertiser (WA: 1897–1950)
The Argus (Melbourne, Vic.: 1848–1957)
The Australian Woman's Mirror (1936)
The Australian Women's Weekly (1933–1982)
The Australian Worker (Sydney, NSW: 1913–1950)
Barrier Miner (Broken Hill, NSW: 1888–1954)
Border Watch (Mount Gambier, SA: 1861–1954)

The Brisbane Courier (Qld.: 1864–1933)
The Capricornian (Rockhampton, Qld: 1875–1929)
The Canberra Times (ACT: 1926–1995)
The Courier-Mail (Brisbane, Qld: 1933–1954)
The Daily News (Perth, WA: 1882–1950)
Examiner (Launceston, Tas.: 1900–1954)
Geraldton Guardian and Express (WA: 1929–1947)
Kalgoorlie Miner (WA: 1895–1950)
The Mercury (Hobart, Tas.: 1860–1954)
The Midlands Advertiser (Moora, WA: 1907–1930)
Mirror (Perth, WA: 1921–1956)
Northern Star (Lismore, NSW: 1876–1954)
Parents and Citizens' Broadcaster (Perth, WA: 1939)
Queensland Times (Ipswich, Qld: 1909–1954)
Recorder (Port Pirie, SA: 1919–1954)
The Register (Adelaide, SA: 1901–1929)
The Register News Pictorial (Adelaide, SA: 1929–1931)
The Sunday Times (Perth, WA: 1902–1954)
The Sunday Mirror (Perth, WA: 1920–1921)
The Sydney Morning Herald (NSW: 1842–1954)
Toodyay Herald (WA: 1912–1954)
The Townsville Daily Bulletin (Qld.: 1885–1954)
The West Australian (Perth, WA: 1879–1954)
Western Argus (Kalgoorlie, WA: 1916–1938)
Western Mail (Perth, WA: 1885–1954)
Westralian Worker (Perth, WA: 1900–1951)
The Worker (Brisbane, Qld: 1890–1955)

Images

Portrait of May Holman p. 120 courtesy of the Western Australian branch of the Australian Labor Party.
Portrait of May Holman p. 181 from <en.wikipedia.org/wiki/May_Holman#/media/File:Holman,_Mary_Alice_%27May%27_(1893-1939).jpg>.
All other images from documents and photographs held in the Sheila Moiler private collection, courtesy Sheila Moiler.

References

Australian Dictionary of Biography, Melbourne, MUP. <http://adb.anu.edu.au/biography>
Dixon, R. (2009). 'Australian Fiction and the World Republic of Letters, 1890–1950', in Peter Pierce et al. (eds), *The Cambridge History of Australian Literature*, pp. 223–254. Australia: CUP.
Hansard, WA Legislative Assembly Parliamentary Debates (1926–1939). Perth: Government Printers.

Hopkins, Lekkie (1999–2001). 'Katharine Susannah Prichard: a Biography', in Anne Commire and Deborah Klezmer (eds), *Women in World History*, 16 vols. Waterford: Yorkin Publications.
Hopkins, Lekkie and Lynn Roarty (2010). *Among the Chosen. The life story of Pat Giles*. Fremantle: Fremantle Press.
Karrakatta Club Incorporated: History 1894–1954. <www.karrakattaclub.org.au>
Magarey, Susan (2001). *Passions of the First Wave Feminists*. Sydney: UNSW Press.
Modjeska, Drusilla (1981). *Exiles at Home. Australian Women Writers 1925–1945*. Sydney: Angus and Robertson.
Nile, Richard (1990). 'The Making of a Really Modern Witch: Katharine Susannah Prichard 1919–1969'. *Working Papers in Australian Studies*, University of London, Working Paper no. 56. London: Sir Robert Menzies Centre for Australian Studies, University of London.
Oliver, Bobbie (2001). '"In the Thick of Every Battle for the Cause of Labor": The Voluntary Work of the Labor Women's Organisations in Western Australia, 1900–70', *Labour History*, vol. 81, November 2001, pp. 93–108.
Palmer, Nettie. *Nettie Palmer: Her Private Journal, Fourteen Years, Poems, Reviews and Literary Essays*. Vivian Smith (ed.) (1988). St Lucia: UQP.
Daphne Popham (ed.)(1978). 'May Holman', *Reflections: Profiles of 150 women who helped make Western Australia's history*. Perth: Carroll's.
Prichard, Katharine Susannah (1963). *Child of the Hurricane. An Autobiography*. Sydney: Angus and Robertson.
Saunders, Kay and Raymond Evans (eds) (1992). *Gender Relations in Australia*. Sydney: HBJ.
Sawer, Marian (1992). 'Housekeeping the State: Women and parliamentary politics in Australia' in *Trust the Women: Women in the Federal Parliament*, Papers on Parliament 17, September. Canberra: Department of the Senate.
Solomon, R. J. (1988). *The Richest Lode: Broken Hill 1883–1988*. Sydney: Hale & Iremonger.
Spearritt, Katie (1992). 'New Dawns: First Wave Feminism in Australia 1880–1914', in Saunders, Kay and Raymond Evans (eds), *Gender Relations in Australia*. Sydney: HBJ.
Throssel, Ric (2012). *Wild Weeds and Windflowers: The life and letters of Katharine Susannah Prichard*. Sydney: Allen & Unwin.
Watson, Judyth (ed.) (1995). *Remarks of an Inexperienced Traveller Abroad*. Perth, WA: J. Watson.
Watson, Judyth (ed.) (1994). *We Hold Up Half the Sky: The voices of Western Australian ALP women in Parliament*. Perth: Australian Labor Party.
Windsors: Victoria Mary of Teck <http://www.britroyals.com>

ACKNOWLEDGEMENTS

Judyth Watson's passion for honouring the life of May Holman has been the driving force behind the production of this book. I thank her for giving me the opportunity to take up the project where she left off and to see it through to completion.

I am deeply indebted to Susan Midalia, long-time friend and editor extraordinaire, for her generous engagement with draft after draft of the manuscript; and I thank the many other friends and colleagues, including the Magdalena women, who have expressed interest throughout. In particular, I am grateful to my ever-expanding extended family for their ongoing support of the work I do.

Finally, I acknowledge the professionalism and expertise of all at Fremantle Press, especially my editor, Georgia Richter. It has been a delight to work with you all again.

The Labor Women

Their cause is ours; our cause is theirs;
  We move towards our common goal;
And we have done with doubts and fears,
  Since one great purpose makes us whole.

Whatever we may gain or miss,
  Year after year, and mile on mile,
Our greatest triumph must be this:
  That they have found us worth their while.

The help that they so richly lend
  Gives us assurance in our claims,
Brings us respect from foe and friend,
  And gives clear guidance to our aims.

The deeper knowledge they reveal
  Is ours to draw on in our need.
They are the temper of the steel
  That cuts through ignorance and greed.

Till wrong shall vanish like a wraith,
  Till petty interests cease to fuss,
May we be worthy of the faith
  The Labor Women have in us.

Our cause can never know defeat;
  While the need lasts it shall endure—
Their faith has made our faith complete;
  Their aid has made our victory sure.

—Oscar Walters.

Inside cover, Souvenir 1935, published by the Westralian Worker.

First published 2016 by
FREMANTLE PRESS

Reprinted 2025.

Fremantle Press Inc. trading as Fremantle Press
PO Box 158, North Fremantle, Western Australia, 6159
fremantlepress.com.au

Copyright © Lekkie Hopkins, 2016.
Foreword copyright © Carmen Lawrence, 2016; preface © Judyth Watson, 2016.

The moral rights of the authors have been asserted.

This book is copyright. Apart from any fair dealing for the purpose of private study, research, criticism or review, as permitted under the Copyright Act, no part may be reproduced by any process without written permission. Enquiries should be made to the publisher.

Consultant editor Georgia Richter
Cover design Carolyn Brown, furrylogic.com.au
Cover photograph Sheila Moiler private collection

 A catalogue record for this book is available from the National Library of Australia

ISBN 9781925163353 (paperback)
ISBN 9781925163377 (ebook)

Fremantle Press is supported by the Western Australian State Government through the Department of Cultural Industries, Tourism and Sport.

Publication of this title was assisted by the Commonwealth Government through Creative Australia, its arts funding and advisory body.

Fremantle Press respectfully acknowledges the Whadjuk people of the Noongar nation as the Traditional Owners and Custodians of the land where we work in Walyalup.

www.ingramcontent.com/pod-product-compliance
Lightning Source LLC
Chambersburg PA
CBHW021147160426
43194CB00007B/720